Untangling the knot
Belugas & Bears

Published by
Whittles Publishing Ltd.,
Dunbeath,
Caithness, KW6 6EG,
Scotland, UK

www.whittlespublishing.com

ISBN 978-184995-444-0

Printed and bound by
Severn, Gloucester

Untangling the Knot
Belugas & Bears

My Natural World on Film

Mike Potts

Whittles Publishing

Contents

ACKNOWLEDGEMENTS

First and foremost I'd like to thank and pay tribute to Dr Clive Minton, my mentor, for training me as a bird ringer; he was responsible for so much more in my teenage years. He sadly passed away very recently but was an inspirational figure to me and many others. Through him I met many kindred spirits that have remained great friends to this day, particularly Derek Stanyard, Peter Challinor, Rob Wilson and Michael George. During my early years at the RSPB Film Unit Editor David Reed and Producer Dan Freeman also became great friends.

Many people have helped with my filming career particularly Maurice Tibbles, who sadly passed away in 2001. He had great faith in my early abilities and I owe him a great deal. I'd like to thank BBC producers, Dr Roger Jones, Robin Prytherch, Dr Steve Nicholls, Mike Salisbury, Richard Brock and particularly Paul Reddish, with whom I have shared untold memorable moments over the many programmes that we have worked on together. Also, from the BBC, Ian Grey, Miles Barton, Adam White, Nigel Marvin, Conrad Maufe and Tom Hugh Jones. I would like to thank Bruce Pearson and Jo Stewart Smith who I worked with on several projects and to Martin Davies for his invaluable help in Cuba. Filming in Alaska was an exciting era in my life and I would like to thank bush pilots Dennis Miller and Bruce Connant who flew us around the country with great skill, safety and knowledge, also John Hechtel for his essential expertise on Brown Bears. I'd also like to thank Jim King for his kindness and friendship and John Hyde, a great photographer. Dr Guy Morrison and Dr Nick Davidson introduced me to the wonders of Arctic Canada and gave me invaluable tuition on riding ATVs, whilst Jason Roberts kept me safe from Polar Bears in Svalbard. I must thank especially Dr Cliff Frith and Dr Dawn Frith for their expert knowledge and great company whilst filming Birds of Paradise in New Guinea and Bowerbirds in Australia and Phil Hurrell for getting us safely up and down trees. I would also like to thank Sir David Attenborough for the pleasure and privilege of working with him on those programmes.

There have been many people over the years that I have worked with in the field and if I have not mentioned you by name then my apologies; without your expertise many sequences would not have been possible.

To other good friends and colleagues who are sadly no longer with us but who all had a strong influence on my life and are greatly missed: Ned Kelly, Eamon de Buitlear, Lance Tickell, Mike Kendal, James Roberts, Ian Langford, Tony Cook and David Cobham.

I am grateful to Keith Whittles at Whittles Publishing for having faith in this book project. Also thanks to Moira Hickey, Kerrie Moncur and Sue Steven.

I must thank my wife Elaine for her support over the many years that I was travelling the world. She is always here for me.

Publisher's note

Browsing the literature, and depending upon the type of book, one can find different styles adopted for the use of initial capitals in animal names. In this volume the publishers have, for clarity and ease of reading, used capitals sparingly.

PREFACE

My interest in the natural world began over 60 years ago when I was a small boy and there was barely a thought given to losing habitats or species. I took for granted all the common birds such as turtle doves, skylarks and lapwings that could be found everywhere. Skylarks nested on old slag heaps in the industrial Midlands where my interest in the natural world was forged. Over those early years my interest in wildlife, and especially birds, became more focused and as a teenager I spent much of my spare time ringing birds for long-term migration studies. Mute swans, swallows and shorebirds such as Knot, Dunlin, Turnstone and Grey plover were caught and ringed in large numbers in the 1960s, leading to new discoveries on migration routes and wintering grounds. At the same time I developed an interest in photography, with some early forays with a cine camera producing my first black and white wildlife images, though somewhat distant and shaky. It was not until my early thirties that I made the leap from hobby photographer to professional wildlife cameraman. I spent several years at the RSPB film unit which set me on the road to a 35-year career, documenting the wonders of our natural world for television. What wonderful things I have seen and experienced. Hummingbirds in the tropical forests of Brazil and Ecuador, birds of paradise in the mountains of New Guinea, locust swarms in the Sahara Desert and massive migrations of caribou across the Arctic tundra of Alaska. Working with dedicated biologists in the field I have captured on film behaviour barely seen before, even documenting totally new behaviour of which scientists had no previous knowledge.

Flying with specialist fixed wing aircraft and helicopter pilots to get us into places where roads did not exist, was always exciting, if sometimes nerve-wracking. For most of my career I captured images on film and only latterly did I use digital cameras for the slow motion capture of hummingbirds in flight, which was the last production I worked on and, I like to think, one of the best. Now everything is produced on digital media.

I hope this book gives you an insight into the life of a wildlife cameraman, the hundreds of hours spent often in extreme locations to capture the many sequences needed for a natural history film, all part of the excitement of this very special career.

Over my lifetime I have seen drastic changes to wildlife populations and to the habitats that they depend upon. More than ever I think wildlife films have a vital part to play in raising awareness of the state of our planet and the many issues that threaten it.

Showing people what wonderful species and places we stand to lose may stimulate more to care and, only if we care, will we take the urgent action to do something about it. I hope this book will provide one such stimulus.

Mike Potts

1 EARLY DAYS

From an early age, even though I lived in the industrial Midlands of England, I had a strong interest in the natural world. When I was about 12, in the late 1950s, my best school friend Peter Baker's parents had a little house by a canal in the countryside, to which I was often invited at weekends. To my eyes it was idyllic, and I couldn't wait for those Sundays when Pete's parents would shut their newsagent's shop and head off with us to 'the bungalow', in reality a very characterful wooden cottage. Pete had a double aluminium canoe and we would set off on expeditions down the overgrown canals, seeing great numbers of water voles, kingfishers and moorhens. The local farmer gave us permission to enter his woodland, where we watched rabbits dig burrows in the sandy soils among the bluebells. There were green woodpeckers and tawny owls in the mature trees, and we were over the moon when the farmer gave us permission to build a five-metre tower hide to watch them more closely. We would sometimes spend the night in the woods, listening to and calling back to the tawny owls. Those were such happy times, and formed the basis for a lifetime of watching and photographing wildlife.

Even at that early age, the first tiny seeds of interest in filming wildlife were waking from dormancy. I had bought a small Bolex Super 8 film camera and scraped together enough money to buy some rather expensive black-and-white film, producing my very first distant – and somewhat shaky – wildlife images.

In our early teenage years, Pete and I began to take an interest in bird ringing, trapping birds to fit them with small rings to study how far they travelled and how long they lived. To start with, we did this using small cage traps in the bungalow garden, catching common birds like blue tits, robins and hedge sparrows and fitting them with colour rings for our own small studies. We knew this wasn't really achieving much, though, so through the West Midland Bird Club we got to know a proper ringer called Clive Minton. Clive was licensed to ring birds under the British Trust for Ornithology's ringing scheme, trapping birds with mist nets and fitting them with individually numbered metal rings, each engraved with the tiny inscription 'BTO Tring'. Clive was incredibly enthusiastic and we were soon recruited into his small army of trainee and assistant ringers, getting heavily involved with most of the several

MP paddling hard to intercept a mute swan taking flight

*MP with a captured
mute swan*

large ongoing studies of different birds which he had underway. A mute swan study, for example, involved up to 20 people catching as many as 600 swans every year in an area of 1,000 square kilometres. Specially designed bamboo 'swan poles', five metres long with an aluminium hook just big enough to slip around the swan's neck, were used on rivers, canals and lakes, with the swans enticed within reach by a few tasty morsels of bread.

Pete's double canoe, *Kingcup*, was sometimes brought into service. One very snowy day, on a deep pool near Cannock in the West Midlands, I was paddling in the front seat, with Clive in the rear seat trying to intercept a swan that was just starting to take off. 'More speed! Faster! Faster!' bellowed Clive, as he wielded his five-metre swan pole, anticipating a mid-flight capture. To Clive's disgust, the swan escaped. The more experienced among us, though, were quite capable of catching a swan in full flight, although to land a 15kg bird with a swan pole is not for the faint hearted. One such mid-air catch cost Clive one of his teeth, and on more than one occasion the backs of my hands were badly bruised by a whack from the carpal joint of a swan's wing.

Annual swan roundups, held in July when the birds were flightless, were an eagerly awaited occasion. Towns as far apart as Stratford upon Avon and Burton upon Trent had their own riverside swan gatherings, creating much local interest and, of course, consternation that we were catching these 'royal' birds, officially the property of the Queen. Clive was always brilliant at putting people at ease, letting them know what we planned to do and why, explaining in great detail the purpose of the work and sometimes even recruiting bystanders into the team. Other studies involved catching nesting swallows at farms and tracking their journeys to South Africa, and visiting huge winter roosts of hundreds of thousands of starlings in conifer plantations, many of which were winter migrants from northern Europe. I remember leaving a forest in total darkness after one of these starling-catching forays, a sack full of very active starlings over my shoulder, and walking straight into a waiting police officer. We managed to explain ourselves, but it must have looked deeply suspicious.

The most engaging studies involved travelling, virtually every weekend of the year, to the east coast. There, on the Wash, we would catch and ring large numbers of wading birds – knot, dunlin, redshank, godwit and curlew. Initially we used mist nets, set in rows of up to 100 metres long, stretching across the mudflats on the northern shores. These would be set at low tide, usually in late afternoon, and as the incoming tide displaced the birds from their feeding areas, in gathering darkness, they would be caught in the nets. Sometimes we would be up to two miles out from the sea bank, wading in water up to a metre deep, hidden channels ready to plunge the unwary in over their heads with potentially fatal consequences.

One November evening, that potential danger became very real for me and a friend, Chris Challinor. As usual, we had left a flashing beacon on the sea bank to act as a guiding light, but a heavy fog had descended and totally obscured the beam. We were completely disorientated, with no idea of the direction we should take. We were very close to the nets on a rising tide, already wading in a metre of water, and it was still more than an hour until high tide. To try to get back in total darkness and thick fog was far too risky: it could have led us out to sea and plunged us into a deep creek with fast-flowing currents. We decided that our only option was to stay by the nets, clinging to the bamboo poles which supported them. The tide would rise, at most, by another metre, but it would be a close-run thing. The two of us clung on, the incoming tide first swirling around us, then pouring into our thigh boots, then rising above our waists. It was very cold. At that time we both smoked, so were carrying matches. Every few minutes we would throw one into the water to see if the current had changed direction, indicating that high tide had passed. It hadn't. Silently, the water crept up to chest level. I began to feel myself become buoyant, and knew that soon I wouldn't be able to keep my feet on the ground. I didn't want to think about what could happen next.

Everything was beginning to go numb. We had been standing in freezing water for nearly two hours. Surely the tide must be nearly full? Another match, and still no change. We couldn't hang on much longer. At the back of our minds was the fact that, just a fortnight before, two wildfowlers had been drowned in this area, and we didn't want to join them.

Then, at last, a moment of elation: the floating matchstick indicated that the tide had turned at last. Now all we had to do was wait another two hours until we could safely determine where the creeks were and start to pick our way back to the sea bank. The fog was lifting and we were getting occasional glimpses of our beacon, so at last we had some indication of the direction in which we should walk but, soaking wet and very cold, we were fighting the real risk of exposure. We were determined not to succumb at this stage, though, and continued to tell stories, smoke and even sing to keep our spirits up. Gradually we began to see the faint outlines of the creek edges as the tide receded and could start to pick our way safely back to the sea bank. We had made it.

Eventually the group started to use cannon nets to catch large numbers of waders at high tide roosts. These nets, developed by the Wildfowl Trust for catching geese, were originally called rocket nets and propelled by a charge of cordite, left over from army stores, but when this became difficult to obtain, cannon nets took over. They use a cartridge with black powder firing a projectile from a barrel, with four projectiles needed to carry out a net of approximately 30 x 15 metres. A good catch could net several hundred birds and needed a big team of very experienced and licensed ringers to extract and process the birds. These studies have led to amazing discoveries about the routes used by migrant wading birds, where they breed and how long they live. These studies are still going strong, as is Clive Minton, now living in Australia and still studying shore birds at over 80 years old.

My working career started when I was 15 years old. I had left school without any qualifications and went straight to work on a farm, with the vague intention of going on to agricultural college. This illusion was quickly shattered by two weeks of hard labour: early starts to catch a bus to the farm at 6.30 a.m., 48 hours a week, for the miserly sum of £2.50. After handing in my notice I managed to secure a lowly job as a gardener at Dudley Zoo but fortunately, within a few weeks, a job on the keeping staff became available. I applied and got it, going on to spend two years working with animals, including giraffes, big cats –leopards, lions and a rare black panther – and polar bears. My main interest, though, of course, was birds. I worked with many species: toucans, parrots, macaws and turacos, but my main interest became the waterfowl collection, which I was in charge of. When the curator at Dudley, Frank Reitz, moved to Peter Scott's Wildfowl Trust at Slimbridge(changed to the Wildfowl and Wetlands Trust in 1988) I expressed an interest in working there too, should a job ever arise, and some months later Frank got in touch to say that a post had become available. To my great delight I got the job, firstly at Slimbridge for a few weeks of training, working in the world-famous collections, then at the Trust's site at Peakirk, near Peterborough, where I was involved with breeding and generally looking after the collection. Here I met a lovely man called Tony Cook, who ran the nearby Borough Fen duck decoy, a centuries-old device for catching waterfowl. It is one of the oldest in Britain, established by the Williams family in 1670 and originally used for catching birds for the London markets. This was the case right up to 1951, when it was taken over by the Wildfowl Trust for catching ducks for ringing. I loved going down to the decoy with Tony and his dog Piper. At the entrance to the decoy wood was an ancient little hut, its felt roof sagging, full of the paraphernalia of duck catching: hand nets, hessian sacks, bags of grain, and thigh boots hung on the walls. The wooden floor had been worn thin by the feet of generations of decoy men, and the place had an intoxicating smell of bygone times, a mixture of hemp, tar and duck feathers.

A decoy is basically a pond of an acre or so, usually set in a woodland, with eight large netted pipes leading off it. These pipes were around seven metres in height and width at the entrance, then bent round a corner and reduced right down to less than half a metre. At the sides of the pipes were screens and little hurdles over which a dog would be sent to jump before disappearing again behind the screens. In this way, inquisitive ducks would be given a tantalising glimpse of the decoy dog and would gradually swim up the pipe. Halfway along, the decoy man would appear behind them at the entrance to the pipe, flushing the birds down into a detachable catching net at the end. It was a simple but effective technique. With eight pipes, wind direction was of no importance: birds could be lured into whichever one would allow them to take off into the wind and up the pipe._

Decoyman Tony Cook breaking the ice at Borough Fen decoy

In the winter months, grain would be scattered at the entrance to the pipes to encourage the birds in, and tame decoy ducks would sometimes be used. In the 1800s, many hundreds of ducks could be caught on a good day, but by the time we were ringing, a good day meant maybe only 50 birds. Although I thoroughly enjoyed working in the collections and helping with the decoy, it was poorly paid, with no great prospects for the future. I decided I needed a change of direction and to get a reasonably paid job, keeping my ringing activities, reluctantly, as a leisure pursuit. I took a job as an apprentice laboratory glassblower, a highly skilled profession, and I learnt the trade for nearly three years in the research department of a large chemical company. It was well paid and gave me a skill in high demand, both in industry and in university research departments at home and abroad, but it wasn't really what I wanted to be doing for the rest of my life.

One of the Wash wader-ringing weekends, to which I was still going on a regular basis, led to a life-changing event for me. I came from a humble background – my dad was a caretaker at the secondary school where I was educated – and I had never gone down the university degree route, so the chances of getting a good job in natural history were slim indeed. One weekend we were joined by the Ministry of Agriculture, Fisheries and Food oystercatcher study team. They had been working on the feeding habits of oystercatchers on the Burry Inlet in south Wales, where there was a conflict of interest between the birds and traditional cockle fishermen. At the time there were 18,000 oystercatchers on the inlet, eating over 600 tons of cockles a year, almost as many as the fishermen were harvesting. The MAFF team were cannon netting birds to ring them, to see where they came from and where they went to, leading to the link up with the Wash team. Was there, they wondered, an interchange of birds between the Wash and the Inlet in south Wales? The MAFF team were looking for a field assistant with a cannon netting and ringing licence, able to drive and to move to north Wales. I didn't need much persuading and more or less took the job on the spot. I headed back to Oldbury in the West Midlands, where I couldn't wait to hand in my month's notice.

As I drove over Conwy Bridge a month later, I couldn't believe what I was seeing. Before me lay a sparkling estuary with an ancient bridge and even older castle, built by King Edward I between 1283 and 1289. I was going to live and work here? It couldn't have been further from the grime and noise of the industrial Midlands.

My job involved travelling to south Wales for several days every fortnight, on the spring tides, to capture and ring oystercatchers using cannon nets; we also studied their feeding behaviour through telescopes, in order to get an accurate understanding of the species of shellfish on which the birds were feeding and how many they were eating. As waders feed by tidal cycles, rather than according to night and day, we also did these studies at night, using infrared lights and special binoculars. This contract was only for six months, and I was then told that the team was being transferred to Burnham in Essex. I had just met my future wife and was reluctant to move, as the extension to my contract may only have been for another six months. A few months later, after a not particularly enjoyable period working on a mink farm, I was offered a job with the White Fish Authority, just next door to MAFF, as a laboratory technician developing techniques for hatching and rearing oysters with the aim of restocking depleted beds. At the time there was also a lot of commercial interest in setting up new areas of oyster cultivation. I spent three happy years in Conwy before joining a commercial operation called Seed Oysters UK, based on the banks of the Menai Straits in Anglesey. Here I was in charge of producing oyster larvae on a very large scale: eight 1,000- litre tanks each held up to a million larvae, growing in highly filtered, heated and sterilized sea water. This was infused with specially cultured algae before the larvae, after around 21 days of growth, would metamorphose into tiny oysters. These would then be grown on in controlled laboratory conditions and hardened off, ready for further growth in the sea in protective mesh bags. Before this critical introduction to the ravages of tidal waters, the 'spat' oysters had to be around one centimetre in size. Any smaller, and their gills could clog with silt, and they would also be vulnerable to the ravages of shore crabs.

Though many of the pitfalls of breeding oysters could be controlled, we could not prevent an almost annual algal bloom of Phaeocystis. This removed many of the nutrients from the seawater and also had a foaming effect, which could block seawater filters and the gills of small oysters. Large losses of production ensued and contributed to the eventual closure of the hatchery.

Whilst working on Anglesey I had been honing my camera skills and the dormant seeds of cinematography had resurfaced. I had purchased a clockwork Bolex 16 mm camera and, using a hide, I filmed a moorhen at the nest. Now I was really bitten by the bug. A good friend of mine, Robin Fisher, a very respected bird photographer, had told me of a sparrowhawk nest in willow scrub in a marsh on the island. I investigated and, sure enough, there was the nest, with eggs. We built a hide, piece by piece so as not to disturb the bird, and soon I was filming the incubation, hatching and rearing of the chicks. This was done over several months in the summer of 1977 and was the beginning of a career that would last over 35 years.

A contact at the BBC in Bristol put me in touch with their film library and an extremely helpful and enthusiastic man, Mike Kendal. I visited Bristol and Mike introduced me to various producers who might want freelance footage for inserts into their natural history programmes. This did lead to some days' work and gave me an understanding of what was required. Mike also knew of an Irish filmmaker, Éamon de Buitléar, who was making a programme on Irish birds of prey and was looking for footage of a sparrowhawk. I contacted him immediately and arranged for the footage to be sent over to Ireland. Éamon loved it and I was paid the princely sum of £500 for my summer's work. Some months later I was invited to the premier of *Cry of the Mountain* in Dublin, the first time I had seen my material on a big screen, and I was thrilled to bits.

One thing led to another and I was commissioned to make a short ten-minute film for the RSPB called *Silver Meadows*, about the work that the society was doing to restore wetlands such as the Somerset Levels and the Ouse Washes in Cambridgeshire. At around the same time, the RSPB's staff cameraman, Hugh Miles, was leaving and I was offered the job, which I gratefully accepted. I was with the society for four years and worked on various productions for them, including *Short Eared Owls; Choughs – The Commendable Crow* and *Pink-Footed Geese*.

The chough film was my first big project and to this day remains one of the most demanding I've ever taken on. Choughs nest in sea caves or old mines in the mountains or quarries of Snowdonia. The site I chose was an old tunnel which seemed to have been rich in copper. Choughs nest in total darkness, so there lay the first challenge: a generator had to be hauled several hundred metres up into the hills, close to the nest site. We then had to lay out cables to the cave to light it. I had to build a hide in the cave, of course, in which to conceal myself and the camera, but that wasn't so easy with eight metres of water on the cave floor and the nest on a ledge five metres up the wall. This meant having to build a scaffold down through the water and up to the nest to support a platform to carry the hide. A further complication came from the fact that choughs often use the same nest site and go to roost in it each evening. Because of this, we had to build the platform piece by piece then wait until darkness fell. Only when the birds flew into roost would we know that what we had done that day had been accepted. It was a nail-biting time. We wanted to film the entire process from nest refurbishment, using sheep's wool, right through egg laying to hatching and eventual fledging. The lights had to be on a dimmer so that the birds could gradually become accustomed to the brightness required for filming. The first time we ran the generator with me in the hide, just two metres from the nest, was nerve-racking. The birds were bringing in sheep's wool, so to begin with I waited until they were in the cave before, very slowly, raising the light levels. They could so easily have taken exception and left the cave in a panic, but they didn't and got used to the set-up. I had to be extremely careful with the lighting: two 800-watt lamps just a couple of metres from the nest gave out a fair bit of heat, so it was critical not to run them for more than a few minutes, especially when the four chicks were quite small.

Interior of nesting cave with lights

Choughs at nest with four young

I spent two months on this project, visiting almost every day, seeing the eventual successful fledging of four big, healthy youngsters: a hugely satisfying outcome for a terrific amount of hard work. The final result was a very detailed and well-received 30-minute programme on choughs, which is still shown to this day. I had quickly found out that a natural history cameraman has to be not only a naturalist and photographer but also an engineer, a carpenter, an electrician and a lot of other things besides.

After four very productive years with the RSPB, I decided that it was time to step out into the big wide freelance world. I was offered a position as cameraman with Partridge Films, an independent production company making a series of six 50-minute wildlife programmes for ITV. Mine was an ambitious project on mangroves, based in Borneo and called *Siaru – The Tidal Forest*. For me and my wife it meant a move to Brunei, where I spent ten months filming a wide range of wildlife—birds, monkeys, crabs, snakes, fruit bats, fish and insects. It was a fantastic experience which very quickly broadened my knowledge of film making, and stood me in good stead for a future in the profession.

After returning from Brunei in May 1983 I didn't know where my next filming work would come from, but it wasn't long before I started to pick up contracts with the BBC Natural History Unit, shooting sequences for innovative series such as *The Living Isles* and *The World of Birds*. *Seal Morning* was a drama based on the book by Rowena Farre and produced by David Cobham for what was then Central Television. I was commissioned to shoot the natural history inserts on the beautiful north Norfolk coast. Another project of David's on which I was invited to work was a three-part series called In the *Shadow of Fujisan*, involving two long trips to Japan in spring and winter. These were busy years, but all these jobs were shooting sequences with other specialist cameramen for bigger productions. I really wanted to get my teeth into projects on which I would be responsible for all of the filming on a particular programme.

One of the producers with whom I had worked on *The Living Isles* was Paul Reddish, who was now going to be one of the producers on a major new series for the BBC called *Land of the Eagle*. There were to be eight programmes, one of which would be filmed in Alaska and called *The First and Last Frontier*. Paul asked me if I would be interested, and it didn't take me long to say, 'Yes!', as I would be the sole cameraman.

This was to be the first television series to produce an account of North America's natural and human history. Alaska, the northernmost mainland of America, was the gateway for native peoples who crossed the land bridge from Asia around 13,000 years ago and began to change the landscape and its wildlife. This involved several long trips to many remote areas of Alaska and was the beginning of a love affair with the country. I have been back many times since and have made some very special friends there. To this day it is my favourite location in the world.

I have been fortunate enough in my lifetime to experience many of the world's natural wonders. The birds of paradise of the rainforests of New Guinea, hummingbirds of South America, the mighty caribou herds of Alaska, pristine rivers full of salmon and the great bears that feed on them. At the same time, though, I have seen continuous reductions in the common birds of my childhood— the uplifting song of the skylark, the aerial displays of the lapwing and the evocative call of the curlew are just a few of the joys of nature that are slipping away as those species decline. Future generations should still be able to experience the wonders of our natural world, if today's politicians and industrialists can resolve the massive problems of deforestation and global warming. I hope that my filming over the years has made a contribution to people's awareness and understanding of the beauty around us, for without those, we cannot care. If enough people do care, we will perhaps be able to turn the tide towards a better future for us and for the natural world.

2 ALASKA AND THE BERING SEA

WINTER CARIBOU MIGRATION

Manoeuvring two trolleys piled high with film equipment through the chaos of Heathrow airport is often the first price I pay for a filming trip to some far-flung – but not necessarily exotic – location. One trolley is bound to have a wonky wheel, making it hell-bent on veering off into the crowd, earning me hard stares from other stressed travellers.

This trip is much longer than usual, requiring mountains of gear; I have spent the last few weeks making sure that everything is working as it should. The dozen or so aluminium cases are full of lenses and cameras, tripods in plastic tubes, camping gear and personal effects, all of which need to be scrutinised by Customs and ticked off against a carnet before we are allowed to check in the baggage. Fortunately I am meeting up and travelling with a BBC producer and good friend of mine, Paul Reddish, who is able to smooth some of the Customs and travel issues. Now, there is just one final hurdle: the payment of the excruciatingly painful excess baggage bill, often amounting to many hundreds – if not thousands – of pounds. This particular cloud, though, has a very substantial silver lining, in the form of a possible seat in business class. Paul is very good at persuading the check-in staff that, because we have parted with such a large amount of money, the least they can do is upgrade us. It doesn't always work, but on this occasion it does. Eventually all is done to the satisfaction of the various officials and we make our way on board our British Airways flight to Anchorage, due to take off at 1.30 p.m.

We have drawn the long straw and are going on a three-month trip to Alaska to film a 50-minute programme for a series on the discovery of North America and the effects on its wildlife, called Land of the Eagle. The flight is spectacular: north over Scotland, across Iceland, Greenland and Arctic Canada before dropping down through Alaska to arrive in Anchorage on time, and at the same time as we took off. We've flown for eight hours and gained eight hours by flying west.

Alaska is a large state, six times the size of Great Britain yet with a population of only 750,000. It has huge mountains, stunning glaciers, old growth rainforest, wild rivers and over 45,000 km of varied coastline. Massive caribou herds range over thousands of kilometres, brown bears and killer whales fish for migrating salmon, alongside great rafts of sea otters and millions of migrating wildfowl and shorebirds. These are just a few of the animals that we are hoping to film and which make Alaska so special. Of all the places in which I have filmed wildlife, I think Alaska has given me more satisfaction and excitement – not to mention brushes with danger – than anywhere in the world.

That same afternoon, as we continue our journey in an Alaska Airlines 737 under clear blue skies, we pass very close to the western edge of Denali, North America's highest mountain at over 6,000 metres.

With the slopes cloaked in snow and ice, climbers are clearly visible on the final summit ridge. It's a quite stunning sight.

Shortly after we land, our minds full of images from this jaw-dropping flight, we are met in Fairbanks by Kathy Turco, our Alaska fixer, who takes us to our accommodation, a cabin in the woods on the outskirts of town. We are shattered as it's now 4 a.m. UK time, so we go straight to bed. Tomorrow is another big travel day.

Alaska has several huge caribou herds which undergo incredible annual migrations, taking them over many hundreds of kilometres. We are going to film the Porcupine herd, which is around 100,000 strong and makes a circular migration of over 2,500 km. This herd spends some of the winter in a remote part of northwest Canada called Eagle Plains, which is where we are heading.

Denali, North America's highest mountain at 6,190 metres

At first light we make our way down to the airstrip to pack all our gear into a Cessna 206, a six-seater single engine aircraft with a good freight capacity. It needs to have, as we have 15 cases of gear between us. As the plane climbs steadily, we fly east to Eagle on the mighty Yukon river, then on to Dawson City, an old Gold Rush town in Canada. We meet up with the researchers from the Canadian Wildlife Service and the Alaska Fish and Wildlife Service, who have been studying this herd for many years and have a pretty good handle on its movements. Picking up our massive Suburban truck with its five-litre engine, we head north up the Dempster Highway, a dirt road still covered in snow and ice. We cross the Arctic Circle, driving through pristine lands of rolling hills and mountains dotted with pine forests and frozen lakes.

Finally, shattered, we arrive at the Eagle Plains hotel at 8.15 p.m. We have missed dinner, but manage to get some sandwiches and a well-deserved beer. Tomorrow we have a day off to discuss plans and prepare filming equipment, and a helicopter and light aircraft are flying in, to take us to look for caribou in the mountains and eventually assist with collaring the caribou for satellite tracking. This will give us the ability to get aerial sequences of the herds within the landscape and, we hope, allow us to get on the ground near the animals.

It's 6.30 a.m. and a big day for us, one which would be impossible without the helicopter and light aircraft which are being checked and prepared as we have breakfast. It's cold here, −20°C, so the engines need special heating before start-up. I'm flying with a very experienced pilot, Dennis Miller, in his two- seater Piper Supercub, a small canvas-clad aircraft, on this occasion fitted with skis which enable it to land virtually anywhere. Paul, the producer, is going in the helicopter, a Bell Jet Ranger, travelling with the research guys who may be darting and collaring caribou if they get the chance.

I squeeze myself and the film camera into the back seat and we prepare for take-off. The local road doubles as the airstrip so we make a final check for juggernauts coming over the brow of the hill before roaring down the tarmac at full throttle, narrowly missing snow poles and road signs. We climb steeply into a clear Arctic sky. We have radio contact with the helicopter and exchange information on sightings of caribou.

MP in plane with camera

*Radio antennae on wing
for tracking caribou*

The Supercub on a frozen lake

Dennis has radio antennae on the wings of our Supercub and we are soon picking up signals from collared animals. By the intensity of the beeps, it is possible to work out the range and direction of the caribou's movements and we soon have a small herd in our sights. Dropping smartly from 7,000 metres to just 150 metres, Dennis lowers the flaps and we fly at 50 knots along the snow-covered ridge where the caribou are feeding. I run the camera in slow motion to smooth out any turbulence and we get some great tracking shots. These will be very useful to cut into any material shot later on the ground as the animals feed.

A voice from the radio tells us that the helicopter team have darted a caribou and have landed to fit a collar and take blood samples, as well as physical measurements. Dennis takes the Supercub down to make a faultless landing on a frozen lake to wait for the helicopter to come in.

We eat our packed lunch at –20°C in the sunshine, chat a little but mostly enjoy the perfect calm of this pristine region. After half an hour or so, the distant clatter of rotor blades breaks the silence and the bright red helicopter appears over a ridge to land in a cloud of snow. The darting team have found a nice herd a short flight away, so we swop passengers and I jump into the helicopter.

After a few minutes in the air, we spot the animals on a ridge and I'm dropped with my film gear about 800 yards downwind of them. The idea is to get some safety footage from this distance and let the animals get used to my presence before I move in slowly, picking off more shots as I go.

The helicopter has headed off and left me alone for a couple of hours. Reassuringly, I have been left with a satellite tracker which I can activate if, for any reason, our aircraft becomes 'unserviceable' and cannot pick me up.

I eventually get within 100 metres of the herd, which I'm pleased about. The images at this distance on a 600mm lens are adequate to show that the caribou are using their hooves to scrape away the hard, wind-blown snow to get to the nourishing lichens and mosses below. This will cut nicely with the shots we got from the Supercub, and will make a great start to the sequence of the animals' behaviour on the wintering grounds, though soon they will be on the move, heading up towards the calving areas on the Arctic coastal plain of Alaska.

Above: MP filming caribou
Below: Caribou herd

MP getting into the helicopter with camera

It's 6 p.m. by the time I get a radio message that the helicopter is on its way back to collect me and it's just as well, as the temperature has plunged to −30°C. The journey back to the hotel in Eagle Plains is breathtaking, the snow bathed a pale orange from the setting sun, every contour accentuated. Yet again we land too late for supper. Tonight, though, is a big event.

An outdoor curling match has been organised between the Canadian and US research biologists, and Paul and I have been roped in too. It should be interesting, as neither of us has played before. It's so cold that the beer we are drinking from bottles is freezing to a slush but I'm distracted by finding that I'm actually quite good at launching the stone down the ice. We have the special brooms they use to sweep the surface ahead of the stone to make it go faster, and it all gets quite heated, with loud cries of 'Sweep! Sweep!' and 'Don't sweep! Stop sweeping!' coming at us from all directions. It's all great fun, the score doesn't matter, and it's a great way for pilots, researchers and film-makers to relax at the end of the day.

I sleep well, and think that the jet lag is catching up with me. After an early breakfast, I'm due to go in the helicopter with two US Fish and Wildlife research biologists, Steve Fancy and Ken Witton. We're heading out to the McKenzie Mountains to catch up with the caribou herds and – we hope – to dart a caribou for satellite collaring.

After 30 minutes flying, we spot several big groups and move in closer so that Ken can pick his target. The helicopter needs to be about 40 yards from the caribou to get an accurate shot. The Jet Ranger hovers for a second or two and Ken finds his mark. We hold back so as not to panic the animals, and watch as the darted animal staggers on for 20 metres or so before dropping softly onto the snow. The helicopter lands 100 metres away and the pilot shuts the engines down.

I'm due to film the fitting of the collar for the BBC programme called The First and Last Frontier, but I'm also shooting a sequence for the French company that produces the satellite tracking systems. I prepare the filming gear while Ken and Steve get the satellite collar and various bits of sampling and measuring kit, then we move quietly to where the caribou is lying. It's fantastic to see such a wonderfully adapted Arctic animal up close, with its dense coat of hollow hairs, one of the warmest known, and its sharp hooves, adapted for digging through the snow to reach the lichens upon which the caribou depend and which form a major part of their winter diet.

Once the filming is done, we wait for the caribou to regain its feet. With a shake of its coat it moves off the short distance to rejoin the herd, providing a very satisfying outcome for all.

After a few more productive days in Eagle Plains, we feel that the sequence has come together well. It's time to move on, but in less than two months, we will be catching up with the caribou on their breeding grounds on the Arctic coastal plain.

THE BERING SEA ISLANDS

In the middle of the Bering Sea, straddling the international dateline, lie two very remote and desolate islands. Just five km apart, Little Diomede belongs to the USA and Great Diomede belongs to Russia. The islanders of Little Diomede are traditional Inupiat hunters, catching migrating ducks but with walrus their main quarry, hunted from a traditional skin boat called an umiak, made from the split hides of the walrus themselves.

We have just had a pretty nail biting flight into Cape Prince of Wales on the extreme west coast of Alaska, flying on a Piper Navahoe twin-engine aircraft. Low cloud and strong winds buffeted us violently as we came in over the churning sea. Behind me, a woman in some distress was crying, her knees pressed hard into the back of my seat. Apparently she had recently been on an even more dramatic flight and didn't expect her luck to hold twice. Fortunately for us all, the pilot won the battle with the elements and brought us down to a perfect landing. Alaskan pilots are the best.

It's from this remote spot on the Bering Sea coast that we hope to get a helicopter out to Little Diomede. We spend the next day preparing gear and shopping for essential stores and then are delighted to hear that the flight is scheduled to come in at about lunchtime the following day.

This area of the Bering Sea is renowned for its bad weather. It's cold, it's windy and it's grey, with sea

Loading gear for the flight to Little Diomede

Little Diomede from the air

fogs common, often delaying flights for days on end. We are fortunate that the Bölkow helicopter is on time and we load all our gear for the 20-minute flight to the island.

Flying high above the pack ice, we see the Diomede Islands and, amazingly close, the Russian mainland just beyond.

We land on the sea ice at the base of the island. Even though it's nearly the end of May, the ice is still right up against the shore, but leads are opening up all the time and there's open water beyond. After the gear has been unloaded, it's taken up through the little shanty village which clings to the rocky hillside. Everywhere, we see parts of haunted animals: colourful King Eider ducks hang in bunches from houses, huge walrus heads with bulging eyes and awesome tusks sit stacked with chunks of seal blubber on verandahs, while polar bear skins dry on lines like the Monday morning wash. It is still legal to hunt polar bears as part of the subsistence allowance. The whole place reeks of blubber and husky dogs bark incessantly. I have a bad feeling about this trip.

Little Diomede - a hillside village   *Ice tunnel leading to our cabin in the hillside*

Eventually we are shown the entrance to our room. It's a rickety door in a stony hillside which, when opened, leads into a rock-lined passageway about seven metres long, the floor and walls glazed with sparkling ice.

At the end of the passage, above our heads, is a small trapdoor which, when pushed upwards, reveals a room about four metres square. This is where three of us will cook, eat and sleep for the next two weeks. There is a small window in the roof, now glazed with glass rather than a tightly stretched dried walrus stomach, as once would have been the case. This room used to be home to a family, and more recently – and more gruesomely – was used to store polar bear and walrus carcases. A little door in the ice tunnel reveals our toilet, a canister lined with a plastic bin bag, and it's bitterly cold in there. A pungent smell is coming from a large wooden barrel in the corner, and a peep under the lid reveals spring greens preserved in seal oil. I resolve not to hang around in here with a copy of the Bering Sea Bugle.

We soon have our room looking a bit more like home, though: all our personal gear we manage to put on benches round the edge, and a little paraffin stove on the table is ready for cooking. Vegetables and meat can be stored in the ice tunnel, which serves nicely as a fridge, and all the camera gear will be kept at the Fish and Wildlife office.

The wind is blowing hard from the north, which is not good news for going out in a walrus-hunting boat, unless we want to end up in Russian territory. I fear there will be a lot of waiting around for the right conditions.

While I have some spare time, I walk down to the sea ice with my still camera and binoculars; judging from the number of skins hanging out to dry, I'm slightly concerned about polar bear numbers. I am reassured by one of the elders that it is quite safe, as by this time of year they have all left the area. At the south end of the island there is open sea – wild, deep blue waters with dazzling white ice floes dotted through it. Huge pressure ridges have been pushed up in the ice near the shore, bowhead whales, looking

The edge of the pack ice

like Polaris submarines, nudge through the ice and flights of sandhill cranes pass high overhead. Sheltering along the ice edge are superb king eiders in breeding plumage, along with displaying long-tailed and harlequin ducks, a mouth- watering sight for a waterfowl addict like myself. This very arctic scene is completed by little flocks of snow buntings, foraging in the rock scree exposed by the wind.

It's time to head back to the cabin. Kathy, our Alaskan fixer, who's preparing a supper of tuna and pasta, is also a sound recordist and researcher; having spent time before on Little Diomede Island, she has the confidence of some of the elders, which is essential when filming an emotive subject like walrus hunting. Other film crews have painted the islanders in a less-than-favourable light, so it's not surprising that they can be wary. We chat a while and Kathy mentions in passing that another polar bear was shot on the edge of the ice today. I go to bed, but don't sleep particularly well.

We've hit a run of really nasty weather. Several days have passed with nothing but strong winds, grey skies and snow flurries. It's very frustrating for everyone; the hunters know that while they are stuck on shore, the walrus are passing through on their way north. There's not much for us to do while we wait. It's difficult to walk anywhere without falling down a hole, as the island is covered in a layer of scree topped by a layer of snow. We pass some of the time chatting with elders of the village about walrus hunting and how it used to be, using harpoons from the skin boats. Now, of course, they use high-powered rifles, and when a walrus is shot they have to grab it quickly or it will soon sink.

The weather is beginning to get depressing as we spend more time sitting around reading books and watching videos. I don't think I've ever watched so many movies in

An upturned umiak
made of walrus hide

my life. The weather is still against us, with high winds, drizzle and very poor light for filming. Frustratingly, some boats have been out and some walrus have been taken, but we were not told. The communication is not good and we are feeling that the politics of this place are going to be too much for us to get a sequence. We are beginning to run out of time.

It's now 6 June and we're due out of here in two days' time. We can hardly wait. The weather continues to be awful, with rain, wind and poor visibility. The chances of getting out on a walrus hunt are almost nil. We keep it in perspective, though: over the last few days a group of hunters in an *umiak* have failed to come home from a trip, and after more than four days missing at sea, hopes that they would return are beginning to fade. Then the news comes in that they've been rescued, alive and well, near St Lawrence Island in the Bering Sea, some 150 km to the south.

Cabin life has become very routine. All the water has to be carried up in jerry cans, as does the paraffin for the stoves. The toilet bag has to be dumped on the sea ice along with everyone else's and, as the ice melts, the whole disgusting mass sinks into the ocean or floats away to foul some other coastline. Looking back at my diaries, I can see my mood flatten and I can't imagine how I would have felt if we hadn't made it out when we did.

Tuesday 7 June: another miserable day, no chance to film so it's watching more movies and drinking coffee. There's no alcohol allowed on the island. There are no fruits or vegetables.

Wednesday 8 June: we're up at 8.00 a.m. which is early for us. We pack up all our gear ready for the helicopter due in at 11.30 a.m. At 1 p.m. we hear that the helicopter can't make it due to bad weather in Nome and Cape Prince of Wales – a massive disappointment.

We are dogged by more rain, mist and low cloud for the next two days. We are getting cabin fever and are starting to smell, having not been able to wash clothes or ourselves for nearly two weeks. Food levels in the shop are very low and we are down to crackers and jam.

Friday 10 June: the helicopter is on hold again and the flight is cancelled for the umpteenth time. It's back to the video shop for more movies. They're doing good business from us.

Saturday 11 June: another misty morning. Let's hope we get off today or we'll all go barmy. After much hassling on the radio from our end, the helicopter arrives at 12.30 p.m. We lift off just after 1.00 p.m. and in no time we are in thick fog again and flying just above the sea ice. The pilot is flying very slowly, almost hovering at times, so poor is his forward vision.

In the end, it was a pretty hairy flight out and we breathed a huge sigh of relief when we saw the airstrip appear out of the mist at Cape Prince of Wales. But we weren't going to get away that easily. We'd unloaded all our gear onto the strip to await the flight to Nome with Bering Air, but it didn't turn up because they thought the weather was bad. Eventually they got to us at about

6 p.m. We unloaded the plane – no baggage handlers here – and reloaded it with our gear and the three of us, and took off at 6.20 p.m.

It was touch and go whether we made the 7.25 p.m. Alaska Airlines flight to Anchorage, but once we did (with the help of a truck to rush our baggage over to the waiting Alaskan 737) the soft leather seats of economy felt just as good as first class. After days of surviving on tinned food, no alcohol, no bread and pilot crackers (a bit like ship's biscuits), we sat back and enjoyed several gin and tonics, a stack of sandwiches and a real sense of liberation.

THE YUKON DELTA

My love of shorebirds and waterfowl, and my past work for Peter Scott at the Wildfowl Trust, now the Wildfowl and Wetlands Trust, set me up perfectly for my next job. Given my passion for Anatidae (ducks, geese and swans) and the wild places that they inhabit, it's not hard to imagine my excitement when I was told by producer Paul Reddish that we would be filming for a fortnight in the Yukon Delta, a mecca for breeding waterfowl. This was to be another major sequence in the BBC programme 'The First and Last

Aerial of Yukon Delta

Frontier'. The Yukon is one of the largest deltas in North America and, at 19,624,000 acres, covers an area bigger than Ireland. It is formed by the Yukon and Kuskokwim rivers where they empty into the Bering Sea on Alaska's west coast, has virtually no roads, and is accessible only by float plane or boat in the summer. It is possibly the most important waterfowl breeding area in the whole of North America, with 120,000 swans, 1.4 million geese, 4 million ducks and 100 million shore- and waterbirds breeding there. There are at least 170 species of birds and 43 species of mammals.

Bethel, a small town in Western Alaska, is the gateway to the delta. The fully-laden Beaver float plane takes off and climbs steadily, headed for Hooper Bay. It's a fantastic, sunny evening with great visibility and we aim to make the best of it. I have the film camera all set up, ready to do aerial shots of the delta, and we climb through 150 metres, eventually reaching 2,000 metres, from where the myriad of ponds , lakes and rivers can be clearly seen.

I get some great shots from the different altitudes, which will really help to put the enormity of the delta into context. I can see now, given its colossal size, how it is possible for all those millions of waterfowl and shorebirds to breed here. We eventually touch down at Hooper Bay at around 8 p.m., met by two researchers who are studying the Pacific black brant geese and emperor geese.

They have a well-established camp here, so we just need to get our tents up and put away our foodstuff for our two-week stay. Paul elects to put up the tents while I film a brood of western sandpipers which have hatched nearby; they are very tame and we have to make the best of this amazing weather, as sunshine can be quite a rarity in the west of Alaska.

The research camp on the Yukon Delta

MP's tiny sleeping tent at Delta camp

Birds are calling and flying everywhere as we set off to look at a colony of Pacific black brant, nesting nearby. There are lots of nests with eggs, some starting to hatch, but we can't film them as there are too many Arctic foxes sniffing around. We head back to camp at one o'clock in the morning, the sun still shining, but we do have to go to bed, as it's been a long day.

Monday 20 June: another beautiful, clear, sunny morning. After breakfast we head off to check out another black brant colony, on an island and in a good situation. Paul leaves me there with all the gear and a hide, just in case the birds will tolerate it, though past experience tells us that most geese at the nest are extremely wary. Apart from the geese, there's a colony of common eiders and glaucous gulls; the gulls, though sometimes predating the goose eggs, are beneficial to the goose colony by driving off Arctic foxes. I have a productive day, shooting 400 feet (130 metres) of film but, as I thought, the geese won't accept a hide at close range. I do get some nice material on the 600 mm lens though, which gives reasonable close-ups of the birds and their nests. Paul comes back at around 5 p.m. and on the way back to camp we put up a hide on a Pacific white-fronted goose nest. The technique is to place the hide at some distance – maybe 25 metres – from the nest, then to move it in to around seven metres over the course of several days. It does depend to a large extent on the species involved; in general, the bigger the bird, the more sensitive it is. Small passerines at the nest, such as finches and warblers, will tolerate a hide being put straight in at three metres and will be back in minutes. I always like to spend time, where possible, watching the bird's reaction to a hide and be prepared to remove it completely to let the bird return to its nest. Birds away from the nest are a different story: they have the option to return to a particular spot or not, with no harm done.

We get back to camp at about 8 p.m., Paul cooks up some meat and vegetables for supper and we go over the day's achievements, looking at the possibilities for tomorrow. One of the researchers has found, just across the lake, an Emperor goose nest. Now that would be a dream bird to film. The emperor is a beautiful marine goose and the Yukon Delta is its main breeding area, although it also breeds on the Bering Sea coasts of Russia.

It's a cool but sunny morning, so we have a quick breakfast, grab all the film gear and set off on the several-kilometre trek to the white-front nest. Thigh boots are essential as everywhere is boggy, with shallow lakes and streams to cross. As we approach the nest, the adults leave the area and we can see immediately that the eggs have hatched. Now we have to work fast. This is a critical stage for the birds: unattended, the tiny goslings can soon get chilled or, even worse, be predated by foxes. We quickly move the hide in to ten metres, not too close, as the adult birds seem to be quite edgy. I get settled into the hide and Paul walks away, as is standard procedure with hide work. Birds – apart from crows, who can count – see someone leave the area and think the danger has gone.

We agree to give it 30 minutes and, if the birds don't return, to take away the hide and leave. I watch the goslings intently in the nest; they seem fine, and the weather is sunny and dry so they are not getting chilled. The adults are nearby but they seem reluctant to come back to the nest. We can't risk them deserting, so we make the decision to take out the hide completely and watch from a distance. We go as far away as we can while still being able to see the nest – about 250 metres – and await events. Slowly, the adults edge back to the nest and within minutes are brooding their downy youngsters. That's a big relief for all of us. In a situation like that, the birds must always come first. After all, it's only television.

We're going to check on the emperor nest now, and hope she's more cooperative. On the way we find nests of black turnstone, Sabine's gull, dunlin, western sandpiper and – best of all – a spectacled eider with three chicks. They are the rarest of the four species of eider and the delta is their main breeding site.

As we approach, the emperor goose slips quietly off her nest, but seems less troubled than the white-front had been. We put up the hide at 25 metres and move quickly away from the area, but she is already on the way back to the nest and is soon nestled back down on the eggs. This looks very promising. We have a well-earned G and T back at camp before dinner with, as midnight approaches, a fantastic background chorus of drumming snipe, the haunting calls of loons and twittering sandpipers.

I crawl from my tent at around 8am. It's a dull morning. Fritz and I cross the lake in the little boat and head for the emperor nest. She is still sitting and is reluctant to leave as we approach, a sure sign that the eggs are close to hatching. We move the hide in to about eight metres and I get in and set up the camera. I have a good feeling about this one. Fritz walks off and within minutes she is back to the nest and shuffling down on her three eggs. It's so rewarding and exciting when a bird accepts you. At this range I have a perfect view of her and the nest. I have a Nikon 50–300 zoom lens on the Arriflex high- speed film camera, a great combination. If I put on the 600 mm lens I can fill frame with just the eggs and the head of the bird. I'm in for a long session as Fritz isn't coming back until 5 p.m., but I'm used to spending eight hours at a stretch cooped up in a little canvas box.

The emperor is quite comfortable with the hide and I pick off a variety of shot sizes. Her occasional shuffling leads me to believe the eggs may be hatching. She stands to turn the eggs and I see the first little downy gosling. How wonderful it is to be here just on hatching, and I'm conscious that not many people have had the chance to see this moment. I manage to get a few close-up shots of the gosling before the goose settles back down. Unfortunately it's quite a dull morning so the image quality isn't as good as it could be – at f4.5 there is very little depth of field.

As I sit quietly in the hide I consider how fortunate I am to be here, in one of the most productive wetland areas in the world. Just a couple of metres in front of me is one of the most beautiful of geese with the next generation hatching, surrounded by dozens of other species that many birdwatchers would pay dearly to see, while I'm being paid to be here. How lucky am I?

By early afternoon, two goslings are peeping out from the dense down of the female, so we have got the timing just right. They won't stay in the nest for long, maybe 48 hours. At 5 p.m. Jeff comes to let me out of the hide and the female doesn't leave the nest, so I creep quietly in to about four metres and get stunning close-ups of the little grey goslings. They're beautiful.

Heading back to the camp, I can see there is so much happening all at once now. There's so much to do, and so little time. It's a really brief season for these birds to breed. There are western sandpipers with young right by our tents and Paul has found a dunlin nest with three eggs. There is also a tundra swan nest close by with five eggs, three of which have hatched into the most gorgeous, downy cygnets. We'll keep an eye on the other eggs. There are courting long-tailed ducks on some of the ponds and the plaintive call of loons echoes across the lakes as I slip into my goosedown (what else?) sleeping bag.

Next day sees another dull, breezy morning and an early start out to the emperor nest.

As we draw close we can see the female is still brooding the young. After getting a few more shots from a safe distance, we withdraw quietly and leave her in peace. We think they may be there for another day. During the afternoon we put a hide on the dunlin nest that Paul found yesterday, and decide to give that a try. The bird is soon back and settling on to her clutch of three eggs. She's looking superb in the early evening light and I very soon have all the shots I need, so we remove the hide and head back for an early supper.

On the way back, we see a female spectacled eider with three tiny duck-lings and, less poetically, I get smacked on the back of the head by an irate Arctic tern whose nest we obviously strayed too close to. It's a cold and windy night even though it's midsummer, but the meal Paul cooks – sausages with fried potatoes and onions with cauliflower– tastes as delicious as food always does in the open air.

Producer Paul Reddish carrying a hide

I decide to go and take a look at the tundra swan nest down at the lake edge. The adults and their three cygnets are way out on the lake, but left in the nest are a cold egg and one that's just hatched. What should I do? It's cold and windy, and this cygnet

Three newly hatched emperor goose goslings

will surely die if the adults don't come back and brood it. I decide to get away from the nest and watch from a safe distance to see if they return. After 30 minutes there's no sign of the adults returning – in fact, they've swum further away. I make the decision to take the tiny cygnet from the nest back to camp with me.

We find a little grocery box for it to sleep in overnight and turn in after another eventful day.

24 June: the little cygnet has survived the night and seems quite happy. I take him to a nearby pool for a drink and he readily picks at seeds and floating vegetation, and also shows a liking for scraps of lettuce. He stays in camp with the researchers as we set off to the Emperor goose nest. We arrive just in time – the goslings are out of the nest, all dried out and ready for the off. It's another dull and windy morning but I get some nice shots of the family.

The female is very confiding and I manage a few more shots as they set off across the lake, giving the nesting sequence a natural ending. As we head back to camp for lunch we flush a short-eared owl with seven eggs. We are not going to attempt to film it, as it would be too risky with the number of Arctic foxes on the lookout for an easy meal. Back at camp, I feed the cygnet, who follows me now that I'm mum. He loves to go down to the water and peck at insects and plant matter and I think he's going to make it. We are due to leave here in a couple of days, though, so what will happen to him then?

Above: Emperor goose with hatching goslings
Inset: Emperor goose brooding hatching goslings

The awful pattern of cool, cloudy and often wet weather continues. It's very frustrating when there's so much going on that we could be filming, but we're stuck with it. After lunch, Paul goes off on a long hike with Jeff and Fritz to check on some distant black brant colonies to see if any nests are hatching, while I stay in camp and tend to Sunshine, as the cygnet is now called. I check out some of the local ponds and see red-necked phalaropes with tiny chicks, groups of scaup and shovellers, courting groups of long-tailed ducks and canvasbacks and more western sandpipers with broods of tiny, gorgeous chicks. Paul and the others return early in the evening but had no joy with the black brant colony. There's nothing to do but have dinner and turn in for another night under canvas.

26 June: a foul, windy and grey day, so we all have a lie-in until midday. It's going to be – yet another – non-filming day, so we stay around the camp, reading or doing a bit of birdwatching. I take Sunshine down to the water for his swim and a feed.

He is the most charming creature, becoming strong and confident now, able to swim quite well and take insects off the water. There is now a plan for his future. We've talked via Bethel radio to a retired waterfowl aerial survey pilot and biologist, Jim King, who lives in Juneau, southeast Alaska. He has a collection of waterfowl, including emperor geese and tundra swans, and has agreed to take Sunshine from us, which is great news.

Sunshine, the cygnet

Our last couple of days in the delta are busy. The weather gets warmer and brighter and we work 16-hour days to make the most of it. From a hide we film a great sequence of black turnstone at the nest, and dunlin and western sandpipers bathing in gorgeous late-evening light. We get a flying visit from two high-powered officials from the Fish and Wildlife Department in Washington, who control the budgets for these huge and incredibly important wetland reserves. They stay two or three hours and chat with the researchers, while I talk airplanes and drink coffee with George, the pilot, a fascinating man. Their float plane roars off into the early-afternoon sky and we are left in our total isolation, although not for much longer. We have heard by radio from Bethel that our aircraft is coming to pick us up tomorrow at 4 p.m.

We spend the evening finishing off sequences (I'm still filming at half past midnight) then it's back for our last evening in camp and a few well-earned rum and cokes. Sunshine is ravenous, so I take him down to the water for a feed of insects, of which there are plenty now that it's warmed up. It's his last night in the delta, too.

Tuesday 28 June is our final morning in this wetland paradise. We have a bacon-and-egg breakfast and head off to film black brants and emperors on the river flats. Some have broods of well-grown goslings, but they're nervous and keep their distance. Now that we have sunshine, we also have heat haze, which is always a problem with big telephoto lenses, so we have limited success and really have to get back to camp. Thanks to the morning sun we get to pack dry tents and sleeping bags and by 4 p.m. we're all ready to go. Sunshine is sitting snoozing in the warm sun, and after a swim and a good feed, he's tucked between a rucksack and the tripod case. The Turbo Beaver lands at 4.15 p.m. and we load our mountain of gear into its cavernous hold, say our goodbyes to Fritz and Jeff and take off in beautiful sunshine for Bethel. It's always exciting to move on to new locations but I'm sad to be leaving one of the most productive wetlands left on the planet.

We land in Bethel at 5.40 p.m. in pouring rain. Our flight to Anchorage on Markair is cancelled due to a pressurisation problem, but we manage to get on an Alaskan Airlines flight which gets us to Anchorage at about 10 o'clock that evening. Our precious package was allowed to come into the flight cabin with us.

All the arrangements have been put in place to get our little swan down to Jim King's collection in Juneau. He is going to travel via Gold Streak service on Alaska Airlines and his status as 'special cargo' means that he'll be travelling with the captain on the flight deck. It's quite traumatic seeing him off at the airport, but we know that he is going to a good home in natural surroundings with other tundra swans for company. We hear a few hours later that he has arrived safely and that Jim has named him BB, after the BBC. Wouldn't it be something to return one day and see him as a full-grown swan?

THE ARCTIC COASTAL PLAIN

It's the end of May and I'm flying north with producer Ned Kelly to catch up with the huge caribou herds that will very soon be calving on the Arctic coastal plain of Alaska. Just south of the Brooks Range, at 2,500 metres, we narrowly miss a flock of eider ducks off the right-hand wing, I tell the pilot with some urgency and he swiftly climbs another 500 metres in case there are any more. Hitting a 3kg duck at 250 km an hour could be catastrophic.

Crossing the Brooks Range at 4,500 metres, we start the gradual descent over the 50 km-wide coastal plain, passing through cloud and fog to land at Barter Island on the Beaufort Sea coast. We're met by researchers from the Alaska Department of Fish and Game, including our old friends Steve Fancy and Ken Whitton. They take us to their modern, heated bunkhouse, our very comfortable base for the next two weeks or so, though we will be spending much of our time camping on the tundra.

Frustratingly, sea fog and 35 knots of wind are forecast to last for two days. The helicopter that would take us and all our gear out onto the calving areas is grounded. I take myself off for a tundra walk near the rather desolate little town of Kaktovik. Above the barking of chained huskies, I can hear snow buntings singing, while Lapland buntings are gathering nesting material. On the tundra pools there are green-winged teal, northern pintail and pomarine skuas.

Near the village is a tiny cemetery looking out over the partly frozen Beaufort Sea It's a bleak and lonely place.

A big herd of caribou on the Arctic coastal plain

The Porcupine caribou herd is one of the biggest in Alaska, at present around 100,000 animals and all here, in the 20 million-acre Arctic National Wildlife Refuge, to have their calves at the same time. The vast majority of the calves will be born in this first week of June, a strategy designed to swamp the brown bears and wolves which will prey on them. A calf that's born as 1 in 100,000 has a far greater chance of surviving than it would have in a smaller herd.

My old friend Dennis Miller, with whom I flew in Canada, is here too. He will be taking me up to do aerial filming of the herds and also landing me on the tundra, in strategic positions for river crossings.

On the evening of 31 May, the fog lifts and the wind drops. It's now a beautiful, clear evening and the Fish and Game helicopter is loaded with our considerable amount of gear. We are going 25 miles inland, to a spot on the Hulahula River, where Ned and I are going to camp for ten days in the hope of getting a good sequence on herds crossing the river, and maybe even a birth.

Our camp on the tundra

The food tent

The helicopter touches down and we quickly unload all our gear, as the pilot won't be shutting down the engines. In minutes, he is up and away back to the Barter Island base. We have three tents to put up, one for each of us for sleeping and one for food storage; bears have an excellent sense of smell, so it's vital that nothing in the way of foodstuffs or even soap or toothpaste is kept in the tent. Most foods are kept in bear-proof containers and in a tent that's 50 metres from the sleeping area.

On a previous visit to this area, also to film caribou calving, I had a nasty experience with bears.

MP prepared for a filming foray

Producer Paul Reddish unloading the helicopter at the tundra camp

Producer Paul Reddish and I had been dropped off by helicopter and were setting up camp when I noticed in the distance two bears, heading straight towards us. One seemed to chase the other away but then continued in our direction; Steve, one of the Fish and Game researchers, had given us a .45 magnum pistol for extreme situations, which Paul had then passed on to me. 'You know about guns, don't you?' he'd said – although it was less of a question and more of a statement – and promptly thrust it into my keeping. Now the bear was only 50 metres away and coming in fast. My stomach was beginning to churn. Even if you haven't been threatened by a bear, you'll know the feeling when something horrible is about to happen. At some point we were going to have to react. I took the heavy weapon from its case, dreading having to fire it. I'd heard from rangers how difficult it is to kill a charging bear at close range. Even a trained person can need three or four shots, so what chance did I have? The bear was now only 20 yards away, huffing and grinding its teeth – never a good sign.

Then something remarkable happened. The bear suddenly stopped dead and stood high on its hind legs, looking hard in our direction, sniffing the air, before suddenly turning and running at full speed away from us, not stopping until it was over 100 metres away. What had happened? Up until that point it had been upwind of us and not caught our scent, and once it was downwind and caught our scent, it was away. Now I was left with a question: could I have fired the beast of a gun and stopped a charging bear? I decided to put it to the test.

We put a cardboard grocery box, about 50 cm square, on the tundra at about 10 metres. I took the .45 from its holster and took careful aim (something, to be fair, that I wouldn't have been able to do with a bear charging at 30 m.p.h.). With both hands on the gun, I fired. When I recovered from the shock of the recoil, I could see that the box hadn't moved an inch but – half a metre away – a hole the size of a bucket had appeared in the tundra.

From then on, we were very vigilant around camp. A lot of bears and wolves follow the caribou as the calves make for easy pickings. We felt uneasy about sleeping in tents while bears were on the move outside – people have been killed that way before – so we set up a watch system, sleeping in shifts. I would sit up from 8 p.m. until 1am and Ned would get a good sleep, knowing that someone was keeping watch. I would then go to bed until 6 a.m. while he watched. There was actually something wonderful about sitting out on a little seat at midnight, as I noted in my diary on 1 June:

Around 8 p.m. a cow caribou and her tiny calf feed in very close, I shoot 130 metres of film (10 mins) of the calf following its mother, then suckling and settling in the dwarf willow. The light gets really good and the calf's delicate little legs are accentuated by the backlight. If I could get a birth, that would be amazing. It's now 11.10 p.m., sat out by the cook tent, the sound of the river in the background, the low sun brilliant in a clear sky, caribou are grazing nearby, Lapland buntings are singing and the odd ptarmigan fires itself into the sky then glides down into the dwarf willow, my shadow is 8 metres long.

It's difficult to sleep, anyway, with so much to see and hear. This is such a remote spot. We are 25 km from Barter Island and 160 km from Prudoe Bay, from where it's hundreds of kilometres south and east before any other habitation. Ned gets up at 11.45 p.m., we brew up some coffee on our little stove and chat for half an hour about the evening's sightings before I reluctantly go to bed, an exciting day in prospect tomorrow.

Dawn is disappointingly cold and misty so, frustratingly, there can be no filming for a while. As the morning progresses we get a few clear patches so I do manage to get establishing shots of the river with the dramatic mountains of the Brooks Range in the distance. By evening, the fog has really closed in again, Ned goes to bed at 8.45 p.m. and I sit up on bear-and-caribou watch in the entrance to the tent. About 9.15 p.m. I hear the clatter of helicopter blades approaching. I call the pilot on the radio. 'I'm flying very low and must be very close to your camp,' he says. 'Sounds like you're nearly overhead!' I just have time to reply before, seconds later, he appears out of the fog, 20 metres off the ground heading straight for the tent. He banks off and follows the course of the river, telling me he's going to follow it to the sea and then along the coast to Barter Island. I don't envy him that flight. With no passengers on board, I assume that he's just dropped off some researchers at a camp. Our pilot, Glen, has been flying for 21 years, including helicopter gunships in Vietnam and taking provisions into the Amazon forest in Colombia, but says Alaska is the most challenging flying he's ever done.

Caribou crossing the river

Over the next few days we get several good spells of sunny weather. The caribou sequence builds up nicely: we film good-sized groups of cows and calves swimming the river, which has become a raging torrent with the snow melt from the mountains, and I get beautiful backlit images of the caribou emerging from the river in slow motion, shaking off the freezing water from their moulting hides. In spite of the variable weather it's been a productive few days and, after we break camp, the helicopter comes in to take us back to Barter Island. It's good to get our washing done and get back to decent cooked meals, rather than the freeze-dried camp meals on which we have been surviving.

The priority now is to get up in Dennis's Supercub, a go-anywhere little aeroplane, to get aerial shots of the huge post-calving herds which are beginning to gather along the rivers. We endure one frustrating day of low cloud and snow flurries when flying is out of the question. I spend the day cleaning cameras and lenses, writing up filming notes, even watching some TV. The following day is equally dull and 5 cm of snow has fallen overnight, but by late morning it's brightening and we decide to get airborne. The light is good now, so I shoot aerials from different altitudes of caribou crossing rivers. These shots are invaluable in cutting the sequence together and giving scale to the masses of animals drifting across the coastal plain. I see an amazing scene below: snow has blown against a bluff along the river edge as it winds its way to the ocean. I ask Dennis if we can land and he picks out a gravel bar in the braided river. After a couple of low passes (low, as in seven metres low) to check for unwanted boulders, we come in to a bouncy landing.

The scale of the cliff becomes more apparent once we're on the ground. The snow, where it has blown against the bluff, is two metres thick and over 20 metres high, stretching away for hundreds of metres toward the sea. I set up the tripod three metres from the base of the cliff on the wide-angle end of the zoom, the shot being a pan off to reveal the braided river swollen with snow melt. As I am checking the framing through the viewfinder, I hear a horrendous cracking sound and look up to see a massive piece of the cliff breaking away. In an instant my legs are whipped from beneath me and I and the camera are thrown into the river. On the spot where I'd been standing seconds before, there is a now a pile of ice the size of a house. My initial reaction is that the camera is ruined and the shoot is over. I stare disbelievingly at the heavy metal tripod legs which are bent like a banana, while my legs are bruised from the block of ice that, fortunately, hurled me and the camera into the river. Dennis comes running over: he'd heard the crash and seen the pile of ice, and thought he would be calling for a helicopter with a body bag. I begin to realise how lucky I've been; had my reactions been a bit slower I could easily have been crushed by tons of ice.

The camera is covered in glacial silt and needs stripping if there's going to be any chance of it working again. We pile everything into the Cub and take off, back to Barter Island base. What, we wondered, had caused the ice fall? Had the turbulence and vibration from the landing aircraft been enough to destabilise that section, or was it pure coincidence that we were there when it happened? It seemed strange that just that 30-metre strip out of hundreds of metres had come away.

Back at base I set to with the camera and lens. Nothing was actually broken but the fine silt had got into the lens focus mechanism, so the next five hours was spent stripping everything down, cleaning and lubricating, until everything seemed to work OK, leaving just bruised legs and a severely bent tripod. We needed to know whether or not the camera had suffered any damage, so I shot a test roll of film which was sent for rapid processing to a laboratory in Hollywood California. Three days later – to our enormous relief – we heard that all was well

Over the next few days we spent a lot of time in the air looking for the arrival of the bull caribou, which come to the coastal plain about three weeks later than the cows. It's quite a spectacular sight, so everyone is looking out for them. Dennis has the big bush wheels on the Cub so we can land pretty much anywhere on the tundra or on gravel bars in the big, braided rivers. I manage – just – to squeeze in my spare wooden tripod and a long lens in case we are able to approach any caribou herds on the ground.

We search the foothills of the Brooks Range and the Kongakut, Aichilik and Jago Rivers, but see hardly any bulls. Dennis is baffled – maybe they haven't come through the Brooks Range yet? We hit some really nasty turbulence created by converging winds from the valleys meeting the plains easterlies, and can do little more than head back to Barter Island to refuel and wait for better conditions.

But better days were waiting for us, and 22 June was one of them. Dennis and I take off, as we had done many times over the last week, at 7.30 in the morning. There is thick fog which we break through at 100 metres and which stretches just 8 km inland. Beyond lies clear, arctic sky.

Caribou are everywhere along the winding Hulahula River, named by Hawaiian whalers who travelled past its mouth in the 1890s, so we do aerial shots using a small film camera mounted on the wing to give a downward-pointing perspective. We see many more animals heading for the river and it looks like the build-up to a big crossing. We have to get on the ground, which is not always easy, the terrain peppered with ground squirrel holes and grassy tussocks. Dennis makes several very low passes, only about two metres off the ground, to assess the chances of a landing, eventually going in, clipping a few tussocks on the way and bouncing to a halt on the big tundra tyres.

A caribou herd from the air on the delta of the Jago river

A caribou herd surrounds our plane

Caribou groups crossing the river

We think it would be good to go back for Ned, so I get all my film gear out of the Cub, along with a shotgun, just in case any overly inquisitive bears came by.

With Dennis gone for Ned, I find myself totally alone in this awesome wilderness. Animals are already beginning to cross, with the river running deep and fast, swollen with meltwater from the snows of the Brooks Range some 50 km away.

Dennis and Ned are back in an hour, bringing more film stock as ours was getting critically low. More and more animals are building up along the river, cows and calves being washed downstream towards me in the roaring torrent but somehow getting ashore, struggling from one gravel bar to the next. This is one of the most dramatic and spectacular sights I've ever seen. Still more animals come, thousands of them, cows and calves, yearlings and some bulls now arriving and, amazingly, all the calves seem to make it. The cows are very protective of them and steer them into shallower water, putting their own bodies upstream of the calves to protect them from the full force of the torrent. The light is crisp and clear, and there's a stiff, cold breeze to keep the coastal haze – and the mosquitoes – at bay.

I get lovely establishing shots of the whole aggregation of many thousands of animals, with the majestic Brooks Range beyond. This has been one of those days when everything falls into place: fantastic weather in a pristine location with amazing animal behaviour happening right in front of the lens. Dennis and I fly back to Barter Island base for 7.30 p.m., and I have to spend time unloading and reloading the film magazines, writing up camera notes and charging batteries while Dennis flies back for Ned.

Two days later and we're back up looking for the bulls, heading for the Aichilik Gap in the foothills of the Brooks Range. The early morning light is spectacular now that the fog has cleared, and we fly slowly up the valley, passing over a wolf den in a willow thicket. Just ahead we spot a big group of bulls on the hillside. At last, they're here. We shoot some aerials but need to be on the ground, but it's far too risky to land here, the surface rocky and uneven. We report back to Barter on the radio and Ned arranges to share the cost of a helicopter with Steve Fancy, a senior caribou researcher, who needs to retrieve from dead caribou four satellite collars, worth $2,000 each.

We arrive back at Barter at 10.30 a.m., I do a quick repack and transfer with Ned and Steve to the Bell JetRanger while Dennis takes off to do some radio tracking. On our way back to the Aichilik, we pick up the valuable collars and press on to the valley where we saw the bulls. They are still there but now in bigger numbers, heading down the valley towards the coastal plain. We do more establishing shots of these bigger numbers, then drop back down the valley, as we need to get on the ground ahead of the herd. The helicopter sets us down on the edge of a willow thicket, about 1 km ahead of the approaching bulls, then takes off and leaves us.

Ned, Steve and I nestle in to the edge of the willow thicket, which gives us good cover. The distant sound of the approaching herd gets louder by the minute. I can

Caribou researcher Steve Fancy and producer Ned Kelly. The helicopter drops us off for the approaching caribou bulls

Below: The herd of caribou bulls approaches

Inset: Jimmy Carter's fishing group with a film crew and Debbie Miller

just see them coming straight towards us, almost all adult bulls with superb antlers in velvet, and if I keep completely still I'm sure they'll come right past me. I'm lying in the willows surrounded by the sweet smell of dozens of species of arctic flowers and now I'm being enveloped by the sound and smell of thousands of bull caribou at the end of a 1,600 km journey.

This is a journey that's probably been made through this valley by bull caribou for thousands of years, as they head to join their cows and calves on the Arctic coast of Alaska. So few people can ever have witnessed this spectacle, the animals flooding past within 15 metres, the sound of their grunting and murmuring to each other, the clicking of their hooves on rocks, the smell and heat from their bodies, their palpable excitement at rejoining the herd and all the new-born calves. Their urge to reach their goal makes our presence irrelevant, but I'm sure they know we're here. I get some spectacular images as the powerful bulls press past us, on down the valley and spilling out onto the plains.

A few days later Dennis and I are flying at 1,000 feet, filming a big caribou herd which, strangely, has a 100-yard hole in the middle of it, and a brown speck at its centre turns out to be a grizzly bear. Sadly, we can't land as the ground is too boggy – well, we could have landed, but we wouldn't have got off again.

It's now 11.15 a.m. and we hear on the aircraft radio that ex-president Jimmy Carter is in the area and staying in a cabin at Peters Lake. A film is being made about him and he's read a book written by Debbie, Dennis' wife, on ANWR, the Arctic National Wildlife Refuge, which he was responsible for setting up. He's keen to meet Debbie at her camp in the Brooks Range and is going there for 11.30 a.m., so Dennis contacts the helicopter, a big Hughes 212, a 12-seater, and talks to the pilots. They're happy for us to follow them in to camp, which is really exciting. We land and I hang back, letting the politics unfold. Everyone seems relaxed and friendly, I chat with the cameraman who is following the Carter travels, Debbie is talking with Jimmy Carter about 100 metres away and I stroll in their direction. Soon enough he's shaking hands with me, asking me who I am and seeming genuinely interested in our filming work.

Everyone – security men, pilots, cameramen and a President – is enjoying this informal gathering, sitting and chatting in an Arctic haven. But for his foresight, we could be looking down at a landscape of wellheads and pipelines rather than a pristine wilderness. The crew films the President talking with Debbie before they go fishing on the lake, while I do some filming myself, of the great drifts of cotton grass. By late afternoon, the wind is starting to pick up so Dennis thinks we should go while we can, given that Arctic weather can change quickly and dramatically from idyllic to atrocious. We take off straight into the wind off a riverbank, which proves a bit hairy, Dennis holding the stick on the Cub right down until the last second to save us stalling and ending up in deep water. We head toward the Jago River and land on the so-called Biddy Strip (a short gravel runway). It's incredibly hot at 23°C, the mosquitoes are horrendous, but the flowers, especially the dwarf blue lupins, are stunning. The mosquitoes can become a real menace to the caribou; they are so ferocious and persistent that they cause animals to panic and charge around. They can lose pints of blood to these huge Arctic versions of the little insect we know from temperate or tropical climes. Large groups of caribou can be seen standing on snow patches where it's too cold for the insects. When they're really bad, the animals head for the sea and stand up to their necks in the water. I'm getting eaten alive – the mosquito's extra-long proboscis can penetrate the thickest clothing – and Dennis takes loads of pictures of me thrashing the air. After a very short time I've had enough and we squeeze everything back into the Cub. There's not much wind but the powerful little plane springs into the air and we're up and far away from the winged menace on the ground.

Our time in the Arctic National Wildlife Refuge is drawing to a close. It's been fantastic to spend time with the caribou on this stage of their incredible journey, and we have some wonderful footage of the spectacle of the great herds, the river crossings and the arrival of the bulls, which should all help to make a memorable programme in the BBC's Natural World series. Soon they will begin to move south, back to their wintering grounds in Canada, their great migration having taken them over 3,000 km in the last 12 months.

WALRUS, WHALES AND OTTERS

Just after dawn on a still morning in late August, I'm sitting outside my little tent. That's not a dramatic start to a story. But this little tent is on a tiny island in the remote Bering Sea, and below me are 2,000 walrus, all packed onto a tiny beach.

These are all males, as the females have gone north to give birth to their calves on the sea ice. Producer Paul Reddish and I are here for a week to film this amazing aggregation. Round Island is about 4 km long by 1.5 km wide, with a precipitous rocky spine up the middle and steep and slippery grassy slopes down to the beach, so filming these lumbering giants will not be as easy as it might seem. Weighed down with heavy packs, film cameras and tripods, we're going up to the north end of the island which has the biggest aggregations, picking our way up through the waist-high grass along crumbling, rocky trails to the knife-edge ridge which forms the top of the island. We can see the great pink masses of thousands of walrus spread along the beaches, though getting to a position from which we can film them could be a problem. We have to pick our way carefully down the trail and twice I fall, tumbling head over heels down the slope, fortunately without doing any damage to myself or the gear.

Round Island

Big group of male walrus on the shingle beach

As we approach the walrus we have to be careful. We cannot go onto the beaches and must film from above, although finding a vantage point is difficult. Male walrus are huge, weighing up to 1.5 tons, and are easily disturbed. If panicked, the great mass of animals charging into the water can cause severe damage to each other with their 60 cm-long tusks. We manage to tuck ourselves into a rocky outcrop about 30 metres above the great burping, gaseous, writhing mass of pink blubber. There is an onshore breeze and the smell coming up from below is memorable. Walrus are benthic (bottom) feeders and although their main diet consists of large clams and other bivalve molluscs, they also eat shrimps, sea cucumbers and crabs. They don't use their tusks for feeding but find prey such as clams with their sensitive whiskers, sucking out the flesh by vacuum with their piston-like tongue. Walrus do not dive to great depths for their prey as do other Pinepeds, like seals and sea lions, and go only up to 60 metres, but can stay down for up to half an hour. When they resurface they can be almost pure white, as the blood vessels in the skin contract to reduce heat loss in the cold, deep water.

There is so much going on beneath us: the walrus are all packed close together on the shingle and, with such large animals, I'm getting stunning close-ups of the

The spine of Round Island

Two male walrus showing their sensitive whiskers for detecting food items on the seabed

heads and tusks with my 600 mm lens, the biggest practical lens for filming. At this height above the sea we can see the ghostly 'white' walrus coming up from the depths and on to the beaches to join the others. Such arrivals and departures cause a great upheaval among the animals, with much stabbing at each other with their tusks. While I am filming Paul is recording sound, which will be crucial to the sequence. This island is fantastic not only for walrus, though: the rich surrounding seas support huge populations of seabirds which nest here, with up to 50,000 kittiwakes on a single cliff. There are also horned and tufted puffins, some nesting just below our camp on the cliffs.

By late afternoon the sun has passed over the east-facing beach and we begin to pick our way back up the track to our camp. I've not been looking forward to this bit, but this time we get back without any more involuntary somersaults off the path. We are not the only residents on the island: Bob and Judy are the Fish and Game Department rangers living here for the summer, carrying out research on the walrus and seabirds, and we spend many pleasant evenings in their little cabin on the cliff top. The weather is amazingly settled for Bristol Bay, but it could change at any time, so I work long hours in the evening, filming the horned and tufted puffins returning from sea with beaks packed full of little fish for their young. I love this kind of situation, being totally immersed in the place, tucked into the cliff with birds whizzing past at great speed. It's a terrific challenge to try and follow them in flight and keep them in focus at the same time.

In the tiny little harbour just below our camp is a rock called, funnily enough, Walrus Rock. It often has small groups of walrus hauled out on it and it's possible to get near to it undetected, allowing great opportunities for low-level filming and shots of interesting behaviour. The rock is covered in barnacles and the huge male walrus will sometimes come and rub their skins against it, using it as a giant pumice stone. We are keen to try and get some underwater footage of them, so we try to hang a camera off the rock. While I am positioning it, a huge walrus emerges from the water just below me and exhales a great cloud of fishy breath. I can see every whisker on his huge head: they are called the vibrissae, are very sensitive and used for detecting prey on the seabed. We get one or two shots underwater, nothing very usable, but it was great fun trying.

In the remaining days on this remote island we get more material of the walrus from Bob and Judy's zodiac. By cruising slowly offshore and parallel to the beaches it's possible to get tracking shots, showing the massive animals from the water. At one point we even manage to land and get the camera on a tripod for shots at beach level. About 100 metres is as close as I dare to get, though, before the walrus start to shuffle uncomfortably and I know to retreat to the zodiac.

It's our last night here and we have a gourmet meal of tinned salmon, packet potato and stir-fried vegetables sitting outside our little tents, gazing out on a flat calm sea with the sun setting and walrus cruising by.

The boatman, Don Winkleman, is coming to collect us at 11.30 a.m., so it's an early start for us. We have to get the tents and all the gear packed and down the precipitous track to the little rocky bay in good time. It's just as well we do, as Don comes in early at 11 a.m. and I think the forecast is for deteriorating weather. As we are leaving, a Beaver float plane arrives with day visitors. It's a high-speed boat ride on flat calm seas at 30 knots and takes just over an hour back to Togiak salmon cannery, where there is a tiny gravel runway next to the beach. Just five days ago we landed here in a Cessna Sky Wagon, and I was in the co-pilot's seat as we banked in low over the sea and came in so fast onto this tiny strip that I felt for sure that we would go off the end of it.

All the gear is piled up on the side of the strip ready for the return journey at 3.40 p.m. and, right on time, the Sky Wagon appears, starting as a speck in the sky and banking around onto the final approach to land in a cloud of dust and gravel. We load up the giant hold ready for the 35-minute trip to Dillingham, and soon are up and away. In no time we are cruising over lakes and tundra, already turning autumnal gold.

Having returned to Anchorage, we spend several days taking time to reorganize our logistics and sort out gear and supplies. Frustratingly, we have to wait for a spell of bad weather in the mountains to clear before we can fly east out of Anchorage and through the impressive Chugach Range.

Far below us we see the huge tidewater glaciers which pour out into Prince William Sound. A trawler called Lucky Star is our target but there are dozens of fishing boats to choose from, all looking like toys from up here. We lose height to try and pick out

The trawler Lucky Star   *Our float plane unloading gear and stores*

names and wrongly circle one, which is embarrassing. After several more abortive circuits, the Lucky Star comes into view. Landing nearby, the pilot taxis the float plane over to the 20-metre trawler which is to be our home and filming base for the next week.

We unload all our gear straight onto the boat, which is not easy as there's a large swell running, but we get it all safely stowed away and very soon we're off on what promises to be quite an adventure. Our captain, Craig Matkin, is a fisherman but is also employed to undertake photo identification work on the killer and humpback whales and various dolphin species.

This is a sturdy, practical boat, stable and well-equipped with radar, autopilot and Loran navigation (remember that this is 1987, before the days of satnav.) It also has a variety of small craft, including a 6-metre skiff, fast and able to keep up with the whales. This is essential as the *Lucky Star* can only do 8 knots, while killer whales can cruise at 11 knots. There's also a sea kayak and a little zodiac, ideal for short excursions ashore looking for sea otters – and, it turns out, for pudding ingredients.

The sequence we're hoping to film will show how productive Prince William Sound is, with an abundance of marine mammals depending on its rich waters, although we will be concentrating on killer whales and sea otters.

Most people are familiar with Prince William Sound from the catastrophic grounding in 1989 of the oil tanker, the Exxon Valdez. Eleven million gallons of crude oil were spilled into the sound, causing untold environmental damage, especially to marine mammals and birds. The sound was first charted by Captain James Cook in 1778 and was initially called Sandwich Sound after the Earl of Sandwich, one of his patrons. It was renamed later that year after the third son of King George III, Prince William Henry.

Today's weather is not great for spotting whales, as the sea is too choppy and the skies are overcast, but we are able to cruise slowly across the sound to a sheltered bay to anchor for the night. Paul, the producer, and I take to the skiff and go looking for sea otters and soon find several: it seems that they're not uncommon here. They're feeding on mussels and one is lying on his back, casually munching through a large starfish. I think we should be able to shoot a good sequence on these over the coming days.

We head back to the *Lucky Star*, where Craig and Eva have cooked up a super spread in the galley: black bean soup followed by huge deepwater shrimps caught in Craig's pots an hour before, fried up with onions, mushrooms and garlic, followed by pork chops and red cabbage coleslaw. Thank goodness there's no sweet. It's been a long day so I retire to my cosy bunk at half past ten.

The next morning is clear with a beautiful sunrise. We have a breakfast of pancakes and bacon with coffee and up anchor at 7.30 a.m. Craig seems to have a sense of where killer whales might be, and soon finds a pod of four or five. This is the first time I've been so close to them and had a sense of how powerful and awesome they are. They surface within five metres of the boat and I get one or two shots, but it's difficult as the sea is too choppy to keep the camera steady. Eventually we have to give up as they are moving away at some speed.

Killer whales, sometimes called orcas, are highly intelligent and sociable animals. Old whalers called them 'the whales that kill other whales'. The males grow up to eight metres in length, weigh 6,000 kg and have a dorsal fin which can be up to two metres long, while females are much smaller. There are two types of pod, made up of residents and transients. Residents tend to live in smaller, more vocal groups and feed on fish, mostly salmon. The transients are in bigger pods of up to 10–15 animals, move more quietly and hunt sea mammals such as sea lions, though they will also hunt down young whales. With the break-up of sea ice in the Northern Bering Sea, the whales are beginning to penetrate more deeply into these regions and starting to attack narwhals and walrus, which can be seen as a worrying consequence of global warming.

Having moved on, we found pairs of huge humpback whales, over 20 metres long. I get shots of them surfacing, blowing and submersing with their tail flukes in the air, but it's a little frustrating, as I have the same problem with choppy water. It's been an unproductive morning. We were in the skiff in heavy seas and having to hand-hold the camera made it difficult to get technically acceptable shots. We just have to be patient and wait for better conditions.

After lunch we refuel from a large salmon fishing trawler which has caught 5,000 lb of salmon and is pumping it onto a larger boat to be taken off to the cannery. We're now going to cruise back to a good killer whale area. The forecast for tomorrow is good, with much less wind and sunny periods.

We're up at half past six and, as forecast, it's a clear and sunny morning. We breakfast as we go and killer whales are soon spotted on the surface, so we get into the skiff for a cautious approach. The water is still choppy so I'm quite restricted in the shots I can get, and limit myself to wide-angle establishers with the mountains as backdrop. It's possible to take a few mid-shots of the whales using a higher frame-rate to smooth out the motion a little, but it's clouding over, so it's back to the *Lucky Star*.

Craig and Eva go off to do some photo ID of the whales. The pictures they get show small differences between individuals, such as nicks in the fins or slightly different tail or body patterns, which make it possible to identify individuals. This, over time, gives them valuable data as to how far the animals are ranging, who they associate with, how long they live and so on.

Paul and I bring up the rear in the *Lucky Star*. It's not every day that you're given charge of a 20-metre trawler so that's another surprising addition to the list of wonderful things about being a wildlife cameraman.

The Lucky Star *heads out into the sound*

We feasted on prawns most evenings

Craig comes over the radio, reporting that they have killer whales around them, just a few kilometres away, so it's full steam – well, eight knots – ahead. I grab the camera gear and get into the skiff, while Craig and Eva take the *Lucky Star*. Two killer whales – a female with her calf – are following the skiff and come right alongside, before passing under our 6-metre boat, turning over to show their pure white bellies, surfacing very close and blowing out as they do so. Paul has a camera in an underwater housing and is hanging over the side, holding it just below the surface. Falling in would not be wise, so I keep a tight hold on his legs, and just one or two shots is all we need to help cut the sequence. These are such powerful animals, and it's a privilege to be so close to them. As we're travelling so slowly, the propeller is producing lots of bubbles which one particular calf loves to roll around in. Amazingly, no one has ever been killed by an orca in the wild, though there have been fatalities in the few large facilities that keep them.

The light has become poor due to yet another front coming in from the North Pacific. Fortunately, the sound is protected from storms by the large barrier Islands – Montague, Hinchinbrook and Hawkins – to the east. Anchoring safely in a sheltered bay, Craig and Eva go off in the sea kayak while Paul and I go ashore and pick big juicy blueberries in the rain, at the same time keeping an eye out and an ear cocked for brown bears, who also love these berries. Back at the *Lucky Star* I make a pie with the juicy fruits and we have the usual feast of prawns, which come up from a baited pot at 200 metres.

We spend the evening chatting and listening to underwater recordings of the whales, made that day by Eva. It's been such an exhilarating and productive day, and I can hardly wait to see what tomorrow brings.

2nd September is dull and wet. It's disappointing, but gives us a good excuse for a leisurely breakfast with real blueberry pancakes. We see a couple of humpback whales and follow them so that Craig can photo-ID them. We are cruising slowly as the weather is poor, and I'm standing by the stove drinking coffee, gazing idly through the galley window, when suddenly the surface of the water is torn apart as a massive humpback whale, black and gleaming, surfaces not ten metres from the boat. It's come right underneath us: it's breathtaking and jaw-droppingly huge.

The rest of the day is quiet with poor weather again. We cook a beef stew and eat it as we are cruising, ending up by early evening at Port San Juan, which has the biggest pink salmon hatchery in the world with a capacity of over 200 million eggs. There are tens of thousands of salmon in the bay, in dense shoals desperate to get upstream but held back by nets. When the nets are removed they are caught, killed, stripped of their eggs and their flesh canned. These fish would have died spawning anyway and the hatchery production puts back many more salmon fry than could ever be produced from the natural streams, which have high predation rates of eggs and fry by bears, eagles and ravens. It seems that tomorrow there may be an 'opener', a three-hour 'season' for seine netters to come in and mop up any salmon that may still be in the bay –and there are a lot. We return to the *Lucky Star* and have a fantastic supper of deepwater prawns cooked with ginger and onions and washed down with beer. Gales are forecast for tomorrow.

By 8 a.m., the wind has dropped and it's stopped raining, but it's still heavily overcast. We head to the fish hatchery to watch the seine netting which starts at the firing of a gun, at exactly 9 o'clock. It's like a grand prix, with more than 20 boats revving their engines, throwing out clouds of diesel smoke and jostling for position before they're off, trying to get the best positions to set their nets, boats bumping and fouling the nets of others, and leading to a fair bit of trawler rage. From our position, we can see the great shoals of salmon enter the open end of the seine, then hear the skipper bellowing orders to the skiff drivers to close off the net before they escape again. Apparently, as it's the end of the season, a lot of the crews have been hastily gathered and they're not that experienced, so it's all very entertaining. The weather is clearing so we head back into the sound looking for whales. We spend the whole afternoon searching but, disappointingly, get no sightings.

It's a pity to not be shooting something in these good conditions so we take the zodiac and land on an attractive little wooded island. I set the camera up on the tripod and, while filming establishing scenic shots, we spot several sea otters that are feeding in the dense kelp beds nearby, bringing up shellfish. The otters were virtually wiped out a century ago by Russian and US hunters for their fur. Theirs is the densest, warmest and most luxurious pelt of any animal and fetched huge prices. In 1911 an international agreement banned such hunting and the populations have gradually recovered to over 26,000 in southeast Alaska, with sea otters found right down the west coast to California, where there are over 3,000.

Sea otter feeding on mussels

These individuals are quite confiding, so I'm able to move in close to get those really frame-filling close-ups. One of the otters is cracking open mussels with its powerful teeth and very soon I have variety of shots to make a good sequence. It's been an immensely satisfying day as we cruise slowly back to Lucky Bay, as we now call it, picking up our super-productive prawn pots on the way. One has a kilo of large prawns in it, the other a very fat octopus...which has scoffed all the prawns. We anchor in Lucky Bay and have an early night.

5th September dawns a beautiful, sunny, crisp morning. We're up and away by 7 o'clock and looking for killer whales, as we need more material to complete the sequence. Within half an hour we've found a good sized pod and follow them in the skiff. The mother and calf are there and they give us more great footage as they play behind the boat, while the main group of six animals cruises alongside us and I get wide-angle shots, with the mountains beyond, and tighter shots as their powerful bodies slice through the water.

We head back to the *Lucky Star* for a late-morning coffee, which gives me a chance to get camera batteries on charge and reload film magazines. Craig and Eva need to go out in the skiff to do more photo ID work, so Paul and I stay on the boat until mid-afternoon. We see killer whales resting on the surface, barely moving, so when Craig and Eva get back we follow them, at a discreet distance so as not to disturb them. From the *Lucky Star* and then from the skiff we get smooth tracking shots of the group on the move, in beautiful light and calm water.

Below: Orcas in Prince William Sound
Inset: Dead salmon along
the bank of a stream

By late afternoon it's clouding over and the sea is getting choppy, so we return to the *Lucky Star* and find a perfect, sheltered bay in which to drop anchor for the night. After dinner, Paul and I row ashore in the dinghy. It's so calm and peaceful that it feels as if no one else has ever been here and maybe, in fact, they haven't. We see two pairs of river otters feeding on dead pink salmon along the tideline. One little stream nearby is packed out with heaving, struggling fish trying desperately, in just a few inches of water, to get upstream to spawn. Many are dead or dying on the stream edges, some half-eaten by otters and others with their eyes picked out by ravens. It somehow seems very wasteful for all these fish to die as they struggle frantically to do this one last thing in life. We head back to the *Lucky Star* at dusk, after an exhilarating and productive day.

The *Lucky Star*, though slow, is a powerful little ship and pushes effortlessly out into a choppy sea and across the sound. Craig soon spots killer whales but sadly, yet again, it's too rough to film. We stay on board while Craig and Eva go off to do photo ID. Paul needs to get hold of Bush Pilots to talk about our flight out, but for some reason we can't access the marine operator. We head for the calm of Port San Juan from where we're able to phone about flights, but there's no chance of getting out today, as weather conditions in the mountains are too bad. In fact, Monday is a write-off too, with no flights due to continuing bad weather, and we remind ourselves that this is Alaska. On a previous trip to the Copper River delta, across the sound from here, where over 600 cm of rain falls a year, we spent ten days waiting for it to stop.

On Tuesday morning we're up early, the weather has cleared and it looks good. A phone call to Bush Pilots confirms they'll pick us up at 10.30. We pack all our gear and take it onto the pontoons, ready to load the float plane when it arrives, and say our goodbyes. It's been a memorable few days, with so many once-in-a-lifetime shared experiences and, though it was a struggle at times, we have ended up with unique footage for the film.

En route we pick up three Alaskan natives and their baby, then travel on via Whittier to Anchorage. It's not a flight for the fainthearted: our pilot keeps the plane low all the way, just under the cloud base, following passes through the mountains and skimming over ridges. It's been a shocking weekend, with eight light aircraft crashes in the mountains due to the severe weather, but fortunately our pilot Henry seems to be a survivor. There's an old saying in flying circles, 'There's old pilots and there's bold pilots, but there's no old, bold pilots.' I'm glad to say that we landed safely on Lake Hood and transferred to our usual residence when in Anchorage, the Airport International Inn. We are flying home tomorrow after nearly two months away but I'll be back: Alaska's in my blood.

RIVER OF BEARS

Brown bears are found in many countries in the Northern hemisphere – Europe, Russia, China, Japan, Canada and North America – but by far the biggest populations are in Alaska. People often get confused between brown and grizzly bears, but they are in fact the same species, *Ursus arctos*, but with many subspecies.

The southern coastal regions of Alaska have high densities of big bears, due to a seasonal abundance of salmon. Their cousins further north and in the interior are somewhat smaller and at lower densities, due to the colder climate and scarcer food resources.

There are several really good places to see bears in Alaska and I have been fortunate enough to have visited most of them – mainly filming for a programme called *Great Bears of Alaska* but also for the *Land of the Eagle* series, both for the BBC – and, as is often the case, in the company of some of the country's top experts on bear safety and biology. The McNeil River on the Katmai Peninsula is one of the hotspots where bears gather for the annual salmon runs, with sometimes up to 70 bears at the falls at one time.

Dr Roger Jones, a BBC producer, John Hechtel, a bear biologist, and I flew out to McNeil with Kachemak Air, a one-hour flight from Homer on the Kenai Peninsula in a big radial-engined Otter float plane. Larry Aumiller, the Fish and Game ranger here, meets us in the bay at McNeil and helps us with all our gear to the camp area. He knows as much about brown bears as anybody.

There is a very small campground here and a wooden cook shack where all food stuff is kept and prepared, to avoid unwanted bear attention. Larry and Derek, a

Rusty – an old male and a real character

Large numbers of bears at McNeil Falls

Unloading the Otter float plane

volunteer ranger for the summer, have built me luxury accommodation: a framed white canvas tent with a plywood floor and bunk and a little Yukon stove, a cast-iron wood burner. Sadly, two 'hooligan' bears – the name given to inquisitive young ones who push the bear boundaries somewhat – have done a wrecking job on it on the day we arrive and it will now have to be repaired with weld mesh reinforcement in the walls. Initially, though, we can sleep in the cook shack as there are no other visitors for a day or two.

My tent at McNeil River

Our first evening here is stunning, with the volcano Mount Augustine clearly visible, 70 km out to sea. We chat in the cook shack about all the possibilities the next weeks might bring. It's still early in the season and we are keen to show the feeding behaviour of the bears as their numbers increase. The male bears are first out of hibernation, in late April, followed by sows with cubs later in May. Because of the density of bears, they have developed quite a complex social language to minimise fights, which can seriously damage the combatants. Male bears are hugely powerful, weighing up to 700 kg, and can run in short bursts at up to 60 km/h. They all have very individual characters and Larry knows by name most of the eighty or more bears that can visit in a season.

Our first day here is dry and bright and we must make the most of it. We take our camera gear and follow the Mikfik River up to the sedge flats, a walk of about 2 km. We film a sow bear with cubs grazing along the riverbank on sedge, a major and highly nutritious part of their early spring diet. As they graze, they keep a sharp eye on the river for any sign of salmon movement, and can change in an instant from a cow-like grazer to an explosive, powerful predator launching themselves into the river at 50 km/h. One of the cubs, poor thing, has porcupine quills lodged in its face and seems quite disabled. They move off into the willow thickets and disappear from view.

More bears are beginning to appear as we head back downstream and I manage to get more grazing shots, as well as interactions between newcomers to the area. I've shot more than two rolls of film (20 mins) so have made a useful start. This turns out to be just as well, as it rains and blows at up to 35 knots for the next three days and we barely go out.

One saving grace is the wood-fired sauna which Larry built, situated on the edge of a little pool with a veranda. I light the fire in there, fill up the tub on the stove to get hot water and, after an hour, it's really cosy in there, with lots of hot water for washing clothes. Roger gets the big stove going in the cook shack, too, so that becomes the centre of social activity. I spend a lot of time reading and chatting with Roger, John, Larry and Derek. You really get to know people well in these situations, and we swapped many stories and shared experiences of all things Alaskan.

Thursday, 6 June is a misty, cloudy, damp sort of morning, but at least the gales and rain have stopped. By mid-morning we decide to go up to Mikfik sedge flats and it's actually quite atmospheric, the mist coming and going and a few glimpses of sunlight revealing the distant hills. We find a bear called Mindy and her pair of two-year-old cubs. An adolescent cub trying to join them causes some commotion, then a lone female comes onto the scene, and the family runs away. Then another three-year-old appears, another adolescent 'hooligan', so there was quite a bit of interaction, including little play chases, sniffing and circling. I'm amazed at how unnervingly close we're working to these impressive animals, which are quite capable of killing us with one swipe of their huge paw, yet which tolerate us filming them at five metres, sometimes moving closer to us than that. It certainly delivers a massive adrenalin rush and I keep reminding myself that no-one has been killed in this bear sanctuary in its 15 years. It's been a good day, I tell myself, as we plod wearily back to camp, and tonight I'll be in the luxury of my own tent, with no more snoring to contend with.

Around 9 p.m. we hear the drone of a big radial aircraft engine, and it's the Otter bringing in paying guests, a couple from Florida and their guide. Dinner makes me smile: as the guests drink their red wine and eat their fresh food, we continue with our diet of freeze-dried rations and Budweiser.

We now have two hooligans around camp, near John's tent, so he chases them off. They start to feed on sedges behind the camp so I get some useful footage of them there. Later, back at the sedge flats, we catch up with Mindy and her cubs, who are still grazing sedge when the hooligans appear. One pushes its luck a bit too far and Mindy charges, catching the cub and pinning it to the ground. It struggles to its feet and they stand growling at each other. I get some of the action but it all happened very quickly. Mindy and the cubs move away from the area then she plops down, not seven metres from us, and the cubs begin to suckle. I think this is a stress reaction, showing that the cubs are distressed and need reassurance. I feel a bit edgy, too, as Mindy looks as if she could charge. I carry on filming.

Roger Jones, John Hechtel and MP outside the cookshack

I get a complete sequence of them suckling, including big close-ups of noses on teats, little paws digging into mum's hair and wide-angles of the family with distant hills and mountains. Larry and John are with us, keeping a close eye on the behavioural aspects. We back off a little to reduce any stress caused by our presence, and eventually the cubs doze off and all is well.

The weather is starting to deteriorate by half past three so we head back to camp. I'm now well settled in my new tent and I fire up the little Yukon stove for the evening with some birch logs. It's a home from home and toasty warm. I unload and reload some film magazines and recharge camera batteries on the little 650-watt generator that we brought with us for the job. The float plane brought in more visitors today but, more importantly, it brought a consignment of fresh bread and – more importantly still – doughnuts.

Sunday, 9 June is a beautiful sunny Alaskan morning with a chilly breeze. We set off for the sedge flats at about half past nine, and find Melody and Manny up there with their two-year-old cubs, but on the other side of the river, so there's not much happening. We sit down and all end up dozing in the warm spring sunshine, Derek keeping an eye out for bears as they can appear quite suddenly, as if from nowhere. By half past two we decide to walk further upstream to see if there are any fish running. We choose a spot on the west bank and, with the afternoon sun behind us and the air crisp and clear, the scene is set. All we need is some action. As the tide falls, a few red salmon are starting to run through. The numbers increase and before long there are hundreds of them, powering through the shallow water. It's fantastic to see them at last and we know that now the action will really start. Manny and her cubs have been grazing sedge nearby and she spots the movement. Exploding into the river, she launches herself into the mass of now panicking fish, with the cubs right behind her. Within seconds they've got their first fish of the season which they carry, still thrashing, onto the riverbank. The action attracts more bears and before long there's a real bunfight going on. I shoot several rolls of film in quick time, there's so much action, bears launching themselves at full tilt onto the fish leaping everywhere. I'm running a lot of the shots at 150 fps which is six times slower than normal and looks fantastic when played back at normal speed of 25 fps. Bald eagles are now joining the bonanza, landing really close to the bears and grabbing any scraps of flesh they leave. As the bears get satiated they waste a lot of the salmon, taking just the fatty skin, the brains and eggs from the ripe fish.

This is the beginning of a salmon feast that may last for two months, as they need to put on as much fat as possible to prepare for hibernation in the autumn. The sows are usually the first to den and the last out, with their cubs, in the spring. The cubs are normally born in January, prematurely and only weighing half a kilo or so, but by the time they leave the den in May they will weigh seven kilos. Filming carries on well into the evening, the light is beautiful, low and soft, it's been a really productive day and it has gone 10 o'clock when we get to camp.

Waiting by the Riffles for the first salmon run

The next day brings another early start as we want to carry on where we left off. The weather is still good and we need to capitalise on the action. We set off at just after 10 o'clock and go straight to the Riffles, a shallow area in the river where the salmon are easily caught. There are far fewer salmon going through, maybe due to it being high tide, but Manny and her cubs are here, watching the river. Some of the visiting photographers have gone up to the Mikfik Falls and the word is that there are some salmon and bears up there, with some fish leaping the falls, something else to try in the next few days. More and more bears are appearing: the latest on the scene is Shultz, a four-year-old and quite funny to watch. He's very persistent in approaching Manny and her cubs, and she

Mandy with cubs

MP filming Mandy

launches a full charge against him, covering 100 metres in about 8 seconds and forcing him right away across the river. Strangely, she could have charged right through us but instead walked around us at a distance of about three metres and then launched the charge, proving herself to be a very considerate bear.

Mandy settles down to nurse the cubs and I get more close-up suckling shots. She's very confiding and I do feel safe around her, although it's weird to find myself so close to an 400 kg carnivore. The cubs begin to play, rolling on their backs with their little paws in the air, biting and tumbling. The whole thing is backlit and looks beautiful.

Roger has set up an underwater camera in the Riffles to get shots of fish swimming through and, hopefully, bears charging around after them. White, a 23-year-old female with two one-year-old cubs, walks downstream and right past the camera which Roger triggers with an infrared release. It could be a great shot.

The big problem with film, of course, is that you don't know until maybe four weeks after the event, when you're watching the rushes back in Bristol, whether or not it's all technically OK. This can be a bit nerve-racking. Video has changed all that, of course, offering instant playback.

It's late evening and time for our long plod back to camp, which is getting later each night. We celebrate our good day with a couple of beers, as we have fresh supplies arriving tomorrow, then it's a quick supper of freeze-dried chicken and vegetables before retiring to the comfort of my cosy tent at midnight.

The run of brilliant weather continues and we make hay while the sun shines. We concentrate more of our efforts upstream, near to Mikfik Falls, where there are impressive numbers of red salmon coming through. I'm able to get in position right next to the top of the falls, so that leaping fish are flying right past or landing in front of the lens, before powering through the shallows. More bears are appearing here now, but it's more difficult to film them, with lots of bushes and blind spots in hollows. We have to be careful, as bears sometimes sleep in amongst the bushes and accidents happen if they're surprised at close range.

One morning Roger and I are walking along one of the narrow tracks through the willow scrub when we hear something charging up behind us. We spin round to see 400 kg of bear charging at 30 km/h in our direction. It charges right past, almost bowling us over, followed seconds later by a similarly supercharged 400 kg bear in hot pursuit. Needless to say, we were left standing, mouths open in disbelief that we were still in one piece. With one bear intent on sorting out another, though, we might just as well have been invisible.

A bear with a fine, ripe salmon, its first catch of the day, at the upper Mikfik Falls

There's a lot of activity at the upper Mikfik Falls now, with hundreds of fish going through and lots of new bears turning up, a pair named Barney and McDougall going through pre-breeding courtship, then White with her cubs and Manny and Melody with their cubs. It's quite a gathering and they're having a long-drawn-out feast. Lots of fish are being wasted and the eagles are cashing in, too. Those wasted fish slip to the bottom of the pool at the base of the falls and there's an injured bear which can't catch live fish, but sits in the pool and scoops them off the bottom. We want to get the underwater camera into that pool, but with so many bears about, it's difficult. Eventually, Roger manages to scramble down the bank to the pool and get the camera in position: there are bears everywhere and he has to be in and out sharpish, as we don't want any nasty confrontations. The camera eventually produces a few shots which could be invaluable in cutting the fishing sequence together.

With this calm, warm weather the mosquitoes have become – if you'll forgive the pun - unbearable. I don't find repellent that effective and the best option is to wear clothing that the insects just can't penetrate, which of course can become very uncomfortable in warm conditions.

The next few days continue to be productive and we add steadily to all the sequences we need to tell the stories within the film. For a courtship sequence, we get a mating, which has never been filmed before, while we also catch feeding behaviour and tell the story of the various salmon species that migrate up these rivers to spawn.

By 17 June, the weather starts to break down and the warm sunny days are replaced with continuous strong winds, low cloud and rain. The shooting rate drops dramatically but I think we have most sequences quite well covered.

Because of the foul weather, Kachemak Air's Otter can't get in with provisions and we are very kindly invited to dinner by Colleen, Larry's wife, at their simple wooden cabin near the campsite. We chat a lot about bears and the problems they face, not least the hunters who think that they should be able to shoot them here. I tell Larry that of all the amazing wildlife spectacles I have filmed worldwide, this is one of the greatest, and that they should do everything in their power to protect it. When we leave, I make a dash for my tent, cosy with the little Yukon stove gently exuding sweet-smelling heat and the wind and rain beating on the canvas.

The next couple of days are bad, with continuous rain and wind. I spend time labelling up 30 cans of rushes. Some brave souls head up to the falls, but for us there's no point: you can hardly stand, let alone keep big lenses steady. Some of the campers have leaky tents and have to dry out their sleeping bags in the cook shack. I light up the stove in my tent and spend some time reading, while the rain and wind continues and starts to play havoc with the flight schedules. The Otter took off to come here but conditions were so bad that it had to turn back. There are a few of us in the same boat, as over the days there have been some interesting visitors here: quite a few photographers, some biologists and a chap from Vancouver who talks a lot about his terror of being attacked by bears. I wonder why he came.

It's getting to the point now where we have to think about getting out of here and there's no sign of the weather improving. I'm meeting up with my wife for a break in Seattle on 24 June and I have flights booked. Apparently the Otter tried to get here again yesterday, the pilot circled Mount Augustus for half an hour in the hope that low cloud and fog would clear, but it didn't and he had to turn back to Homer.

21 June: the weather looks better, but just in case the Otter can't make it again we book Windy's Air Service from King Salmon. The weather is better on that side and they're confident that they can get us out at about 3.30 p.m. We pack everything up ready for a flight and get it down to the beach. We're not leaving for good, as we're due back here on 14 July, with a special permit to visit the big falls on the McNeil River when the chum salmon have their main migration. Up to 60 bears could be at the falls then, so it's a very exciting prospect. It's already on my mind as we climb away into a clearing sky.

3 UNTANGLING THE KNOT, BELUGAS AND BEARS

The red knot, to most people, is one of those wonderful winter waders that swarm in great grey clouds across our wildest estuaries, like the Wash and Morecambe Bay. Few people see them in their rich chestnut breeding colours and even fewer see them on their high Arctic breeding grounds. I have been given the enviable task of filming them there. It will form an important sequence in a film about their remarkable migrations from South America to the high Arctic, entitled *Untangling the Knot*.

We have chosen the most northerly of their nesting locations, on Ellesmere Island in Arctic Canada, where they are being intensively studied by the Canadian Wildlife Service, and will be working from the Canadian radio communications base at Alert, right up in the northeast corner of the island. This 'island' is the tenth biggest in the world, 520 miles long and covering 75,000 square miles. From there, it's possible to see the coast of northwest Greenland, and the North Pole is only 500 miles to the north.

The journey into Alert is not an easy one. I meet up at Ottawa Airport with the two researchers with whom I will be filming: Dr Guy Morrison from the CWS and Dr Nick Davidson, a shorebird researcher from the UK. A jet takes us to Resolute Bay for at least one overnight, depending on Arctic weather, at the Polar Shelf station. This is a kind of clearing house and outfitters for polar researchers, scientists, explorers and the like, able to supply, from a huge warehouse, skidoos, skis, polar clothing, rifles, GPS systems, tents, cooking equipment, dried foods, anything and everything, in fact, that you might need to survive in this very remote region. Most people spend the night here to plan their onward journeys and get a handle on the weather for the coming days. We're fortunate to have hit a quiet spell and we are scheduled to fly out the next morning.

Having loaded up the Twin Otter aircraft, we're soon up and away into a clear Arctic sky, in fantastic flying conditions with exceptional visibility as we pass over a patchwork of ice, islands and clear blue leads of open water. Our only stop is at Eureka and we land into Alert at 2.30 p.m. The runway here is a dirt strip able to take flights of the huge C41 Galaxy transport planes. We are met by a pick-up truck which whisks us and our considerable amount of gear to our hut. It's more than adequate: we each have

Three red knot in summer plumage, feeding

a single room with a comfy bed and a washbasin. I like the feel of the place, and it's good to be in a very special and remote location and yet have home comforts to return to after a long, hard day in the field. We have dinner at 5.00 p.m. in the good-sized cafeteria with an enormous selection of hearty food. Working in these cold latitudes, you need to be well fed.

Our main mode of transport is going to be ATVs (all-terrain vehicles). These have been stored in a shed so it's time to get them out and have them checked over. We start them up and pump up the tyres. I've never ridden one before so Guy gives me some instruction on how to handle them. They seem very stable and the front and rear racks will enable me to carry my camera gear packed in protective cases.

Near to the base is a stream which pours out into a muddy bay, and the knot love it. There are three beautiful adult birds feeding there in full summer plumage, with rusty-red breast and belly and a spangled red-and-grey back. They are confiding and I'm able to get within 20 metres of them, close enough with the 600 mm lens to get good frame-filling images. These are good establishing shots and will help to build the sequence.

It's time to get back to base and prepare for tomorrow, when we're hoping to get out on the ATVs to do an extensive recce of the area. Knot at the nest is the key sequence that we are hoping for from this, their most northerly breeding area.

Later, as I am having supper with Nick, Guy appears, very excited. He has cannon netted a knot and a turnstone and fitted them both with radio-tracking devices. This is going to make our chances of finding a nest much greater; the shorebirds here nest in very low densities, probably less than one pair per square kilometre, so trying to find them by luck is almost impossible. They are superbly camouflaged and blend seamlessly with the red mosses and grey stony ground.

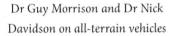

Dr Guy Morrison and Dr Nick
Davidson on all-terrain vehicles

MP on ATV with camera gear

On a crisp, sunny afternoon, we load up the ATVs and head off. It's 3°C. The terrain is rough going and we have to contend with rock fields, snow banks and rivers swollen with meltwater. Surprisingly, you can drive into a river and – most of the time – make it to the other side, as long as you keep the wheels turning. The purple saxifrage is in full bloom and the huge Arctic hares are very active and confiding. Nick and Guy check out an area where they found turnstones nesting last year and, sure enough, a bird is feeding in a small marsh nearby. We find the beautiful nest with four eggs and Nick and Guy manage to trap the adult at the nest and ring it.

The radio signals we're picking up from the few birds with radio transmitters turn out to be only from birds feeding. They could be off-duty nesting birds or non-breeders and it's not going to be easy to find a bird at the nest. We must, though, keep on trying. If Guy can fit more birds with transmitters, that should increase our chances of success. It's now 8.30 p.m. and we ought to be heading back, as we've come quite a distance and it will take nearly 90 minutes of rough riding to get home, crossing rivers of uncertain depth, traversing treacherous snow banks and descending rocky, rutted gullies streaming with icy water.

Coming off a snow bank at speed I lose control of the ATV and bury the front wheels in a drift, my Nikon camera flying into the air and whacking me on the forehead. It hurt a bit, but no great damage was done. We arrive back at base just before 10 p.m. and manage to get a much-needed steak supper from the canteen.

It's such a clear, sunny evening that I decide to make the most of it and venture out to the edge of the frozen sea, a jumble of massive pieces of ice forced into the air from pressure ridges. The air is so crystal clear that I can easily see the mountains of

Greenland, over 50 miles away, and the silence is eerie and absolute. Being alone out here is a strange feeling, in total quiet and endless space. I do some panning shots off the ice to reveal the base and its isolated position, with various details of aircraft and signage.

The next few days are exciting. We cover many miles over snow-covered hills and ridges and plunge through torrents of rushing meltwater, with the ATVs certainly living up to their name. We follow up signals from knot with radio transmitters, but none provide us with a steady signal that could indicate a sitting bird. We get lots of false alarms: a static signal comes in, we think, 'Yes, this is it!' then it starts to move again, showing that it's a feeding bird. We see lots of nests of fabulous Arctic birds in our far-ranging searches, but still no knot. We knew it wouldn't be easy with only one breeding bird per square kilometre and the terrain so difficult, and on some days we can't even get out as the arctic fog has rolled in.

Guy points the radio antennae across the tundra, blazing with coloured mosses and little arctic flowers. He has done this many times and picked up signals which have come to nothing. This time the signal is very distant and weak, right on the edge of the receiver's range, but it's steady: the wearer of this tiny transmitter appears to be static. We take a bearing and approach the signal cautiously. It starts to get stronger and it's still not moving. Closer still we go, and still it doesn't move. We dare to believe that this could be a sitting bird. The buzz from the transmitter indicates that we are very close, within metres, so we turn down the receiver and start to look intently to the ground. Wherever it is, we must almost be stepping on it. The ground is covered with red mosses and shattered grey stone, exactly the colours of the knot's plumage.

A mossy stream, typical nesting habitat for knot

A knot on its nest

A remote camera at a knot's nest

Then, bingo! Guy spots the sitting bird just a couple of metres from where we are standing, brilliantly blending into its surroundings. We're all so excited to be seeing this, the most northerly nesting red knot.

She doesn't leave the nest and we take lots of photographs of the bird sitting tightly. Guy then eases her gently away, as he needs to weigh and measure the eggs, this being a rare opportunity to gather important nest data. I prepare the film camera which, until now, has been carefully packed away on the ATV. I put on a wide-angle lens and a remote release, then place the camera just 12 inches from the nest, set against a stunning Arctic panorama. I feel the bird will come straight back to the nest with no fear of the camera, and we retreat to a distance of a few yards. Sure enough, within a minute she is back to the nest. I get great shots as she shuffles back onto the four eggs, the great expanse of Arctic tundra beyond. Over the next hour or so I pick up more shots on the zoom lens, close-ups of the eggs and of the bird settling down to incubate and turning the eggs, as well as beautiful details of her summer plumage. With all the other shots I have picked up – of knot feeding and away from the nest, Arctic scenics and other breeding species – I feel we have all the shots we need to tell the amazing story of the shorebird that breeds at the top of the world.

BELUGAS

As the Twin Otter aircraft approaches Cunningham Inlet in the Canadian Arctic, I can see, in the far distance, a tiny oblong strip. That can't be a runway? As we get closer, with the sea below choked with pack ice, I can see that it is, with a menacing cliff just below the touchdown point. The Otter is skillfully planted onto the runway with a firm thud, a roar of reverse thrust slowing the plane as it rapidly approaches the end of the runway, slewing to a halt in a cloud of dust and gravel.

I am here with an old friend and colleague of mine from my RSPB days, David Reed, to film a very special event: a unique gathering of beluga whales which assemble here at the inlet to moult their skin in the shallow waters. Thousands come here every year and it looks as if we have timed it just right. We have a local Inuit guide, Simeone, who will help us around camp and should provide some security from polar bears, though he only appears to have an ancient .303 rifle. Nearby is a very modern – and expensive – tented tourist camp and its owner, Peter Jess, is very kindly giving us logistical support in the way of ATVs and trailers to get our considerable amount of gear from the airstrip to our camp area. A fleet of these little go-anywhere four-wheelers soon have the job done and, while the camp is being erected on a hillside just 300 metres from the water, I grab the camera gear and get down to the edge of the inlet where the whales are gathered. The sun is shining and the behaviour is right there, just waiting to be filmed, so I have to grab it while I can: fog can come in for days on end. We have 24-hour daylight so I intend to make the most of it. I don't know how approachable the whales are, so while the instinct is to get as close as possible, I know that this could spook them, so go very cautiously at first. They are in very shallow water and vulnerable to attack by polar bears so I, too, have to keep an eye out.

The gravels on the river bed act as an abrasive and the old, peeling skin is removed by the action of the whales, rolling and rubbing on it. There are many hundreds of them here at present but numbers are dictated by tidal movements; as the tide drops, they head into deeper water or risk being stranded. As the tide comes back in, they slowly move into the water nearer to my filming position, the closest animals less than 50 metres away, thrashing and cavorting together in less than two metres of water.

Belugas in the shallows of Cunningham Inlet, rubbing off moulting skin on the stony bottom.

The waters of the Cunningham River are ten degrees warmer than the surrounding seas and produce a natural spa for the animals, which are here not only to moult but to nurse their young and socialise, too. They don't feed much in the inlet but go to the richer, colder waters of the nearby Northwest Passage to feed on squid, krill, octopus and Arctic char.

I've had a brilliant first day of filming and shot 2.5 rolls of film (25 mins) in good light, which could make a couple of minutes in the finished sequence. It's getting on for 7 p.m. so I trudge back to the camp which has sprung up on the hillside in my absence. David, the producer, has produced – people often ask what producers do – a hearty dinner of steak and mashed potatoes with tinned vegetables. It's a stunning, clear evening so I take more establishing shots looking across the inlet from camp. The whales are very vocal, producing a variety of singing calls, trumpeting, bugling and whistling, making a fantastic end to a memorable day. It's clouded over now so I don't feel too bad about finishing filming at 10.30 p.m. All I have left to do is fire up the mini-generator, get batteries charged for tomorrow and reload the film magazines before curling up in my sleeping bag. I hope, as I drift off to sleep, that no polar bears are wandering about.

Next morning is dull and overcast so, to start with, there's no chance of filming. After breakfast we take a stroll to look for other possible viewpoints and marvel at the tiny arctic flowers now in profusion. By early afternoon the cloud is rolling away so it's action stations with the camera gear, down to the water's edge. The tide is pushing the animals close inshore, with one particular adult, which seems very confiding, swimming with its head above water, a youngster in tow. I get

Our camp on the Cunningham Inlet

some great shots using my 600 mm lens, with the head filling the frame, which is always a useful shot for cutaways when editing the sequence. Being white, the beluga is inconspicuous in the sea ice, making it difficult for their main predators – orcas and polar bears – to spot them. Instead of a dorsal fin, which would get damaged under the ice, they have just a bony ridge capable, along with the large head, of breaking through ice 8 cm thick.

There are big numbers of belugas in the river mouth, too, so I can get impressive establishing shots, and the sequence is really starting to take shape. There is so much action: tail flukes and heads out of the water, even some breaching, which I shoot in slow motion at 75 fps. Some of the females have young calves with them which, typically, are dark grey, not turning white for six years.

Sadly, the next couple of days bring more typical high-Arctic weather – heavily overcast, cool and windy. I've been so lucky to have had two days with sunshine. While filming in these murky conditions is possible, it won't give me any usable images, so I have to be patient and hope for a change. We spend our time watching the belugas' behaviour, taking sound recordings and making sure that we're ready to start filming as soon as the sun reappears. The tide is receding, a change in the wind direction has brought sea ice into the shallows, and every single beluga has disappeared. They've retreated to the safety of deeper water, as the grinding of the ice on the gravel bottom can interfere with their sonar, preventing them from detecting a polar bear entering the channel.

Above: MP filming belugas

Right: A very confiding beluga

By 5 p.m. on 31 July the sun has started to break through so, at last, after two days of frustration, I can start to film again. The ice has retreated and the whales are drifting closer as the tide fills the shallows. The great thing about these spectacles is that this is behaviour happening at close quarters, repeated many times over, making it possible to shoot sequences in a short time. The nearest whales are less than 20 metres away, with many hundreds in the background, giving me great establishing shots. We use a stepladder to get a high-angle shot of the big numbers near to shore then, as squalls cross the inlet, fantastic rainbows complete the scene. In the clear arctic air I can see, to the north across Barrow Strait, Cornwallis Island and Resolute Bay. As the evening approaches the rain showers become more persistent, so we head back to camp and another 'boil in the bag' supper.

David has spoken with Bazil, our logistics man back at Resolute Bay, and the decision is to pull us out tomorrow because of deteriorating weather conditions, but fortunately, despite some bad weather days, I think we have a good sequence. The Twin otter is coming at 2 p.m. so we will have to pack up camp in the morning. The bad news is that we'll have to spend four days in Resolute, as we can't get on the flight out of there to Cambridge Bay on Wednesday, and the next one isn't until Saturday. At least we may be able to pick up some background material on the coast there.

1st August is dull and cloudy but dry, so after a quick breakfast we start to take down the camp and pack away all the gear. The fleet of ATVs from the camp are kindly made available to take everything down to the airstrip and, just after 2 o'clock, we see the Otter on its final approach. There's a strong crosswind so the pilot really has to 'crab' the plane in, coming to a rapid stop after touchdown. The pilot refuels the plane from 50-gallon drums, we quickly get our gear aboard and say our goodbyes. After a very short take-off we're up and away over the inlet and flying through thick fog, coming out on the other side to a blue sky before landing in Resolute Bay. I don't think killing time here will be too much of a hardship: there are arctic flowers in profusion, nesting shorebirds and wonderful vistas of floating, sculpted ice.

SVALBARD: POLAR BEARS AND ARCTIC FOXES

Most people, if asked, would have little knowledge of Svalbard, formerly named Spitzbergen by the Dutch. Where is it and who does it belong to? It lies halfway between Norway and the North Pole, the most northerly settlement in the world with a permanent civilian population of little over 2,000, and is actually part of the kingdom of Norway. Originally the first settlers came in the 17th and 18th centuries to establish whaling stations and to hunt walrus, followed by coal-mining operations by Russia and Norway at the beginning of the 20th century. Coal mining is still taking place but the main industries nowadays are Arctic research and tourism, with wildlife one of the biggest attractions. Polar bears especially are found here in large numbers, with around 250 inhabiting the coasts, but as many as ten times that number in the Barents Sea region.

I came to Svalbard in 2001, not to film polar bears – though they did feature in our lives, as we'll see – but to film seabirds for a David Attenborough series called The Life of Mammals. I had been charged with getting a difficult sequence on the guillemots which nest on the high cliffs of the island of Svalbard. These are not normal cliff-nesters, in that – due to rising land levels – the nesting cliff is now one kilometre from the sea. Young guillemots leaving the nest are forced to glide this distance down to the ocean, with any that fall short picked off by patrolling Arctic foxes. It's quite a challenge to film, especially as the cliff is several hundred feet high.

Jason Roberts is based in the capital of Longyearbyen and has helped many cameramen with logistical support and expertise, so I felt safe and confident in his hands. After a night at his base in town, we set off next morning in his small boat, packed to the gunnels with all of our food and filming gear for the next 17 days. It's rough as we travel down the big fjord to the ocean, the boat slamming over the crests into the troughs of the short, steep sea. We are fully kitted up in survival suits so feel nothing of the icy spray crashing over us, though my back is feeling the effects. As we get on to the open sea, things calm down a little, with much gentler but bigger waves. It's a 3.5 hour journey even at 15–20 knots, following the stunningly beautiful coastline to our very remote cabin on the coastal plain. It's gone 10 p.m. as we unload our mass of gear onto the steep shingle beach, with a lot to do yet – it's over 250 metres up to the cabin.

Jason accesses the polar bear damage

Jason is first to the cabin and confirms the fear that had formed from afar: it's been trashed by polar bears, which have apparently done the same to other cabins along the coast. Ours looks as if a bomb has exploded inside, with shattered glass everywhere (they came in through the window), cupboards torn open in the search for food and the place an absolute mess. Everything has to be taken outside and cleaned before we can begin to reassemble the cabin and get our gear safely stowed. The cabin is small, slightly bigger than the average garden shed, with a tiny loft in which I elect to sleep, given that we may get a return visit from our white furry friends. Jason sleeps downstairs with the arsenal of firearms: first line of defence a flare pistol, followed by a .45 magnum pistol and a .350 rifle. It's 5 a.m. by the time we get to bed and I'm shattered.

Reindeer bull feeding on mosses and lichens   *Snow bunting feeding a fledgling*

It's 1.15 p.m. before I emerge into bright sunlight the next day. Jason is staying in his bunk feeling unwell with a flu-type bug. I make coffee on the little coal-fired stove and sit on the step outside, soaking up the grandeur of this spectacular spot. We're surrounded by glaciers and, nearby, the diminutive Svalbard reindeer are feeding on mosses and lush arctic grasses. These are the smallest of all the reindeer and, at around 80 kg, only about half the weight of a caribou. They have very thick winter coats to withstand the harsh arctic winter and are possibly the most northerly of all herbivorous mammals. A dapper male snow bunting is collecting insects from a nearby marsh to feed to its young while a parasitic skua, nesting just outside our cabin, seems to take great delight in trying to smack us on the back of the head at every opportunity.

The seabird cliff behind our cabin, with nesting guillemots

The seabird mountain rears up behind the cabin and it's just possible to see the hordes of auks crammed onto the precipitous ledges. There are no youngsters coming off the ledges yet, which is good news, as it gives us time to recce the area and find out where the foxes have their dens and how approachable they are. We'll also have the chance to build up the background shots to make the sequence. By evening, Jason is feeling slightly better and at about 10 p.m. – it's virtually 24-hour daylight at this time of year – we go for a walk along the base of the scree slope. This is where tens of thousands of little auks nest under the boulders. They are perched all over the rocks and at the approach of a glaucous gull will all take flight, circling around in great waves at high speed and flying right past us. These massive gulls, along with the Arctic fox, seem to be a major predator of the auks and can quite easily take one on the wing and swallow it whole. I was quite shocked the first time I saw it but soon became used to what seemed to be a daily occurrence. It was hardly going to affect the auk's colossal numbers.

As we sit in this cauldron of activity, a few guillemot chicks are leaving the ledges for the most dangerous flight of their young lives. They are accompanied by three or four adults, offering protection from the gulls as they glide down to the sea. We hear the eerie sound of barking foxes in the still arctic night: they, like us, are waiting for the big event.

Back at the cabin by 1 a.m., Jason cooks up some fish and vegetables, just what we need after sitting out in the chill evening. We chat awhile then turn in about an hour later. I'm woken by loud screams after just a couple of hours: a polar bear has tried to get in to the cabin through the window, right where Jason is sleeping. He slaps the window and shouts, and it runs away. I look through the tiny gable-end window and see the family of mother and two massive cubs ambling away, and shout down to Jason that they have gone. It's a good job we nailed down the window, as the bear could have jumped right through, with horrendous consequences for Jason. After this traumatic event I have real difficulty in getting back to sleep, and think that every little sound might mean that the bears are back.

The next few days are frustratingly quiet. The weather is cool (4.5°C) and overcast, with very little happening with the auks and foxes. The polar bear family have been active, trashing other cabins along the coast. Camp Bell and the Governor's cabins have had the windows broken in, so we clear them up as best we can and nail the shutters back up. In the evenings we keep an eye on the colonies for any signs of action, but there is just a trickle of chicks leaving the cliffs, and nothing worth filming yet.

The cabin is very cosy, with the little Jotul stove loaded with coal which we brought with us. The long days are spent reading, keeping my diary up-to-date and watching for the start of any activity. We are beginning to crave company. A Dutch sailing ship, the *Noorderlicht* (North Light) has just gone around the glacier where our boat is moored. Jason knows some of the crew from previous visits and calls them up on the VHF. They are going to anchor in the bay and probably come to visit in the morning for coffee, which is something to look forward to.

26 July is another dull and windy morning so we don't emerge from our cabin till gone midday. The visitors from the *Noorderlicht* come by mid-afternoon. They're mostly Dutch but some are German or English, and are on a wildlife cruise around Svalbard for ten days or so. It's great to chat and hear about their experiences on the cruise. We are invited back to the ship this evening for dinner, which we gratefully accept, and set off just before 6 o'clock.

It's an hour's walk along the coast to where the ship is anchored, and on the way we see beautiful arctic flowers, poppies and saxifrages and a purple sandpiper which is nesting nearby. It is wonderful to see these waders on their breeding grounds in full summer plumage. As we approach the ship, the first mate comes out in a zodiac to pick us up, and as we draw near I realize how big the vessel is, probably 25 metres long and made of steel. We board via a ladder onto the beautiful teak deck with a huge traditional ship's wheel. I stand behind it for a few moments and try to imagine what it would be like to sail this ship in stormy seas. We go below and have a very pleasant evening before the mate drops us back on the coastal plain for the hour's walk back, spent hoping that we don't meet any bears. It's drizzling with rain, overcast, breezy and, happily, uneventful, and our tiny cabin is still warm, as we stoked up the stove before leaving. We watch for any sign of activity with jumping guillemots but still there's nothing, the weather is becoming slightly depressing and we retire to our sleeping bags, hoping for better things tomorrow.

Tomorrow, though, brings nothing better. It's another disappointing morning so we don't emerge until gone half past eleven. We take a long walk after breakfast towards where our boat is moored by the tidewater glacier, watching tugs manoeuvre a massive coal ship, which makes a change from the daily monotony of dull, overcast weather with nothing to film.

As we walk back, at around 8.30 p.m., we see a fox along the bird cliff and a few guillemots gliding down to the sea. We count six that make it but one that doesn't quite. He crash-lands on the grass, then scrambles down a low cliff and into the sea where he instinctively dives. Sadly, when he resurfaces, he is spotted by glaucous gulls and that's the end of his short little life.

It's 28 July and, although it's overcast, the wind has gone. By lunchtime it's beginning to look more promising, with blue sky to the north. The winds have been from the northeast but have now swung west – a good sign. We decide it's worth the big trek up to the seabird cliffs on the mountain, so all the film gear and some food is packed into rucksacks and we set off at 3.30 p.m. It's a long, hard slog up to the boulder scree where the little auks' nests are hidden, tens of thousands of them, then up again, steeper still, to the precipitous cliffs where the auk colonies are. We find a flattish

spot from which we can look across to the nesting ledges packed with guillemots and kittiwakes. At last, we have sunshine and something to film.

I'm able to position myself to get establishing shots of the packed ledges, with mountains and glaciers in the distance and groups of guillemot chicks almost ready to make the shortest, most important flight of their lives: the 1,000 metres from this cliff to the sea. We spot an Arctic fox nearby and I manage to grab a couple of shots of it, as it looks longingly at the masses of birds above it. Then we see cubs appear – there must be a den – so we quickly pack away the gear and head down to the spot. The female barks at us and we soon find the den entrance. This is fantastic, as it should give us good opportunities to get shots of the female returning with auk carcasses, important for building up the sequence.

As it's getting late and we've lost the light, we decide to leave all the gear here, burying it under rocks so that the foxes can't get to it. Jason takes us down a different, rather dramatic and precipitous route. We pass a glaucous gull nest with two large chicks and see a barnacle goose with a large gosling as we pick our way down a ridge, through huge numbers of nesting little auks, onto the coastal plain. As we walk, we hear a whimpering sound from a hole among the rocks, and see another fox's den. There are feathers and bits of bird all over the place, so we retreat to 50 metres and sit quietly. Sure enough, within five minutes, a cub emerges and goes down into some other rocks. This is going to be very useful: it's so much closer and easier to get to than the den up the mountain. It's been a good day – we have some establishing footage of the auks, a few cutaways of foxes and a den with cubs to work with.

The following two days, though, are hopeless for filming, with continuous low cloud and drizzle. We manage to do some sound recording by the fox den and the little auk colony, and decide that we have to make the arduous climb up the scree to recover the gear. It's 12.30 p.m. when we get going, pausing frequently to wonder at the masses of little auks zooming around us at high speed. Reaching the cache of film gear, which is thankfully all intact, we get a little hazy sunshine and I'm able to film more scenics and some behaviour of the auks on the ledge. We sit at a safe distance from the fox den but get no sign of the cubs, and pack everything up for the treacherous descent. At least now I have enough footage and, with luck, we may not need to come up here again. After a short break at the cabin, I repack the gear for a foray down to the sea cliffs, where a few guillemots are making the flight to the sea. Glaucous gulls are patrolling. Unbelievably, one takes a chick and swallows it in mid-air, even though the parents are flying alongside. Another is caught in mid-air, dropped, then caught again and eventually dropped for a second time into the sea, where two gulls have a tug of war with it. I manage to get a few shots and we do see a fox making off with a chick, but it's too far away to film. What little sun there was has disappeared behind the mountain. It's a slow business at the moment: we have just about a week to go and haven't achieved a lot yet, although a couple of days of decent weather and intense activity could change all that. In this game, you have to remain optimistic. It's back to the cabin for a late steak supper and we turn in at about 1 a.m.

We are woken mid-morning by a helicopter landing nearby, carrying workers to repair polar bear damage at the Governor's cabin, just along the coast from here. While there is good light I go down to the sea cliff to do establishing shots and also to film the little herd of Svalbard reindeer that are confiding and in a good situation. It's possible to frame the herd with the seabird mountain behind them, and also looking across the ocean to distant mountains and glaciers. This is all helping to build the sequence, putting our main animals – the auks, foxes and gulls – into context.

A group of reindeer

Bombarded en route by the nesting pomarine skuas , I head back to the cabin for a snack and a repack of the gear and Jason and I set off for the fox den near the little auk colony. We need to make the best of this sunny spell. As we get close to the den, a cub is out exploring, so I set up the gear quickly at a safe distance (about 10–15 metres). Within a few minutes another two cubs come out and I manage to film some useful play fighting.

Jason spots the adult female coming back with a dead guillemot but she disappears among the rocks before I can film her. The weather has socked in again – it's cloudy with a cold wind – though it's been a useful afternoon. I've shot ten minutes on the foxes, and although it's nothing spectacular they are definitely cute. I need some 'meat' now: bringing in a guillemot for the cubs, stashing it, or something similar.

We're back at the cabin just after 6 p.m. It's a miserable evening and we light our little Jokul stove which soon has the tiny cabin cosy. After dinner we take a stroll to the beach and collect driftwood, which we stack at the top of the beach for collection by snowmobile later in the winter. We head off to check the foxes, but there's no action and hardly any birds coming off the ledges. The weather is still atrocious so we head back to the cabin by 11.15 p.m. Time is beginning to run short and the weather forecast for tomorrow is not good, but there's nothing we can do about that, or about anything.

As forecast, it turns out to be another depressingly miserable day. We read, chat and eat to pass the time. This is a very remote place – we are more than 50 miles from the nearest habitation – and it feels all the more isolated with the rain pouring down outside. We peer out periodically to see if anything is flying down to the sea but,

Arctic fox cubs outside their den

fortunately, nothing is. The day passes slowly and it's a relief when bedtime comes. After all, tomorrow could be the day.

We are awoken mid-morning by powerful sunshine streaming through the tiny window. In great excitement we hurriedly put together our packs with film gear and some food and head off to the Arctic fox den. After setting up the camera with the 50-300 zoom lens, about ten metres from the den, it's not long before the action starts. Cubs cautiously emerge and begin exploring and playing together, giving us some really useful material, and then, just after lunchtime, the female comes in with a guillemot chick. I get approach shots as she picks her way carefully through the rocks. She passes the plump chick to a cub, but – frustratingly – right behind a huge rock, so I miss that one. I do get the cub running off with it, then the female setting off again over the scree. Building up the shots to tell a story is a slow process, and a matter of remembering which shots you do have and bearing in mind what you still need to get.

Within an hour or so the female is back with another auk, and this time I miss the approach but do get the pass-over to the cub, which ties in with the previous visit. She digs up a cached auk and passes it to another cub, which runs off with it to prevent its siblings from stealing it. The female sets off again across the little auk scree, a lovely wide-angle shot in the late afternoon light with the auks all zooming around her as she picks her way across the rocks down towards the beach. I don't see her for the rest of the afternoon but there is plenty of action at the den. The cubs are more used to my presence now and are out, playing and exploring, beautiful in the low evening sunshine. I've shot more film in the last six hours than I've shot in the past six days.

By 7 p.m. the light has gone off the steep mountainside so we head down to the coastal plain, as we think tonight could be good for the birds leaving the ledges. I set up the tripod and camera with the 600 mm lens, by a group of rocks for cover, in the middle of the guillemots' flight path to the sea. Jason goes back to the cabin for more film stock and extra food, as it could be a long night. It's not long before the first birds are gliding down overhead, chicks accompanied by three or four adults. Most make it safely straight onto the sea, while others land short and have to run to the cliff edge. They hesitate briefly, then flutter off, crashing onto the beach and dashing to the sea. They start to call loudly and are soon joined by patrolling adults who seem to act as 'minders', crashing in alongside the chicks and discouraging the marauding glaucous gulls from attacking them. In fact, the gulls are barely bothering: they must have eaten a few already and are satiated, unlike the foxes, with hungry families to feed back at the den, which will kill as many as they can and cache them for leaner times. Any birds that don't make it are killed first, with the fox running around and picking them up later. I film one which is running with two chicks and an adult packed into its tiny jaw. When a chick falls short, the adult will land with it to give it protection but sometimes, before they can take off, the fox will kill them both.

The next couple of hours are very productive. I get shots of adults and young overhead as they glide to the sea, then young that have fallen short and are scrambling for their tiny lives over the cliff and into the relative safety of the sea. Big groups of adults and young in rafts are all calling and encouraging others to join them, because there's safety in numbers. The fox is very busy; I get ample shots of it running around in pursuit of fallen birds, then picking up ones it killed earlier and burying them in the rocks at the base of the little auk colony. The final shot is of the fox picking up three birds that it crams at one go into its jaws. I follow it as it heads toward the scree and manage to keep it sharp for about 15 seconds, which isn't easy on a 600 mm lens with the subject running away from you. Eventually, it disappears behind a large boulder and provides me with a natural end to the shot.

It's gone 11 p.m., we've been out for 12 hours and decide to call it a day, especially as the cloud has rolled in. Back at the cabin we light the stove and get the kettle on for a hot drink. I unload all the exposed film magazines, make rushes notes on what has been shot and prepare for tomorrow's filming.

3rd August is miserable; a grey, misty, cold and drizzly day, the highlight of which is a passing cruise ship. Jason knows a couple of people who work on it and we get the chance to top up our supplies of frozen meat, coffee and Cokes. The remainder of the day passes slowly. We've only three days left now and could do with at least one more good filming session.

The following day is equally foul so we stay in our sleeping bags till midday. I become aware of movement outside and peer out through my little gable-end window to see all the reindeer charging towards our cabin. I don't see anything that could have spooked them so I get back into my sleeping bag. I feel uneasy, though, and get the feeling that something is outside. Again I look through my little window and there, just outside the cabin, are two huge polar bears. I thump the floor urgently to alert Jason, who's sleeping below. 'Bears outside!' I scream. There's much commotion as Jason pulls on his trousers and grabs the flare pistol and revolver. We know it's a family of three but we don't see a third bear so Jason slides back the little square trapdoor and peers out. There, tearing into our rubbish bag, is the other bear. The mother and one of these very large cubs have gone across towards the Governor's cabin, so the cub can't see them, and it starts to roar very loudly. They eventually join up and amble off in the direction of the fox den, before settling to sleep on the hillside. Our heart rates eventually return to normal.

The rest of the day is miserable so, to prevent cabin fever, we venture out in the early evening. It looks as if the bears have moved on but we carry the flare pistol and revolver to give us a little security. We see a purple sandpiper in its beautiful summer plumage, its large young feeding in a boggy stream.

We again collect driftwood from the beach and stack it high up on the shore. Jason will move it up to the cabins with his snowmobile in wintertime. On our way back we see a small group of 18 barnacle geese resting on the coastal strip. There are no youngsters with them so they could be failed breeders or young adults that haven't bred. These are the ones that winter on the Solway Firth in Scotland, over 1,500 km away. Polar bears will take the eggs of barnacle geese where they are accessible on the cliffs; in fact, because the bears are getting less food in the summer, with less ice around from which to hunt seals, they go to greater lengths to reach the nests that they normally would not bother with. This is not good news for the barnacle goose colonies.

Jason by the cabin

There's no sign of any guillemots jumping, the weather is still foul and windy and it's after 9 p.m. when we get back to our remote little cabin. We light up the stove for comfort and Jason produces a magnificent meal using our newly-acquired ingredients. We drink coffee and chat for the rest of the evening and, as we turn in for the night, we can see through the gloom and mist that there has been light snowfall on top of the seabird cliffs.

We are rudely awakened at 4.30 a.m: the bears are back. The mother and one cub are visible out front and the other cub is in the rubbish sack again. Jason fires a flare that explodes just in front of the cub and it runs like mad to join the others. Frightened, they all charge off in the direction of the Governor's cabin. We eventually get up mid-morning as the skies are beginning to brighten, and wonder if the weather might be improving at last.

After a hasty breakfast I get my filming gear together. There's a good group of reindeer out front so I get some great establishing shots with the seabird cliffs beyond. We're going up to the fox den and have to pass through gullies and dead ground where the bears could be laid up. We make sure to talk loudly and are carrying our firearms as we pick our way through the boulder-strewn slopes where the little auk colony is; we spot the three bears just disappearing around the distant point beyond the colony and away, hopefully for good.

The weather is good now, so I spend a very productive hour or so getting great slow-motion flight shots of the little auks. They are very approachable so I am able to get really detailed shots of them on the rocks as they court and preen. We press on up to the fox den, and the cubs are soon out playing and enjoying the late afternoon sunshine. I get lovely shots of them cavorting and chasing each other in the grass as they become backlit by the low evening light.

Looking across the sound with glaciers emptying to the sea

It's time to move down to the coastal plain. Conditions are building for a productive evening, the wind has dropped, it's sunny and the guillemots are flying to the sea. I set up in my usual position behind a cluster of rocks and very soon have birds overhead. I concentrate on these shots first, the chicks accompanied by adults gliding to relative safety on the sea. I then change tack and move to shots of the crash-landers and the ensuing drama: running to the sea, many make it with the protection of a parent, then those that don't are efficiently killed by the patrolling foxes. It's a dramatic evening with lots of action. It's sad to see the chicks get killed, but of course there is nothing you can do to interfere. The main thing is that the vast majority do make it and will return here to breed themselves in the years ahead. The sun disappears behind the seabird mountain just before 11 p.m. so we head back to the cabin. By the time we have sorted camera gear, eaten and made notes it's 1 a.m. again.

We're up at 9 o'clock after a disturbed night: Jason's friend Louis, an eider farmer, called at 2.30 a.m. for a coffee. He was on his way home by boat to Akseloya Island (in Bellsund) where he has a cabin and stayed for 90 minutes. I didn't get up.

It's a fabulous morning, calm and sunny, the sea is glassy and the distant glaciers are sparkling. This is one of the most pristine places on earth and today it is spectacular. This is our last full day and we need to start to prepare for leaving in case of a dramatic change in the weather. We get some of the gear that we don't need again down to the beach, I go to get water from the stream, chop kindling wood for the winter then sweep out the cabin. After lunch we head off for a last session with the foxes, but the distant clatter of helicopter blades breaks the arctic silence and a heavy Bell chopper hovers and lands nearby. We go over and chat with various officials from the Governor's office, who are looking for the three problem bears. Apparently they smashed their way into Louis' cabin on the island while he was in town, wrecking his radio, equipment and furniture. The officials kindly offer Jason a lift over to the tidewater glacier where our boat is anchored, so he can bring it back to our beach for the night, which will save us time later.

I go to the fox den for a last session and get more useful shots in the early evening light. This seems to be the time when they are most active. Jason comes up at around 7 p.m., having safely repositioned the boat. A last couple of hours on the coast in clear, sunny conditions produce more useful action shots of the guillemots as they run the gauntlet of the foxes and gulls, and I now feel that we have a good sequence of this unique behaviour. Louis arrives just as we are packing up to go back to the cabin, very upset by the bears having trashed his home.

As Jason cooks dinner, Louis produces a bottle of whisky which we all share, and try to give him some moral support at this difficult time. It's gone midnight when we finish our meal and now face the horrendous task of packing everything and getting it the 400 metres to the beach and into the boat. It's 4 a.m. by the time we've cleared the cabin and packed the boat, and I say my goodbyes to what has been my little home in the Arctic for the last 16 days.

It's a stunning, flat calm and sunny morning as we set off across the bay to Akseloya Island. Wherever I look, I see seabirds scattered across the glassy ocean, the glaciers sparkling in the distance. Louis lives in the most idyllic spot: Arctic terns are nesting in his backyard, a huge and dramatic sea cliff rears up behind the island with nesting puffins, Brünnich's guillemots and kittiwakes, but what a mess the bears have made of his island home. They have ripped through the timber walls like paper, torn apart cans of chainsaw oil that were stored on shelves, drenching the whole crop of eider down, ruining it all. Louis, who's not been a well man recently, is almost suicidal. I go outside for a while to photograph the Arctic terns that are scolding me overhead, leaving Jason to have a quiet and reassuring chat with Louis. We reluctantly say our goodbyes and head off at 30 knots over the still, glassy water, though it gets progressively rougher as we head toward Isfjorden radio station where we stop for a much-needed coffee. Jason seems to know everyone hereabouts, which is certainly useful.

The last leg is up the fjord to Longyearben, and I'm really tired now as we have been on the go for 24 hours. Jason tells me I have been sleeping even though, coming up the fjord, the boat was doing 41 knots over a short, choppy sea. We arrive safely at the dock at 10.30 a.m., having travelled at 30–40 knots for over three hours on a not-always-calm sea in an open boat, blasted by freezing arctic spray: not a trip for the faint-hearted. We unload all the gear, reload it into Jason's truck and head up to his warehouse in town, a treasure house full of all the kit needed for Arctic travel in winter: skidoos, skis, tents, stoves, firearms, special clothing and boots. After storing all my considerable amount of gear, Jason takes me up to the local hotel where I sleep from 1.30 p.m. to 8 p.m. We have a late evening meal followed by a few drinks in a rowdy pub full of mining engineers, with a walk back to the hotel in the midnight sunshine providing a fitting end to my time in this memorable part of the Arctic.

4 IN SEARCH OF BIRDS OF PARADISE

The birds of paradise are a rare family of just 42 species, found mainly on the island of New Guinea. Until recently, very few of them had been seen or studied and certainly hardly any had been filmed or photographed. David Attenborough had filmed birds of paradise in black-and-white with cameraman Charles Lagus back in the 1950s and it had always been a great ambition of his to return to New Guinea to film these beautiful creatures in colour, and with more powerful lenses than were available back then.

The idea for this ambitious project was put forward in 1993 to the BBC Natural History Unit in Bristol by Sir David and producer Paul Reddish. The plan was to shoot a 50-minute film using two cameramen based in different regions of the island, each working with a specialist on birds of paradise. Due to the very difficult nature of the terrain and the secretive behaviour of the birds, it was calculated that each cameraman would need four months in the field to produce the footage required. It would be impossible to cover all of the species, so it was decided that up to eight each would be a realistic target.

I was thrilled to be chosen as one of the cameramen for this exciting project, along with Richard Kirby, a Bristol-based cameraman. I'd be working with Phil Hurrell, a specialist on the birds of southeast Asia and an experienced tree climber, while Richard would be working with David Gibbs, a very experienced tropical birder with a great knowledge of New Guinea and its birds. My first trip of two months would be to Irian Jaya (now West Papua), the Indonesian western side of the island of New Guinea. Arriving at Manchester airport on 12 September 1994 with 16 cases of equipment was just the beginning of a very long journey. As usual, all the gear had to be checked by Customs and the carnets stamped to verify that all was in order. All checked through to Jakarta, via London and Singapore, and that was the last I'd see of it until I arrived.

I'm due to meet up with Richard at London Heathrow for the flight to Singapore and, boarding the flight at 1.15 p.m. for a 2 p.m. take-off, I am a little concerned that there's no sign of him. Eventually, just fifteen minutes before we are due to leave, he appears in the aisle of the aircraft with a heavily strapped wrist; he fell through a glass door at home and had to go to hospital for eight stitches. The twelve-hour flight passes quickly enough, as our different filming schedules give us plenty to talk about. After three hours in Singapore we have a short flight to Jakarta, arriving there at 2.30 p.m. local time and feeling totally shattered. We are met by our local fixers, who have smoothed the Customs process, and we have our 38 cases of filming, camping and climbing equipment. We overnight in Jakarta, a hot, dusty and chaotic city, but we're staying in a real oasis of cool and calm at the President Hotel. It's just what we need, but there's still a lot to do before we see our first bird of paradise.

Our journey to the first filming site has only just begun, and today we have meetings with a Mr Akai and the rather inauspiciously named Mr No No to discuss permits and where we are allowed to travel. By early evening, all is settled and a 40-seater bus arrives to take us and our 38 cases of gear through the chaos that is Jakarta to the airport. We have flights overnight to Jayapura via Ujung Padang in Sulawesi, then another 2.5 hours on to Biak, finally arriving in Jayapura at 7 a.m. local time.

Jayapura is a stinking, hot, humid and frenetic place on the northeast coast of West Papua, very close to the border with Papua New Guinea. One box containing our film has not arrived, but a few enquiries by Mr No No who, we suspect, carries a fair bit of weight, recovers it within half an hour. En route we dropped Richard and all his gear at Biak so are now down to about 18 cases. Somehow we manage to squeeze into two taxis for the short trip to the hotel.

We are only 30 miles from Genyem, which will be our first camp, and have just a few more things to attend to. Wildlife filming is quite a complex logistical exercise. Mr No No goes off to sort out more permits with the police, while Phil goes up to Wamena to pick up climbing gear from another location: some of the species we will be filming display 50 metres above the ground. I'm feeling the effects of jet lag and a whole night of short-hop flights and after consuming the foulest cup of coffee ever – too strong, too sweet and too much – I fall fast asleep and don't wake until 4 p.m., six hours later. Phil is back from Wamena and we spend the evening shopping for our basic groceries: rice, noodles, tuna, sardines, crackers, jam and the like. I'm afraid that, for the next two months, fresh milk and muesli will be things of the past.

Today is the day we may see our first birds of paradise so, cramming the gear into two taxis, we're off. Although it's only 8 o'clock, it's roasting hot, with clear blue skies. We are stopped at an army check point, but Mr No No smooths the way, and at Genyem village we have to check in at the police station. This takes quite a while and involves yet more paperwork. At the end of it all we are allocated a policeman, ostensibly for our security, but possibly to keep an eye on us. We note that he carries a sidearm. We have yet more calls to make but, most importantly of all, we have to pick up Jamil, our local bird finder. These guys are invaluable – they know the area so well and can lead the way to display areas which we could take days to find, if we ever did. Finally, after picking up our cook and yet another police stop, we arrive at our campsite, an old sawmill on the edge of the forest. There's a disused building where our entourage will all sleep while, some distance away –we know how noisy Indonesians can be – Phil and I erect a tarpaulin, under which we pitch our tents without the flysheets. It'll be much cooler and, if it rains, the tarp will keep us dry.

This is a great base. The nearest birds of paradise are just ten minutes from here, and all around are beautiful, exotic bird species that we have never seen before – Blyth's hornbill, yellow-faced mynahs, red-cheeked parrots, orange-bellied fruit doves and the rufous-bellied kookaburra.

When, in the mid-19th century, Alfred Russell Wallace first approached the shores of West Papua, he wrote, 'that he could barely contain his excitement knowing that those dark forests produced the most extraordinary and the most beautiful of the feathered inhabitants of the earth'. I think that is the way I'm feeling now, having caught glimpses of these mysterious and elusive species.

West Papua is still covered by some of the largest tracts of pristine forest on earth, outside Amazonia. First sighted by the Portuguese in 1526, the huge island of New Guinea is second in size only to Greenland. It exhibits huge ecological diversity: in just 100 km, the land rises from the humid mangroves and peat swamp forests of the coast through impenetrable rain and moss forests up to the open alpine grasslands and jagged snow- capped summits of the Jayawijaya Mountains at over 4,700 metres (15,000 ft), the highest peaks between the Andes and the Himalayas.

Lowland rain forest in West Papua

The isolating effect of the rugged terrain has resulted in a cultural and linguistic diversity unparalleled on earth. Here, 0.1% of the earth's population speaks 15% of the known languages. Early Dutch colonial influence barely extended beyond the immediate vicinity of the coast, vast areas remaining totally unknown until the mid-20th century. Most of the tribes, especially those of the Highlands, were not contacted by outsiders until the 1930s or later, and even today some are still unknown to Westerners. Despite the efforts of missionaries and the Indonesian Government to 'civilise' tribes, they remain largely as they were before the arrival of outside influences. There are still stories of cannibalism and we witnessed, first hand, inter-tribal warfare with the burning of villages and the use of home-made weapons replacing, in some instances, the bow and arrow. This is still the weapon of choice for hunting pigs and deer, though, and these primitive weapons are still used for hunting birds of paradise for their plumes, to decorate ceremonial headdresses.

It's been a long, hot and exhausting day. We need to go to the river to fill up several jerry cans to use as counterweights on Phil's ingenious pulley system, for getting me and the equipment to the tops of enormous trees. The river is deep, clean and inviting so we strip to our underpants and plunge into the cool water, much to the amusement of the locals also bathing there. They see it as an opportunity to make a quick buck and ask us for 3,000 rupiah (£1) for the privilege, and Phil jokingly teaches them a little new vocabulary. We are back at camp just on dark, around 6.30 p.m. in the tropics, and while we sort out gear, the cook knocks up a tasty meal of rice and fried corned beef with a spicy sauce, a dish which will, over days and weeks, end up losing its appeal. We retire to our tents and sleep solidly under clear, starry skies.

It's 5 a.m. and just getting light when we set off from camp for the nearby swamp forest. This is where the rarely-seen twelve-wired bird of paradise performs its elaborate display. It's to be my first sighting of a bird of paradise and I'm getting really excited. We park the vehicle and start to walk through the swamp forest, which is buzzing with malarial mosquitoes. As we approach the display perch – an old decayed tree stump – we can see in the half-light that the male is already there. He hops up and down the stump, the twelve curved, springy wires protruding from his tail, his bright lemon-yellow flanks and the metallic green edge to his black, erect breast shield irresistible to the females which are gathering nearby. His lime-green gape adds to the impressive colour scheme as he utters a stream of strange sounds. A female hops onto the stump and the ritualised courtship begins. She backs down the stump and the male, now facing downwards, pokes at her bill in a series of jerky movements, a sort of fencing action. She then flies over his head to the top of the perch and the whole action may start again, or mating may take place. This could be a fantastic sequence if the birds will stay long enough at the perch. As we have just seen, though, the behaviour begins at 5.15 a.m., when it's far too dark to film, and sunrise – usually the trigger for the birds to disappear back into the forest – is another half hour away.

About 20 metres away, Phil has already erected the platform for filming. It is a little over one metre square and in a tree, probably 25 metres off the ground, looking slightly down towards the display perch. The hide, which will cover the platform, is made from canvas, a neutral green colour which blends with the forest canopy.

My camera set up on a typical platform

On the tiny platform I will somehow have to fit a small stool, a fairly big tripod with the camera on top, a case with various lenses and a small pack of essentials such as mosquito repellent, water and a torch. It will be pitch black in the hide when I first get in there at 4.30 a.m., so everything has to be arranged so I can put a hand to it instantly. At 20 metres I am a little further from the action than I would like to be, and even with a 600 mm lens the image size will be less than frame-filling. Until I have spent time in the hide, though, it is difficult to know how the bird will react; they are very sensitive and it's better to be slightly cautious at this stage. In fact, there doesn't seem to be a tree that could be used that's any closer, and building a tower hide in a swamp forest would be a massive engineering undertaking and might not be accepted by the birds.

Back at camp our cook has prepared a tasty breakfast of rice, fried tuna and beans. Phil is going back to the twelve-wired filming site; he needs to scale the tree and set the system of ropes to get me and the gear up the tree safely and swiftly and also erect the canvas hide on the platform. I stay back to get the small portable generator fired up to charge batteries for the camera and sound recorder. I also have to check over the camera, clean lenses and load up film magazines for the first filming session tomorrow morning. It is very hot and even the mosquitoes seem to be hiding. Phil returns from a successful session at the platform and after lunch we drive up the road to look for locations for scenic shots to establish the habitat in which the birds are living. It's very important in a film to put the birds into context with their surroundings; sadly, the tranquility of this largely pristine area is being shattered by huge lorries carrying massive logs from the forest to sawmills on the coast. The destruction has started. Tomorrow is the first filming day and after our usual refreshing plunge in the river and an early supper, we crash out by 8 p.m.

We have an early start at 3.45 a.m. and it's still dark, of course, as we set off for the site of the twelve-wired bird of paradise. We need to get me and the gear up onto the filming platform as quickly and quietly as possible, as any hint of disturbance when the birds are around could be catastrophic. Phil climbs the rope with a system of leg straps and pulleys which propel him slowly up the tree, some 20 metres or so, and he then hauls up the camera gear, tripods and the rest of the gear. Counterweights in the form of several jerry cans of water are then attached, Phil ties himself on at the top and, as he descends, the jerry cans ascend to the platform. I then clip on in place of Phil, give a little kick off the ground, and the jerry cans descend, propelling me magically into the treetop without any effort on my part. I should point out that Phil and I were, fortunately, approximately the same weight and that the weight of the cans of water was also matched, otherwise the potential for disaster would be high.

It was now a case of arranging everything, in the dark, into some kind of order, bearing in mind that I was 20 metres off the ground on a one-metre square platform. Anything that fell from this height (including me) would be damaged beyond repair, so it's important to make everything secure and be able to put a hand to anything required. It's just coming up to 5 a.m. when the rest of the team slip quietly away into the forest and I am left in absolute silence and pitch darkness. The male bird normally comes at 5.10 a.m. so I sit, straining my eyes in the half-light for any sign of it. This will be the first time I will have seen a bird of paradise through a big telephoto lens and these will be the first images to be captured for this exciting project. Many of these species are hardly known to westerners and many – including the twelve-wired - have never been filmed before. Suddenly, there it is, my first bird of paradise, a dark shape hopping up the tree stump, the twelve wires and lemon-yellow flanks clear to see, although it is way too dark to film. Even with 500 ASA film there is nothing like an exposure, so it's very frustrating to see the action but be unable to record it. A female appears and the display becomes more intense, as the male pursues her in his ritualised, jerky, hopping motion, up and down the top of the stump, before finally mating with her. By 5.45 it's all over and they disappear into the forest. I have seen the full display but filmed nothing, so it's going to be a case of plugging away for the next week and hoping we get lucky with the light.

I radio Phil and the lads, who soon arrive to get the gear down the tree. I come down on the descender, a little double-pulley device that attaches to the rope from my harness and enables a safe descent. We head back to camp for our usual breakfast of coffee, rice, beans and tuna.

Even though it's barely 7.30 a.m., it's very hot and humid and the mosquitoes are out in droves, so we have to cover up and use lots of repellent. Malaria is rife here. We rest up a while and enjoy our pristine forest surroundings. It's such a rich area for birds: we see rarities, such as the pale-billed sicklebill, only ever seen by a handful of westerners. A charming little yellow-billed kingfisher is excavating a nest tunnel in a termite mound less than 100 metres from my tent, and is something to keep an eye on. Later in the afternoon we visit our Canadian neighbours, here as missionaries,

MP descending the rope after a filming session

who are very kind to us, Robert often dropping by our camp with cold drinks. They have the luxury of a fridge and also let us use their washing machine. On the way back to camp we go for our swim at the river, and it feels glorious to wash away the sweat and mosquito repellent and ease the irritation of several dozen mosquito and other forest insect bites. I'm taking Larium religiously once a week, to protect me from a particularly nasty form of malaria which is in these parts. It's supper time – another variation on corned beef hash with rice and tinned green beans – and by 8.30 p.m. I'm feeling shattered. It's another pre-dawn start tomorrow, so I retire to the luxury of my airbed.

3.30 a.m. comes very quickly. We pack the film gear into the vehicle and head off to the swamp forest. It's a clear morning and, in great anticipation, I ascend the rope to the tiny platform. The counterweight system makes it so easy and by 4.50 a.m. I'm in my hide with all the filming equipment set up. Twenty minutes later, and precisely on time, the male twelve-wired bird appears and begins his routine up and down the dead stump. It is still frustratingly dark and impossible to film, so I just have to watch and hope that he stays longer than usual. I have the fastest available film (500 ASA) loaded into the camera magazines and can do no more. Time passes, females come and go, but it's still too dark, and by 5.45 a.m. I know that I probably only have five minutes left before the male disappears and all the females with him. I run some film in marginal light – it is possible to make corrections at the post-production stages, and I just have to start building some sort of sequence. Days can pass very quickly and dry weather here is far from guaranteed. We could get days of rain and in those conditions the birds would probably not come to the display perch at all. Sure enough, the male flies off at 5.50 a.m., his short display period over, and – as with all birds of paradise – that's it for the day.

I am beginning to realize that this sequence is going to be hard-won. The last few days have shown that the male bird only stays for a maximum of 40 minutes each morning, of which possibly the last ten minutes may be filmable. Over the next few days I gradually start to acquire various shots, slowly building the story: the male up and down the post, a glimpse of a female through the foliage, another flying in, a close-up of the male display. The daily routine is tiring, getting up at 3.30 a.m. for the walk to the forest with its attendant cloud of hungry mosquitoes, the frustration of seeing behaviour that for the most part is not filmable and the return to the sweltering heat of the campsite and the monotonous diet of rice, canned vegetables and tuna or corned beef. Thank goodness for our missionary neighbours a couple of miles away, where we do have the occasional luxury of a shower, a chicken dinner and a cold drink.

A king bird of paradise that we had hoped to film has been a disappointment, in that it never reached its display potential. It was always in very heavy canopy and difficult to get clear views of so, reluctantly, we decided to take down a hide that we had painstakingly built. We think we may get another chance with this species at a different location later in the trip. Yesterday I was fortunate in that I saw and filmed a mating of the twelve-wired bird of paradise on the display post in the swamp forest. The light was not brilliant but, with all the other shots, I think we may have a sequence. We can now think about moving on to film other sequences in different parts of West Papua.

It's Tuesday 27 September, our last morning at Genyam. In some ways we're sad to leave, but on the other hand glad to be moving on to a new location with different challenges. It takes the whole morning to break camp and pack up all the gear for shipping. Robert the missionary is kindly giving us the use of his truck and a driver to get us to the airport at Jayapura.

A mass of filming gear on a trolley, ready for the aircraft

Having just spent a chilly week in the Highlands at 3,000 metres, filming the bizarre MacGregor's bird of paradise, we are now heading west to the Vogelkop Peninsula. We have flown with Merpati Indonesian Airlines many times and there always seems to be a problem: late flights, no flights, baggage going astray or arriving several days late. Today, we are flying from Biak, an island off the north coast of West Papua, to the little town of Manokwari on the peninsula, in remote North Western Papua. As usual we arrive at the airport with mountains of equipment, not only for filming but for cooking, camping and climbing trees, usually met with a degree of disbelief by the airport staff. We arrive in good time at 7.30 a.m. and are immediately told that the flight is cancelled and that the crew are sick. All of them, of course, and there are no standbys. We'll have to go on the Twin Otter and our baggage will follow on tomorrow's cargo flight. Phil is incandescent and on the verge of hitting someone, as this happens so often. Barely disguising our rage we separate the bags for cargo and insist on keeping with us in the aircraft our personal gear and the priceless rushes. When they eventually find a crew, we take off at 10.45 a.m. The weather is not good – heavy tropical rainstorms with thunder and lightning and consequent heavy turbulence.

Halfway through the short flight, we see the alarmingly young pilots checking through an impressively thick manual as the aircraft's speed seems to falter. We are beginning to have a bad feeling about this whole trip. After an anxious hour, we start the descent to Manokwari and an eventual safe landing. We share a taxi with someone to the Mutiara Hotel and a taxi driver who tries to rip us off is nearly the final straw for Phil.

We are here to film the flame bowerbird, another of the many species of bird of paradise that has never been filmed before. We are meeting up with David Gibbs and Richard Kirby, who have been filming the black sicklebill deep in the Arfak Mountains; this region of montane rainforest is rugged and remote, rising up to 2,500 metres. They are supposed to make contact or meet us here, but we've had no word as yet. After an early supper I crash out, hoping that all the gear arrives tomorrow. It's been a stressful day.

After a grim breakfast, Phil heads off to the airport. I stay at the hotel in case there is contact from David Gibbs; we are totally dependent on him to get us to the filming sites deep in the forest. By 10.30 a.m. Phil is back with all the gear, so that's a huge relief, but sadly no one was there to meet Phil and there were no messages. We have to make contact, as every day lost is one less filming day. We drive 45 minutes to the nearest village to send a note with a runner, up through the forest to David's camp, which would take us all day even if we knew the way. The runner will be there and back within hours.

Back at the hotel we await any news, and meanwhile take exposed film rushes and any film we don't need to the local World Wildlife Fund office, where there is an air-conditioned butterfly room, perfect for safe film storage. That evening, back at the

Porters gather with our equipment

hotel, the bush telegraph seems to have worked, as there is a long note from David Gibbs saying where he is in the forest. He has a camp near to a flame bowerbird and says that we should head up there as soon as we can tomorrow. I go to bed full of anticipation for what lies ahead.

It's 24 October and we arrange our flights back to Biak for 6 November, giving us nearly two weeks to film the bowerbird. We rush to the market for more provisions and pack two taxis with all our gear, driving the 45 minutes to the edge of the forest from where we'll start the long walk in.

There are 13 porters waiting for us, excited to make the journey and to earn a little cash. Many of the carriers are only children but they are tough and eager to be part of the party. Cases are strapped onto backs with headbands to balance the load, and we set off on narrow trails through the forest, onward and upward, the climb becoming ever steeper, we slip and trip, the ground is covered in the roots of huge rainforest trees that form the primary forest through which we are trekking. It is exhausting to carry heavy loads in tropical heat and humidity, but there is compensation in seeing and hearing palm cockatoos, lesser birds of paradise, hornbills and magnificent riflebirds. It takes us nearly three hours and when we get to the camp in a forest clearing, I'm dripping with sweat and exhausted.

David Gibbs and Richard Kirby are there to meet us, and with their guides have built from forest saplings a large day tent, with a raised floor – keeping bugs at bay – and a thick tarpaulin roof. We need somewhere dry to store all the gear and cook,

Our camp in the forest, the base for our filming of the flame bowerbird

as there are very frequent rainstorms here. The camera gear in particular has to be kept dry, as fungal growth on lenses could spell disaster. We set up our own tents for sleeping, widely separated to minimise the effects of snoring, and David takes us to see the bower of the flame bowerbird deep in the forest. A hide is already in place – heavily camouflaged with palm leaves and about ten metres from the bower – to allow the bird to get used to it. We insert our waterproof canvas hide inside it and make sure everything is blended with the forest.

Flame bowerbirds are extremely wary. They are still hunted for their amazing plumes, much sought after by tribesmen for headdresses, so I'll have to be very cautious when working at this bower. It's too late for all the porters to go back to town so a huge meal is being prepared back at camp. There are more than 20 porters with David's group, and after much chatter and catching up with all that's been happening, I slip away to my little tent. I'm excited at the prospect of seeing the flame bowerbird in the morning – only about five Europeans have even laid eyes on it and it's never been filmed.

We are filming bowerbirds to compare the different strategies for attracting females to those of birds of paradise, which rely entirely on stunning plumage. Bowerbirds – although some males like the regent and flame do have colourful plumage – rely on their bowers and the treasures displayed within them, such as berries, fruits, stones, the skulls of small mammals, beetle wing cases and flowers.

I crawl from my tent at 5.45 a.m. The sky has a veil of thin white cloud and I hope it will brighten sufficiently to film, but these bowers have a tendency to be in the gloomiest parts of the forest. I'm into the hide and settled by half past six and there is no sign of the bird, which is good. There's nothing worse than being caught out by the bird as you enter a hide, as that can upset it for the whole day. The porters are a noisy lot and I'm really pleased when their chatter gradually fades as they make their way back to the town of Manokwari.

The bower is a sparse construction of twigs, with two parallel walls about nine inches high and five inches apart. That's not very exciting to a female, but the bower is adorned with various fruits – in this case the size of a large grape and a deep purple colour – arranged just so at the entrance to the bower. I don't know how many visits from the bird I'll get so I need to grab as much as possible when conditions allow. Rain is always a worry. After four hours of nothing I see a flash of orange in the viewfinder – without a sound, the male bird has arrived suddenly at the bower. I can't believe its colours: a brilliant, fiery orange on the head, nape and mantle and bright yellow wings and underparts, made more dramatic by a jet-black facial mask, wing edges and tail. It seems to glow in the darkness of the forest as though spun from glass filaments. It has a large white eye and I get the impression that it is staring straight at the hide. I even have to wait until the bird is looking away before I zoom the lens, as I'm sure it sees the glass elements move inside. It is without doubt one of the most stunning birds I've ever seen and probably the least known – no one has ever found a nest.

It is still too dark to film, but I'm so thrilled to see it at the bower. It stays for just nine minutes, rearranging twigs in the avenue. Many of these avenue-building bowerbirds produce a paint of vegetable matter and charcoal, masticated and mixed with saliva and applied to the bower walls, some even using a small twig as a tool to apply it. The bird slips away into the darkness and I wait expectantly for the next visit. By 12.30 there is no sign of the bird and it's beginning to rain so I decide to leave. Six hours sitting cramped in the one-metre square hide is enough for now. It's a 30-minute walk back to camp and soon after I arrive the rain becomes torrential, so I'm glad to have left when I did. I spend time under the canopy with the rain beating down on the tarp. By 2.45 p.m. it's stopped, so I go back to the hide, now dripping wet and soon to become a haven for mosquitoes. My diary sums up the rest of the day:

Still too dark to film but the adult male comes at 3.10 p.m. for 3–4 mins, then again at 4.00 and 4.10 p.m. for a few minutes each time, an immature male came at 3.50 p.m. and stayed for 5 mins. Phil lets me out of the hide at 4.30 p.m. and back to camp. We have a test run with the 1.4 kW generator, we may need to use it with a Redhead (an 800 watt lamp). I feel very tired, and after a spartan dinner of rice, noodles and fried corned beef, feeling rather sickly, I go to bed.

26th October is a beautiful, clear morning, the air thick with moisture and a heady mixture of tropical smells. There is an outrageously loud and varied dawn chorus as I sit outside my tent and eat two stale doughnuts with coffee. I head to the hide for 7.00 a.m. The stunning adult male comes shortly afterwards, just as the sun breaks through the canopy and lights up the bower. I shoot 30 metres of film (about three mins) in short order, needing to grab these moments as they happen. Getting the bird at the bower just when the sun is on it is a rare event. Bowerbirds spend much of their time housekeeping, clearing away leaves and twigs that have fallen close to the bower, which needs to be in pristine condition for that special moment when a female visits. I manage a variety of shot sizes on the big zoom lens, wide-angles of the bird around the bower, medium close-ups of it rearranging twigs within the bower and close-ups to intercut. Close-ups of the head are always useful, with the bird maybe responding to something off-camera, a reaction shot which helps enormously with the editing, commonly known as a cutaway. I'm now beginning to feel that the sequence is coming together.

It's clouded over by lunchtime so I head back to base. As it stays overcast I stay in camp, preparing a second camera to put next to the bower and operate remotely from the hide. It could give us a wide-angle shot of the bird at its bower from ground level, which would help so much with editing the sequence. Phil is spending the afternoon in the hide just watching the bird, and I hope it doesn't do anything too unusual. I go to let Phil out of the hide at around 2.30 p.m., relieved to hear that nothing of interest has happened, and it's now heavily overcast.

We have an early supper and I fall asleep to the strange sounds of the forest and the more familiar ones of the World Service. Tomorrow, I'll continue with the early morning routine.

I'm back in the hide at 7 a.m., it's a clear morning so I'm hoping that the male flame bowerbird will come early. It doesn't. When it does come, at 8.30 a.m., the sunlight is off the bower.

We have put out some additional purple berries nearby in the hope that the male will pick them up and take them into the bower. He inspects them but disdainfully rejects them, so there's obviously a very precise selection process. Shortly afterwards, a spotted catbird comes along and makes off with them, then reappears and steals purple fruits from the bower, much to the anger of the bowerbird, who is nearby. Later in the morning the bowerbird performs some sort of display which I don't think has been described before, a little zigzag side-to-side dance on the ground, half-opening his wings and arching his back, whilst pointing his beak downwards, at the same time uttering strange hissing and buzzing sounds. Although the light is far from ideal I have to film this, as I may never see it again. I've now shot two rolls of valuable film, 20 minutes of behaviour that has never been seen before, which at the very least should make a two-minute sequence – all we really need –and I still have four days left. I unload the precious film from the magazines, taping it up carefully into cans, batteries are recharged on our little generator and cameras and lenses checked and cleaned.

Over the next few days I manage to shoot more precious material on this fascinating bird and, with the basic sequence in the can, try a few different techniques to improve on it. I put out the remote camera and get some useful ground-level shots. Lighting in the bower fails miserably – the male will not accept it – so I remove it straight away.

It's 5 November and, after a last couple of hours in the hide, it's time to take it down and pack up the camp. That's the end of filming for this trip. It's quite sad to leave our home in this magical forest: we've been here for 12 days and I've been privileged to film one of the least known birds in the world. Over 90 hours spent in the hide has produced 50 minutes of film, which should make a three-minute sequence in our programme. Here we've lived with exotic rifle birds, palm cockatoos, hornbills and tree kangaroos, woken to fantastic dawns with a chorus of some of the most exotic species in the world. There have been frustrations with light and weather over which we had no control but we have our sequence and, after all, where's the satisfaction in doing something easy?

Return to New Guinea

The last year has been a busy one, with trips to Jamaica and Cuba for a series on Central America called Spirits of the Jaguar and to Somerset Island in Arctic Canada for a programme on beluga whales, but all the time I have been anticipating this next trip to New Guinea. I'm looking forward not only to the new species we'll be seeing and the habitats in which we'll be filming, but to the opportunity to work with Sir David Attenborough.

It's 18 October and time to return to Papua New Guinea. I've spent the last two days packing for this trip: 27 cases of film and video equipment, including 60 rolls (over 7,000 metres) of film, a stack of aluminium scaffolding for accessing the forest canopy, ropes and climbing tackle, camping and cooking gear, first aid kits, a generator for charging batteries, and more. The whole lot is packed into a large van and we head off to Manchester airport. It takes six trolleys, a visit to a cunningly hidden Customs office and an eye-watering £10,270 excess baggage bill before we're ready to fly to Port Moresby in New Guinea, our baggage booked through and allowing me to relax a little.

After several exhausting flights I arrive at 6.40 a.m., two days later. I'm met by Brian Baldwin, acting High Commissioner, and Doug Maskelyne from the TNT freight agency. We get straight through Immigration and we're thankful to find that – amazingly – all the gear has arrived in one piece. I head for the Islander Hotel with Brian to get checked in, while Doug sorts the gear with Customs, arriving at the hotel with it only a short time after me. This is a great relief, as Customs sometimes like to hang on to gear for no apparent reason, and we get it locked away in the hotel storeroom for safety. I make some phone calls, snatch some sleep and head to Brian Baldwin's for dinner. Port Moresby has a bad reputation for robberies, muggings and general violence so I'm glad to be picked up and taken to the High Commissioner's house, which has a big fence around it with electrically- operated gates and numerous security guards. I leave with an invitation to go snorkelling on the fantastic reefs of New Guinea, once we have finished filming.

I'm up at 5.20 a.m. I didn't sleep too well as my sleep patterns are haywire. Doug from TNT comes at 6 a.m., we load the gear into a van and get down to the airport. Doug seems to know the right people at Customs and having paid Kina 420 (about £100 sterling) for excess baggage, we get it across to check-in. As the aircraft are small Piper Cherokees, we can only get ten pieces on my flight, and the remainder will come on another, 45 minutes later, via Tari in the Highlands.

It's a 90-minute flight to Daru, a small town on the southwest coast of Papua New Guinea, then another stop, 20 minutes on, for refuelling before the final 45-minute leg to Kiunga. The whole flight has been stunning, flying low all the way over virgin lowland rainforest. Phil Hurrell, who has been in PNG for a few days, is at the airport to meet me, and we pick up the gear and take it to our little guest house in town. At first sight it looks like a warehouse but the rooms are clean and with good air con.

Kiunga is a shabby port town on the Fly River, a hot and humid place with a bad reputation for malaria. We're going to have to be careful to take all the precautions here, with long-sleeved clothing, insect repellent and the appropriate prophylactics. We are using Larium, only taken once weekly but with some unpleasant side effects, such as weird dreams. The rest of the gear has arrived, so we're all set for the next phase of filming. I spend the remainder of the day checking equipment and taking a little sleep. This evening we are going to spend some time in town socialising with guys from the Ok Tedi mine. The mine, open cast and producing copper and gold, is based at Tabooville, over 100 km of dirt road up the Fly River. They may be providing the services of a helicopter for access to the alpine areas to film scenics and to shoot a sync piece with Sir David, so it's good to establish contact and explain what we are about. It's a very social night and we don't get away until one in the morning.

It's 22 October and this morning we're going to look at the greater bird of paradise display site which Phil has found and where he's put up a filming platform in anticipation. It's a 25- minute drive along a decent gravel road, then a 20-minute walk through the untouched forest, a magical place where the huge trees are festooned with bromeliads and orchids and the sounds of riflebirds and parrots ring through the canopy. Arriving at the base of the tree I gaze, slightly nervously, up the 30 metres to where the tiny metre-square platform is strapped to the rainforest giant. The distance from the hide to the display area is 30 metres but the crown of the display tree is 10 metres higher than the platform meaning that over the 30 metre distance between

*A platform hide
in the canopy*

the lens and the displaying birds I will be looking up at an angle of 20°, which won't be ideal. We decide to go with it, though, and Phil climbs the massive tree to set about putting the canvas hide on top of the platform. Once the canvas is stretched over the framework, the whole thing is covered in camouflage netting; it all blends in remarkably well and we hope that the greater birds of paradise accept it. We leave the forest and head back to Kiunga, as we have the usual lens

*Phil Hurrell climbing ropes to
assess a filming position*

cleaning, battery charging and magazine-loading duties to do, to prepare for the first hide session tomorrow. The heat and humidity, combined with the very early starts, are energy-sapping so we take a short afternoon nap, then an early dinner and head to bed by 9 p.m., ready for a 4.30 a.m. start.

It's a cloudy morning and, after picking up our two porters, we are into the forest by 5.20 and at the base of our giant tree by 5.40, which is really a little late, as the birds of paradise are already calling nearby. We haul the gear up to the platform, then I go up on the rope as Phil comes down on a finely-engineered pulley system. I quickly get settled onto my tiny seat and set up the camera on its tripod. It's pitch black in the hide, which doesn't make life easy. I'm all set by 6 a.m. and very soon after that, the birds are on their display perches, calling loudly. Sadly, though, it's still cloudy and the activity is brief. I have filmed nothing by the time the birds have melted away into the forest at 7 a.m. It's a disappointing start but I remind myself that we have plenty of time yet.

Phil belays me and all the gear back to the ground and we head back through the forest, which is ringing with the sound of riflebirds. Back in Kiunga we hit the local bakery and buy fresh bread and cakes, then stop for timber to build a platform hide for a twelve-wired bird of paradise which Phil has found on the river, about 15 minutes upstream. Samuel, our local contact and bird finder, has a five-metre boat which we load up with the timber before heading off at around 3 p.m. It's only slightly cooler than it was at midday, probably still in the high 30s and 95% humidity.

The display site is only 50 metres from the riverbank and the display stump ten metres high. The tree for the platform is about 12 metres away from the display perch so there is good potential for close-ups, which would be a great help in editing the display sequence shot at Genyem last year. As Phil fires the first thin lines from a catapult into the tree, ready to haul up the platform, we hear the male twelve-wired nearby. We must leave the area, so retreat to the riverbank and do some assembly of the platform there. As the male is still around we decide to leave it for now and come back tomorrow. It's almost dark by the time we get back to Kiunga and after dinner I slip away to my bed.

This morning we are going to the greater bird of paradise platform but only to observe. Yesterday the birds seemed a little edgy, so today we will watch from a distance. As we get to the base of the tree, at just after 7 a.m., we can clearly see the birds performing on their favourite perches and all seems well; they stay until 7.30 then, as usual, they silently melt into the forest. We head back to Kiunga and load up Samuel's boat with the remainder of the hide materials, timber, ropes, climbing gear and canvas. It's 9.30 a.m. and already steaming hot by the time we set off up river. We complete the construction and Phil puts on the camouflaged canvas cover; if the bird accepts the hide, we could get some great shots. Back in Kiunga by late morning, we have a spot of lunch and rest up a while, as the heat and humidity are shattering.

By mid-afternoon the heat is almost tolerable and we take the pick-up truck to drive the unsurfaced haul road up to Tabooville, home of the Ok Tedi copper mine. It's pristine forest all the way and we need good scenic shots to establish the birds' habitat, but sadly we have to drive 80 km before we find a viewpoint. We stop there and check out the possibilities; yes, it is untouched primary forest, but we may have more success from the air next week, when a helicopter from the mining company will be available to us.

We see some great forest birds: eclectus parrots, sulphur-crested cockatoos, vulturine parrots and orange-faced mynahs. We drive back to Kiunga in the failing light and it's getting on for 7 p.m. by the time we arrive at the guest house. After a lovely dinner of chicken and banana soup with coconut and roast pork, it's bedtime, as we have another pre-dawn start for the greater birds of paradise tomorrow.

The alarm seems to go off very soon after I go to bed, and after a quick coffee I get all the filming gear together. Phil is soon knocking at my door and we're off in the pick-up to collect Samuel. After another magical walk through the forest we're back at the base of our giant tree by 5.25, slightly earlier than usual. I need to be in the hide and settled before any birds are around, because it could be a disaster if they see me. We haul up the gear, I follow on the pulley as Phil comes down, and I'm in position and settled by 5.50. It's still very dark,

6 a.m. comes, and the first birds are beginning to call. This is always an exciting moment as the anticipation builds and I wonder if I'll be lucky today.

It's a slow start. Ten minutes in, the first silhouettes of the birds are just visible through the viewfinder. I have the 50-30mm zoom lens on, which will enable me to get a variety of shot sizes without changing lenses – after all, taking off a lens and poking another through the front of the hide could very easily spook the birds, so until I know their tolerance levels I want to play very safe. I don't dare move. I watch through the viewfinder the remarkable displays of these fabulous birds, the light levels picking up, and I begin to see the colours and plumage detail as the extravagant males bounce around the branches. There are two fully adult males and five to six females, along with two sub-adult 'brown' males who are watching and imitating the movements of the highly experienced birds. The adult males, with their great cascade of golden tail plumes, attract all of the females' attention as they go through their well-rehearsed routines, making jerky, hopping movements along the branches then flipping over, their head pointing down and wings spread in an arc. Sometimes, the two males perform together, perfectly synchronised, hanging for a few seconds with wings arched and tail feathers puffed up, calling loudly. These birds can be up to 10 years old, but so little is known about them and their nests have never been found. They probably do not mate until their fifth or sixth year when they are fully mature.

By 7 a.m. it's light enough to film and the birds are still very active. Normally I'm struggling for light and having to use high-speed film, which in dull conditions can look

*A greater bird of paradise
from a Gould painting*

grainy. Now, with nice, bright, overcast skies bouncing diffused light into the canopy, I can use my preferred option, Kodak 7245, a slower, fine-grained film which gives superb results. I grab as many shots as possible on the big zoom lens while the light and activity are good; I've soon shot the whole magazine –130 metres – which is ten minutes of screen time. I change film magazines quickly and continue shooting; there are two matings in more or less the same spot on the branch by possibly the same male, and I'm not going to risk changing to the 600 mm lens – there's too much at stake. I need to get as much of this behaviour as I can. This has never been filmed before and it's very exciting; it makes all the early mornings and frustrations with weather worthwhile. Tomorrow I will start off with the 600 mm lens on the camera and concentrate on close-ups to match with today's action. The display finishes abruptly and the birds are gone.

Phil is now able to climb the display tree, which is no mean feat as it's over 30 metres up, and with my guidance from the platform is able to remove any offending twigs and leaves. I now have a perfectly unobscured view of the whole display area, ready for – I hope – a repeat performance tomorrow. Back at the guest house we grab some lunch and I go through the usual routine of checking the gear, unloading magazines, charging batteries, writing up notes on what I've shot and writing my personal diary; exciting though filming is, there is also the routine stuff to attend to. I fail in an attempt to phone the producer Paul Reddish to report on progress as, frustratingly, the phones are down, a regular occurrence.

This morning has been very productive in that it has produced the close-ups of the display that I really needed. Similar bright conditions and the fact that the birds used the same perches and positions will make cutting the action that much easier and I'm feeling more confident about getting a detailed sequence on these charismatic birds. Back at the guest house I pack up the priceless first three rolls, 30 minutes shot on the greater birds of paradise, and get them off to TNT which will fly them back to the UK for processing. I'd hope to get a report back from Paul on their technical and artistic merits in a few days' time.

The next few hide sessions are frustrated by overnight torrential rain lasting into the morning period, but now that the platform for the twelve-wired bird of paradise is complete, I decide to rest the greater site for a day and head upriver to try to add to our existing material on this bird. We go to collect Samuel, our boatman, to take us upriver in his boat but he's still asleep, and then takes ages to bring the boat to the landing stage, so we're late away. We're not happy: just a few minutes can be crucial with these displays. It's 5.35 a.m. so we quickly get me and the gear into the hide, with a bird already calling close by. It's a dull morning and raining a little, it's just 6.15 a.m., and in the half-light the twelve-wired bird thuds onto the post; unbelievably, it has no tail wires and is in wing moult, so it just won't cut with what we shot last year. This is a huge blow as it's such a great location. There's a slim possibility that it's a different bird to the one Phil saw, so Samuel will watch it tomorrow.

There are more frustrations with morning rain, but the weather picks up later in the day and we are able to do tracking scenics of the river and forest from Samuel's boat, essential to establish the birds within their habitat. Another species we are keen to film is the riflebird, but it's difficult to pin down and seems to have several display perches. Richard Kirby, the other cameraman, is also trying for riflebirds and maybe he'll have more luck.

Phil, Samuel and I have been looking for and, fortunately, found a suitable tree in which to do the sync pieces with Sir David when he arrives in a few days' time. This involved finding a rainforest giant, perhaps 50 metres high, in which we could set up ropes and a pulley system to get Sir David right up to canopy level. Now Phil is not only an ornithological expert but also a master of getting himself and other people safely into the tops of very large trees. He uses a crossbow or catapult to fire the initial light line over the selected large limb and then attaches a heavy climbing rope, which is hauled over the limb and anchored back on the ground, forming the basis for all the forays into the canopy, when additional ropes and pulleys can be attached. Safety is of paramount importance as any fall from these heights would be fatal. David, once at the top of the tree, will be filmed doing his piece to camera and describing the displaying birds of paradise in front of him, which is quite a difficult logistical exercise as I have to film it from different angles. I need to be at the top of the tree as David comes up the rope and I also need to be at the top of a nearby tree to film him from a different angle; we also need POV (point of view) shots of what David sees as he ascends into the canopy. Sir David, with producer Paul Reddish, sound man 'Dickie' Bird and producer's assistant Judy Copeland are all arriving tomorrow, so today is spent, between tropical downpours, finishing off the rope and pulley systems on the big tree.

It's 13 November and after yet another early start to check out a riflebird and move a platform before going back for breakfast, it's down to the airport at 10 a.m. to pick up Sir David and the crew. Phil and I have been working together for some weeks now and it's really good to see new faces and, above all, to meet and be working with Sir David at last. We head back to the little guest house and, once everyone is settled into their rooms, have an early lunch. It's great to catch up on all the news and gossip from home. After our meal we take a trip into the forest to show everyone the locations and possibilities for the sync pieces at ground and canopy levels before heading back to the guest house for a few drinks in the evening. Paul has brought with him the VHS tapes of the first 30 minutes of the greater birds of paradise rushes, which look fantastic. Paul and David are more than happy with them and all the exhaustingly early mornings, the drenchings in tropical storms and the onslaughts from a vast array of forest insects seem well worthwhile.

It's a big day. We are all going upstream to Samuel's village to do the first sync piece. As there are now seven of us, we need two boats to carry everyone and all the associated film and sound gear, as well as food and drink. It's very hot and humid so we also need

gallons of water. It's a two-hour journey upstream through fantastic pristine forest and we see wonderful birds from the boat – radjah shelducks, hornbills, cormorants, darters, red-cheeked parrots and palm cockatoos – before we arrive at the village at around 8.45 a.m. Everyone is out to meet us and we're offered quite a reception. We set David up on the veranda of an ancient longhouse. In the background sits a wizened old man in traditional costume, in the foreground David sits stroking an old skin of a greater bird of paradise. Part of his piece to camera will involve describing how the

Sir David with a skin of a greater bird of paradise

Dickie sorts out a problem with the sound gear

birds were first named. Specimens were first brought to Europe in the 16th century, on ships returning from the east. The skins they obtained from native traders had had their legs and wings removed, leading to the belief in Europe that the birds never landed but were kept aloft by their amazing plumes. Antonio Pigafetta on Magellan's ship wrote, 'The people told us that those birds came from the terrestrial paradise and they call them 'bolon diuata', that is, 'birds of god'.

This simple sequence turned into quite a problem one. Chickens crowing loudly and children playing in the background ruined the sound, then high humidity shut down the DAT recorder, much to Dickie's disgust. David having trouble with his lines needed three or four takes, then I needed to reload a film magazine because I'd used it all up on the dud takes. At this point Paul and David were showing some signs of stress, but in the end we managed to get several good takes. The great thing about sync pieces is they do provide maybe two or three minutes of footage in quite a short time, whereas two or three minutes of wildlife behaviour can take a week or more. We finished around midday, it was very hot and humid, so it was good to get into the boat and enjoy the tropical breeze as we zoomed down river.

We stop off to check the bower of a flame bowerbird where we will do a sync piece, but the sky has become very heavy and a storm is on its way, so we carry on back to Kiunga. Phil stayed behind today, as he has had the complicated job of setting up the many ropes and pulleys for the greater bird of paradise sync sequence, to get me and David up and down the huge trees. There's just enough time for a couple of drinks outside before dinner and then we head to bed by 10 p.m., with another 5 a.m. start tomorrow.

I never tire, though, of early morning in the rain forest. It's cool and fresh, often dripping with moisture and smelling of a thousand different plants, all blended into the headiest perfume. Dozens of exotic birds are ringing, singing, calling and shrieking as we make our way through this timeless place. By 6.30 we've reached the area where we're going to do shots of Sir David walking through the forest, talking about the displays of greater birds of paradise before ascending the tree and looking across the canopy to where the birds are displaying. I need

The crew head downstream by boat

to don the Steadicam, a piece of equipment which enables the camera – as the name implies – to be held steadily, to follow the presenter as he delivers his piece to camera.

Wearing the Steadicam is akin to wearing something from the Middle Ages. It's a modern version of a breastplate of metal and leather, designed to prevent death by sword or dagger, but made of metal alloy, plastic and velcro strapped tightly to the chest. It is fitted with a spring-loaded vertical stabilised pillar on which the camera is mounted, enabling the operator to maintain a perfectly level attitude and make smooth vertical craning shots. All this depends on the skill of the operator, of course, and to film while walking through a rainforest is difficult.

MP filming with the Steadicam

The ground is festooned with roots, vines and creepers, only too ready to bring the unwary operator crashing to the ground. We eventually get several takes of David walking and talking, ending up at the base of the big tree, which is where the fun starts. At least I get to take off the Steadicam, as prolonged use can mean serious backache.

Phil has built an ingenious device which we have called the 'flying bike'. It's a lightweight alloy frame with a saddle at one end, on which David sits, with the camera on a pedestal at the other end.

This rig is attached to the rope and the whole thing ascends into the canopy by means of an ingenious counterweight system. The plan is that I will have set the camera running, with Sir David filming himself as he glides effortlessly up through the canopy, the forest magically slipping by in the background. We do several takes, just to be sure. Now we need to change the set-up for the next shot, using several different angles to make the whole sequence work. I have to go to the top of the tree with the camera and strap myself to a limb in the canopy, looking 35 metres vertically downwards.

David ascends on the rope and I film him coming up and arriving in the canopy. Here he pauses and does his sync piece about the display of the birds of paradise, looking at them through binoculars, about 50 metres away. At this point I am thinking that this is quite something: I'm in the top of a rainforest canopy with David Attenborough, just the two of us, and he's talking to my camera about the thing he is most passionate about. It doesn't get any better, does it? With that piece in the can we descend to the forest floor and prepare for the next shot, a wide-angle taken from a platform on another tree about 50 metres away. I am winched up to that platform and

Sir David ascending through the canopy

Sir David and Paul Reddish with the filming rig

Sir David about to ascend into the canopy on the 'flying bike'

set up the camera, before David ascends the main tree again on the rope and I film the whole ascent in wide-angle. David then descends and comes up again and I film it in close-up. This now gives us four different cutting points, which will make for a much more interesting sequence and a happy editor.

It's been a hard morning and the day isn't finished yet. We pack up, leave the forest and head back to the guesthouse for a quick change and a sort out of the gear. We are driving up to the mine site at Tabubil, where tomorrow we're hoping to film aerials from a helicopter, courtesy of the mining company. We're taking two vehicles, and I'm driving one with David and Judy Copeland.

We're away by 3.30 and it's a three-hour drive on a dirt road through rainforest. The road was built and is maintained by the mining company to get vehicles and equipment from the coastal town of Kiunga and is not the safest, being liable to regular flooding and landslips. The journey goes very quickly, as David talks about his old Zoo Quest expeditions and his early climbing days in Snowdonia, and I talk about my early filming career and how I started with the RSPB and Partridge Films before becoming a freelance.

Tabubil is a service town built by the Ok Tedi Mining Company for its employees, with a hotel, international school and engineering facilities. Mount Fubilan is a copper mountain with a gold cap and when production started, in 1984, was thought to be the biggest copper mine in the world. Between 1985 and 1990, over 47 tons (1.5 million ounces) of gold bullion were produced and between 1985 and 2004 over three million tons of copper. Sadly, the pollution from the mine has produced huge problems, silting up the river with toxic tailings and other noxious chemicals, and affecting fish populations and the agricultural lands adjacent to the river upon which the indigenous peoples rely.

We arrive in darkness at around 6.30 p.m. and check into the hotel. After getting out of our sweaty clothes and taking a shower, we gather for a barbeque with some of the people from the company that have helped to set up the helicopter time. It's a pleasant evening but we have an early start the next day – to go flying, we hope.

It's a super, clear morning – and my birthday. We all have breakfast together before heading down to the airfield for 6 a.m. Bill, the Aussie helicopter engineer, has the covers off the Squirrel, doing some maintenance, which upsets Paul and Bruce the pilot, who hadn't been told either. Timing is so critical when filming aerials: just a few minutes can make the difference between an ordinary shot and a magical one. Paul and I go off in the first helicopter with the Steadicam, climbing rapidly over forested hillsides with cascading waterfalls until, at 3,000 metres plus, we start to get into the open alpine moorland with tree ferns, which is where we want to do the establishing scenics for the MacGregor's bird of paradise.

We land and quickly do some safety scenic shots from the tripod, making the most of a beautiful ground mist. We then quickly set up for shots with the Steadicam; it takes 15 min's to rig up and get it all finely balanced with the camera, and we manage it just in time before the others arrive. At this altitude it can cloud over suddenly, not only making it impossible to get shots but also highly dangerous for the helicopters trying to get back down the mountain. We have to move quickly to get all the shots that we need, and immediately do the sync piece with David walking through the tree ferns. This is most important, to establish the story relating to the MacGregor's bird of paradise. Sir David is amazing – he needs just a few minutes walking alone to rehearse what he is going to say and it's usually done in one take. The weather is already starting to change, clouds are forming and the pilots are getting edgy, so Paul decides to get everyone, except David and me, down on the first helicopter. We stay back to grab a few more shots, wide-angles of David walking through the alpine habitat, with giant tree ferns from ground level, then I take off with the pilot and run a few shots from the air as David walks through the same areas, to give us the ability to cut between shots. The cloud is really rolling in now and we have to get out before we're stranded. We land and pick up David, then make a high-speed descent before the cloud envelops us.

Back in Tabubil, where the weather is clear, Paul is keen to do more aerials while the Squirrel is still available to us, so I make a quick change of film, check the camera and it's back into the chopper to take off downriver. We shoot low-level tracking shots of the thick forest, flying downstream at 80 m.p.h. just 15 metres off the water. It's exhilarating and a great way to mark a birthday. Back at the hotel, all the gear and film are packed away, ready for an early start back to Kiunga in the morning.

Once there, we finish off some more shots in the forest and we're just about done with the sync pieces. The crew, apart from Phil and me, are going back tomorrow, so this evening we have a good social and a few beers. We take a look at the rushes shot on video of Phil going up the rope on the 'bike' and some of the shots of Sir David walking through the forest, but the highlight is getting a second look at the rushes of the greater bird of paradise. They are fantastic and it's amazing to have the wild soundtrack playing alongside. This is something never before seen in such detail and will be a memorable sequence in the film, I'm sure. All we need is a few more like it.

Everyone goes to bed early so I return to my room and watch a film on TV before falling asleep. Around 2 a.m. I'm awakened by a noise and see, through the curtains, the silhouette of someone outside, trying the door handle. I get out of bed, go to the window and whip back the curtain. The man has a blank, glazed expression and doesn't reply when I ask him what he wants, so it's a good job the door is locked. My mind races with what might have happened had he got in, and picture him wielding a machete. I tell him to clear off, he rants and raves but eventually leaves, and it takes me quite a while to get back to sleep.

Sir David and the rest of the crew are off on a charter flight to Port Moresby this morning, then heading back to the UK, and we go with them to the airport in Kiunga to say our goodbyes. It's been a busy, productive and very stimulating week, and now Phil and I can go back and relax for a while before spending the rest of the day packing and sorting for our flight to Tari tomorrow.

The Highlands of New Guinea

Tari is a small settlement at over 2,000 metres in the Highlands of New Guinea. As we descend to the airfield we see a shambolic scene below. Hundreds of local tribespeople are pressed up against a barely adequate security fence, some waiting for arriving passengers, others trying to get onto flights to other villages. Many are dressed in traditional costume featuring bird of paradise feathers.

One of the main tribes here is the Huli, famed for their intricate wigs made from human hair. I'm glad that the ancient bus from Ambua Lodge, where we are staying, is there to meet us, as it's quite intimidating here, with lots of stories of hold-ups and general violence. Reassuringly, our driver seems to know a lot of people and we head up out of town towards the lodge. A clan war has been raging for a week or two, bridges have had to be patched up where planks have been removed, and everywhere we see bands of traditionally dressed warriors with bows and arrows and home-made shotguns. We pass a heavily trampled field where a war had been fought and people killed, and the remains of burnt-out villages; as we descend a hill towards a river crossing, a great band of heavily armed tribespeople appear from the bush and start running down behind us. The driver accelerates and they disappear into a cloud of diesel fumes.

The untouched Highland forest approaching Tari

Further along the road we stop to take some pictures of a group with home-made shotguns, of which they were very proud. The driver said it would be fine but in retrospect, it might not have been the cleverest thing for us to do.

We eventually arrive at the lodge and meet up with Dr Cliff Frith, a well-known Australian ornithologist, very experienced at working with birds of paradise in this region. He has been here several times before and has good contacts with local bird finders. You need to have really reliable people who have your interests at heart, as it's disastrous if local hunters get to know where we are working. Cliff is unwell and not in good spirits, but at least we can give him some antibiotics.

Phil and I are staying in the small research block at the lodge and very soon have our gear carried down there. It's a fabulous spot, with great views of the surrounding forest and the lodge garden, which is fantastic for birds; we see a Loria's bird of paradise, a new species for me. As we are in the Highlands here, with altitudes between 1,700 and 2,800 metres, mosquitoes are not a problem and it's quite cold at night, which makes a pleasant change from the hot and humid lowlands. Cliff has been here for a while and has been checking out several birds that we want to film. One of our main target species is the King of Saxony bird of paradise, not an easy bird to pin down, usually displaying very high up in the rainforest trees, and quite a challenge. The other amazing bird here, and one that we are keen to film, is the MacGregor's bowerbird. Cliff takes us to a site that he has found, deep in the forest, where he has built a hide just five metres from the intricate structure that is its bower. A central maypole, two metres high, has been constructed around a sapling using little twigs all locked together, with at the base a shallow dish, constructed of moss up to a metre across, with a rim maybe ten centimetres deep, like a mini velodrome. The lip of this is decorated with little pieces of charcoal, beetle wing cases and dark-coloured berries. Now we have to line the hide with waterproof material – this isn't a moss forest for nothing. The rainfall is enormous, as we are to see for ourselves in the next few days.

A group of local tribesmen with traditional weapons and home-made guns

The first session in the hide is depressingly dull. Apart from there not being enough light to film by, the bird is timid and reluctant to come into the bower. Something is wrong and I think it may be that the hide is too close. Reluctantly, we withdraw it to ten metres, which does make a difference, and over the next few days I begin to pick up

shots of the bird visiting the bower and adding decorative items to the maypole. One of its favourites is caterpillar frass (droppings) which is hung like ladies' earrings from the maypole. Even now that the hide is further away, the bird is still very timid, so I have to be extremely careful with any camera or lens moves. The rain which is plaguing us each afternoon is making the walk in to the hide treacherous; we have to walk along fallen logs coated with moss and lichens which, when wet, are lethal underfoot. It would be so easy to slip off and turn an ankle. Cliff has now gone back to Australia, so our local man Joseph – who has quite a reputation with visiting birders for being able to find the really elusive species – is chief bird finder, and may have found us a really good site for the King of Saxony bird of paradise. Normally, these birds display really high up in the trees, using many different display perches, so it's very difficult to locate them. Joseph thinks he may have a bird that is displaying lower down and has seen it more than once in the same spot, so we cross our fingers that it's what we are looking for.

After an abortive helicopter trip to a location for blue bird of paradise, which failed miserably due to atrocious weather and lack of behaviour, we cut our losses and returned to Ambua Lodge.

We meet up with Joseph and the good news is that the King of Saxony is still displaying. The rain arrives as usual in late afternoon, so we retire to the lodge bar for a few drinks and chat with new arrivals. They're an interesting bunch: a Japanese film crew are making a programme on mining and oil exploration and there are some American birders and divers going to New Britain. After the usual forgettable dinner we have an early night, with another dawn start the next day.

Our van is off the road due to an engine fault so we have to get a lift in the clapped-out hotel bus up the rutted track to the trailhead. It's a long slog through the dense

Cliff Frith next to a MacGregor's bower

The maypole of MacGregor's bowerbird

and very wet forest to the MacGregor's bower, where disaster has struck. The wind has blown down a big, rotten stump and it's fallen right across the bower. Fortunately, it has missed the central maypole but there is no sign of the owner and I fear the worst. We clear the stump and debris and tidy up the bower as best we can, hoping that it has only just happened. These birds invest a huge amount of their time in these elaborate structures so probably won't give them up easily.

I climb into my dark, damp hide and set up the camera and sound-recording gear just in case. It's now half past seven and as time passes, I feel that the bird may have deserted the area. By ten o'clock there's still neither sight nor sound of it and it's all very depressing, particularly since the last few days have been so unproductive. Then, suddenly, there's a great burst of song nearby – the male is back and drops into the dish of the bower, singing his heart out. I can hardly breathe with excitement and cautiously start the sound recorder and begin filming. The bird seems to be overjoyed with its miraculously restored bower and the singing becomes louder and more intense, continuing for 30 minutes. I've never heard such a range of calls: a rapid series of growls, coughing sounds, twangs like an elastic band, screeches and chimes. All the time it tinkers with the bower, readjusting the carefully placed decorations that have been displaced by the tree fall. I have managed to shoot almost a roll of film while all this has been going on, a useful addition to the material already shot, and what we really need now is for a female to come down. The clouds build up and the rains begin by midday, although they're mainly showers. Phil and Joseph come to let me out at 2 p.m. – I've had enough after six and a half hours in a damp hide – but it's been very productive. We head back to the lodge for the usual sort-out of the gear and the ritual of charging batteries and reloading film magazines in preparation for a repeat performance tomorrow.

Over the next few days I get more material on the bower bird, but sadly no female lands in the bower, although I do get shots of one nearby which will help enormously with editing the sequence. We switch our attentions to the King of Saxony, which Joseph has been keeping a close eye on for the last few days, while Phil is close to pinning down the display log used by a superb bird of paradise.

The King of Saxony bird of paradise inhabits the montane forests of New Guinea and West Papua at altitudes of between 1,800 and 2,500 metres. It was first described in 1894 by Adolf Bernhard Meyer of Dresden Museum for Albert, King of Saxony, a province of Germany, and is one of the more bizarre of the birds of paradise, with long electric-blue scalloped plumes attached to its head, several times its body length. It is able to move these around independently as it sings and displays. The moulted plumes are keenly sought after by the Archbold's bowerbird to decorate its bower and also by local people to incorporate into their headdresses. Adult males are territorial and guard their territories from perches high in the trees, from where they sing to compete with adjacent males. This makes them difficult to hunt and extremely difficult to film, so we have quite a task on our hands. We do feel we're getting closer, though, and just need a bit of good luck.

Joseph has been working hard on getting a good display site for the King of Saxony. He is now watching two males: the first one doesn't seem to be faithful to one perch and is in a dark area of forest, but the second is more promising, in a more open and lighter patch of forest, and lower down, too. He has seen this bird display several times on the same perch just three metres off the ground, so we decide to put up a hide. Just after 2 p.m. we make the trek into the forest and are beginning to unpack the gear when, unbelievably, the bird drops out of the forest canopy and starts to display right in front of us. We are amazed. We were hoping for good luck but this is better than we could have dreamed of. We decide not to put up the hide as we will have more options without it and the bird seems oblivious to our presence. Our presence, in fact, seems to have prompted the display. It's now heavily overcast with the first of huge rain droplets beginning to fall, so we decide to call it a day and head back to the lodge. We have our bird now – all we need is enough light to film it.

The previous afternoon's rainstorm has cleared, leaving everywhere fresh and moist with a gloriously clear, blue sky. After a quick breakfast Joseph and I head up to the King of Saxony display site, dropping Phil off on the way to watch the other site from a hide. We may need it if this one doesn't work out. We're in position by the display site at half past nine, just standing in the open. Joseph goes away and within a minute or two the male King of Saxony is on the display perch and – fantastic! – in filmable light, too. I have the 300 mm zoom lens on the camera so I'm able to get a few different shots in a short time, 'safety footage', as it's called in the trade, which is just as well as the bird stays for only a few minutes before flying off. It didn't go into a full display but at least I've made a start and the bird is singing nearby, so I think this is the spot. By 11 o'clock it's starting to rain, so Joseph and I head out of the forest, picking Phil up on the way and heading back to our little thatched rooms. That's it for another day as the torrential rain pours from the dense clouds.

At least we have the comfort of the lodge where we can have a drink and meet up with other guests who are passing through. I unpack and check over my cameras and decide to take a walk into the forest, even though it's pouring with rain – a brolly keeps off most of the downpour. I check out a female MacGregor's bowerbird

A male King of Saxony bird of paradise showing the amazing head plumes (photo by, copyright and courtesy of Clifford and Dawn Frith)

that has a nest nearby, and she's sitting tight on her small chick in the pouring rain. Everywhere is dripping but she's chosen her site well, with huge leaves sheltering the nest. Strolling back to the lodge I hear the clatter of a large helicopter coming in low over the forest: it's a Bell 212, full of engineers coming in from one of the mines. They'll drink the place dry in no time, so I'd better get back.

It's 7.30 a.m. the next morning and the rain is just stopping after 16 hours of continuous downpour. Phil has gone to check on the superb bird of paradise display site. It's depressingly dull and I sit around at the lodge with Joseph, waiting for some sort of break in the weather. By 9 a.m. it's starting to brighten, so we pack the van, now repaired, with our film and sound gear and head up to the forest. I set up on the edge of a clearing, hoping to pick up a King of Saxony as it feeds, but after an hour or so there's no sign of the bird, so we move to the display area deeper in the forest. I quickly set up the camera with the 600 mm lens, just in case the bird comes straight down, but there's nothing. After an hour I'm beginning to think that, yet again, we will go home empty-handed when, suddenly, the male glides through the forest performing the most amazing display flight and accompanied by a female. Unbelievably, they both land on a vine right next to us. The male immediately launches into the full display, bouncing up and down on the springy vine, getting more and more excited with each bounce, his bill slightly agape showing its aqua-green interior and producing a stream of strange hissing, buzzing and whirring sounds. His electric-blue head plumes pointed backwards are sometimes swung over his head. He clings tenaciously to the perch and vigorously flexes his legs to maintain the bounce in the vine, his breast shield and mantle cape erect. The female is perched about half a metre above the male on the same vine so that she is bounced around by his gyrations. At the climax of the display the male hops forward toward the female, slowly at first, breast shield and mantle cape feathers erected to their maximum, head plumes raised and swirling on a slowly rotating upper body. The bizarre sounds increase in volume as he mounts the female for the three-second copulation, they separate and fly off and that's it, all over, in two minutes.

That was stunning. The birds were only about seven metres away and I was on the 600 mm lens all the time, not daring to change. We will never see that again – stunning close-ups of the action and in good light, too.

Unusually, the rain stops in the early evening and I take a walk down to the waterfall trail; as I cross the bouncy rattan bridge over the raging river, it's now beautifully sunny and I get stunning backlit shots of the mist rising through the forest. The giant trees on the steep slopes down to the river are festooned with mosses, orchids and flowering vines, which will all help the programme to paint the picture of this remarkable forest. It's been a good day, so I indulge in a few glasses of wine back at the lodge.

Our last few days in the Highlands of New Guinea are somewhat frustrating. I get more close-up behavioural shots in good light of the King of Saxony, with sound effects to match, which all in all makes an excellent sequence on a bird that's never

A rattan bridge over a forest river

been filmed before. But the superb bird of paradise has largely defeated us. Phil has put in many mornings finding out where this very timid and elusive bird displays. The log on which it performed was deep in the darkest part of the forest and the route in to it was treacherous with slippery pathways crumbling underfoot from all the rain, rickety rattan bridges with a 15-metre drop into the river below, our only light a dim torch so as not to scare these secretive birds. The remarkable display happened very early in the morning when the light was insufficient to film, even with a video camera, and although I saw it from the hide, I could do very little to record it. When he suspects a female is nearby, the male – which appears mostly black with an iridescent turquoise-blue breast shield – erects his nape feathers to form a complete, concave cape around his head, with two central white spots which look like tiny eyes. He then bounces and hops along the log in an attempt to court the female. Over several mornings we at least gathered a few shots, which gave a tantalizing hint of what this strange display was like and produced a rudimentary sequence of this very secretive and little-known bird, but how I wish I'd had today's video technology back then.

It had been a long, hard slog, 28 days in the Highlands with huge amounts of rain most days, which had reduced our filming time considerably. We may have produced 12–15 minutes that will be used in the programme, though, so considering the conditions we felt we maybe hadn't done so badly. We were right to suspect that it wouldn't be easy, but over the two trips, with Richard and me each spending four months in the field, we had gathered the raw material for a unique behavioural film on these remarkable birds. The film it made was indeed very successful, providing many insights into the previously unknown behaviour of birds of paradise, and won a series of international awards.

5 AFRICAN ENCOUNTERS

BEYOND TIMBUKTU

Cattle are grazing on the edge of a village where the houses are made from clay and grass and the people are very poor. In the distance, water shimmers, the surface covered with lilies. Fishermen pole their traditional craft through these lagoons to set their traps, and great clouds of waterfowl erupt from open water. This is Mali, one of the poorest countries in Africa, just south of the great Sahara Desert.

It is January on the Niger flood plain, which at this time of year is inundated with flood waters from the River Niger. The seasonal rains that fell to the north between July and September have taken several months to reach the delta, providing a fishing bonanza – both for people and for many species of birds – and lush grazing for millions of cattle that may have been brought to the region from hundreds of miles away. This life-giving river travels 4,200 km on its journey to the sea.

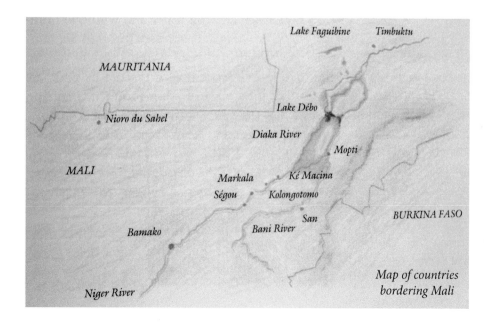

Map of countries bordering Mali

The village of Seria is typical of the region, built on a *toguere*, a little raised island above the flood zone. It's a group of mud and grass houses close to the water, the people here fishermen and pastoralists, their massive herds of cattle driven out to graze on the marshes at dawn and brought back at dusk in a scene unchanged for hundreds of years.

I am here as a wildlife cameraman filming for a BBC Natural World programme entitled *Beyond Timbuktu*, working with artist Bruce Pearson as we follow the lives of European birds that have migrated to Africa for the winter. Apart from me, there is a full sound crew that will film Bruce as he paints various birds and habitats. Working separately, I will concentrate on filming the behaviour of the huge variety of birds, both resident and migrant, that make this place their winter refuge.

For the next week the village of Seria will be my home. The villagers have given us – 'us' being me, my driver, Booba and the interpreter, Curanta – our own compound to use, with five little grass huts. The producer, David Cobham, and researcher, Jo Stewart Smith, are here for a couple of nights before moving on to Youvarou to recce other sites and meet up with the sync crew.

I manage to cram all my equipment into the tiny hut. It's hot, dry and dusty and I quickly discover that I am sharing it with other wildlife. Mice live in the walls and tiny fire finches roost in the roof.

The area around the village is teeming with many species of birds, feeding on the insects disturbed by the cattle: yellow wagtails, sand martins, cattle egrets and pratincoles. Waders – black-winged stilt, ruff, wood sandpiper, little stint, black tailed godwit and greenshanks – are abundant on the marshy pools left by the now receding flood. In the deeper waters there are glossy and sacred ibis, grey and squacco heron and great white egrets. Jacanas are common on the lily pools and there are white-faced and fulvous tree ducks and – most impressively – great clouds of garganey, often put into the air by hunting marsh harriers. It is calculated that up to one million

My bed in the straw hut

Cattle-herding boy

birds of this species, representing 25% of the world population, depend on the flood. There are also white storks in abundance, though sadly some are taken for food by the villagers. They are kind, friendly people who cook for us and often bring us milk, and sometimes fish, to supplement our meagre diet.

It's dawn. I follow the herds of cattle with their young herdsmen as they are driven slowly out to the rich grazing on the bourghou marshes. A low red sun and clouds of dust backlight the abundance of insects, driven from the grasses by thousands of hooves, snapped up by yellow wagtails, egrets and sand martins. White storks, a little more wary, keep their distance. These beautiful images set the scene perfectly, while in the distance I get tantalising glimpses of clouds of waterfowl above the lagoons that over the next few days I must try and portray.

It's 24 January and this morning David, Jo and Jamie are leaving for Youvarou. We will catch up with them in a week's time and we already know that we'll be looking forward to the chance of a bath and a cold beer by then. For now, though, it's down to the real business of getting to grips with the key species. Behind the clay-and- thatch village there is a large lily-fringed lagoon that has great filming potential. The pirogue, a traditional local craft, is the main method of water transport and is perfect for us as, if it is poled silently and expertly, we glide through the lilies without a sound, birds all around us. There are masses of garganey, so the plan will be to return tomorrow and build a hide on the shore. It's very hot today, with less wind, so we head back to the hut for a spot of lunch, then the afternoon is spent filming close-ups of birds around the cattle that are close to the village. By the time I return to my straw hut at 6 p.m., it's thankfully a little cooler. Dinner is rice and a meagre piece of some sort of meat, preceded by a little fish and a leg of white-faced tree duck, which is rather tough.

After filming little green bee-eaters on the edge of some acacia woodland near the village, we load up a pirogue with poles and reed screens, the essentials for hide building. Waterfowl are notoriously suspicious of any new object on the waterside, so

Building a hide to film ducks on the edge of a lagoon

it will need to be well-concealed. We choose a site on the shoreline of the lily lagoon where good numbers of garganey, tree ducks and some pygmy geese have been seen in the last few days. The soil at the water's edge is soft after the flood and it's easy to push in the poles, to which we attach the reed screens to make a box about 1.5 metres square and the same height, leaving a small hole to take the lens. We camouflage the whole structure with grasses and reeds to blend in with the surroundings, then slip quietly away to let the birds get used to it.

The light has not been good over the last few days. Dust storms from the north have filled the air with a haze which makes it difficult to use long lenses on the lagoons. I spend the rest of the afternoon filming the stunningly-coloured bee-eaters, which is difficult, as they are fast and erratic flyers and never seem to use the same perch twice. They catch the bees and similar insects on the wing, then fly back to a perch where they repeatedly smack them to get rid of the sting. Filming them in flight needs to be done in slow motion to have even the slightest chance of keeping them in shot for any length of time. I need to put a perch in a place that may be used on a regular basis.

Booba and Curanta have made a run to the local town for drinks. The water in the village is from a well and of doubtful quality. It tastes foul when a purification tablet has been added, and while boiling is another option, that uses up scarce fuel. It's a joy, then, to see them return with a dozen bottles of Fanta, Coke and tonic water, simple pleasures that you really come to appreciate in such places. This is very basic living: the toilet is a foul pit in the ground with huge numbers of flies, there's dust and rubbish everywhere, herds of cattle, dogs, chickens and goats range freely through the village and general chaos is the norm. It is never quiet, and a continuous chorus of animals throughout the night, along with mice fidgeting around in the thatch of the hut, regularly ensure a poor night's sleep.

Early morning and late afternoon, when the sun is low and the light more atmospheric, are the best times for filming. Having got the herds of cattle grazing at dawn, we need to shoot a sequence of one of the village fishermen going out to set his traps in the lagoons. His pirogue is piled high with fish traps as, dressed in his traditional robes and using a long pole, he glides effortlessly through the maze of channels and lagoons into the wetlands. We are travelling alongside in a very similar pirogue, and I'm hand-holding the camera, which isn't easy in a craft that is less than a metre wide. We see pygmy geese feeding on the tubers of the lilies but it's too unstable and risky to use a long lens, with a real risk of dropping something over the side. The great thing about these pirogues is that you are low to the water, which allows me to get smooth tracking shots as we glide alongside, the traditional bow of the boat cleaving its way through the dense beds of flowering water lilies. Experience leads the fisherman to the best spots to drop in the pots and he will return again tonight to check them.

We head back to the village in incredible heat and a cool Fanta is heavenly. I cook potatoes and onions with sardines, which might not sound that appetising, but which

A local fisherman poling his pirogue to lay traps

makes a change from rice. We bought a sheep at the market the other day, and it's been grazing in our compound. This morning it had its throat cut and is now roasting on a fire. I feel a little sick, probably due to a combination of the heat, poor food and the sight and smell of the sheep so, unusually for me, I go for a lie-down until half past two. Feeling a little better, we go out to the lagoon to set another hide, this time a canvas one, and camouflage it well. I get into it straight away and set up the camera with the big 500 mm lens. By now it's 3.30 p.m. and the light is getting less harsh as the sun starts to drop. It's looking good, I can see birds out on the lagoon, feeding, and hope they'll come closer to me. Sure enough, as time goes on, the pygmy geese, which are less timid than the other wildfowl, gradually come closer. They are actually Africa's smallest species of waterfowl and not a goose at all, but a dabbling duck, weighing a mere 250 grams and very striking to look at. Through my most powerful lens I can see the stubby yellow bill and white face, the iridescent green back and chestnut flanks. A pair is definitely moving closer and I can see they are using that strange bill to break open the seed capsules of the water lilies which provide the bulk of their diet. They also feed on the floating seeds of other water plants and small invertebrates.

In the mid-distance, groups of garganey are starting to feed closer, and to see such huge numbers is very exciting. Normally in the UK they're something of a rarity, just pairs or individuals turning up in spring at locations such as the Ouse Washes in Cambridgeshire. This has been a good afternoon with some useful close-ups of the pygmy geese and the beginnings of a sequence on the garganey. I will come back to this spot again.

Over the next few mornings I work the permanent hide on the lagoon which we built from reed screens, going out at 6 a.m. for the best light. I'm plagued by early cloud, haze and wind so don't achieve much, although the huge clouds of garganey look quite impressive, slightly backlit and harassed by marsh harriers , so I shoot some of that anyhow as safety footage. The visibility remains awful, with the wind whipping up the fine dust and creating a haze that reduces visibility to 500 metres, so it's generally frustrating.

I finish early evening and cook up a nostalgic treat for a delicious supper: mashed potato with a Vesta curry, which isn't bad as a change, fortified with extra sultanas, onions and curry powder.

29 January: on Thursday morning, on my way back from the lily lagoon hide behind the village, I saw a fisherman emptying his nets into an enamel bowl and was horrified to see in the bowl with the fish four garganey that had been caught by their feet in the net, still very much alive and with the wings tied with reed stems, bound for the pot I'm afraid. Beautiful little ducks, their eyes looked knowing of what was to come

Garganey in bowl

Apparently they catch a few every day, although in the great scheme of things I doubt the few dozen they take makes a great difference to the population as a whole. It is the massive schemes for diverting rivers, building dams and draining wetlands that is affecting waterfowl populations worldwide.

It's up at 6.30 a.m. for a final hide session for garganey. It's still very hazy and the sun doesn't get through at all, which is very disappointing, but I do feel that there is enough material to tell the story of these large numbers of birds taking advantage of this seasonal flood. On the way back to the village a group of storks is feeding around the cattle. I get useful shots of them moving out to the marshes and the storks take flight, providing a fitting little closing sequence.

It's time to clean and pack everything into the vehicle for the trip to Youvarou, a small town to the north, and the whole village comes out to see us off. I have that odd feeling I get when I leave a place: it's good to be moving on to meet up with the rest of the crew, and I love the thought of a hot shower and cold beers, but there's also a real sadness at leaving people and a special place in which I have been embedded for some time.

Our heavily laden pirogue makes its slow passage through the maze of channels then, in the hazy distance, we see a pall of smoke above a barely visible shoreline with its teeming mass of people. As we draw closer, we begin to see the mass of humanity packed onto the narrow strip of land. In front of each reed hut are piles of dried and smoked fish to be sorted, weighed and bagged, the air is full of smoke from little fires on the ground and mud brick kilns, smaller fish are drying in the sun and there's a frenetic scene of urgency as more fish arrive from the traps for processing. This is Tielde, a seasonal fishing camp built on the shores of Lake Debo; as soon as the flood starts to subside and enough mud is revealed, the transient city of reed huts starts to grow, with fishermen arriving from many miles away. There can be up to 2,000 people here and they have only six weeks to cash in on this bonanza. It is a grass and reed city, with 'streets' between the huts.

Water running off the flooded delta, where millions of fish have spawned, is concentrated through a narrow channel into Lake Debo, the fish travelling with the flow to escape but being dried out by the falling water levels. Semi-permanent rows of traps are built along the channel to intercept the concentrations of fish pouring off the delta. Close to the camp, thousands of birds are also taking advantage of this bonanza: in the air above the traps are Caspian, gull-billed, whiskered and white-winged black terns. In the water and on the traps are a mass of black herons, little egrets, great white herons and cormorants, spearing fish at will, and in the distance I can see the elusive flocks of garganey and pintail.

Our boys have arranged for our own thatched hut to be built, in among the hundreds of others, and day and night the noise is continuous. With the crying of children, the constant thud of women pounding millet, loud radios and cocks crowing, I wonder if we will ever get any sleep. I am sharing with the producer, David, and assistant producer, Jo, but there's plenty of room for us and all our gear. My stomach is still off, as it has been for most of my stay here, so I don't have the usual rice and sauce with a scrap of chicken, playing safe with bread and a boiled egg. The noise continues into the early hours, then gradually subsides and I slip into a fitful sleep.

The fishing camp at Tielde

A line of fish traps

A mass of egrets with the fishing camp behind

Daybreak – with the attendant noise – comes quickly, and after a coffee and bread and jam for breakfast, I'm only too glad to load the pirogue, grab our boatman and head off along the fish traps to film both people and birds in their frenzied fishing activity. Among the egrets and terns there are black herons, which have a unique fishing technique: by arching their wings into an umbrella shape over their heads, they form a shaded area on the water into which the little fish are attracted, then easily speared by the heron's dagger-like bill.

I'm back at camp for half past five after another exhausting, though quite productive, day. As you would expect, the sanitary facilities here are indescribably poor. Just behind the mass of straw huts, ours included, is an open, dry area where everyone goes to perform their morning constitutional. As the days go by, the smell is worsening alarmingly in the heat, as is the minefield that has to be crossed to find a clean patch. There is no shelter – you just turn your back to the world and get on with it.

The next few days are productive. As well as filming squacco herons and cormorants fishing and roosting on the fish traps, I find a good location for waders, where I manage to put up a hide. The receding water has left exposed areas of mud where the birds are feeding on an abundance of insects and invertebrates. Marsh sandpipers, curlew sandpipers, little stint, ruff and Kittlitz's plover are soon in close to me and I get some very useful shots. Bruce will no doubt be painting many of these when he arrives.

Fortunately, a lot of tracks are now becoming passable as the flood drops and the ground dries. Booba has got through from Youvaru, only half an hour away, with some fairly fresh bread for breakfast. I will probably go back there tonight to get a decent night's sleep with a proper toilet.

Back in Youvarou for the night, I'm feeling somewhat under the weather with a bad stomach and the beginnings of a cold, so an early night seems like a good idea. Until, that is, a vehicle's headlights light up the yard, doors open and close and I hear familiar voices. It's David with Bruce Pearson and the crew, so I feel duty bound to get up and be sociable, and stay up chatting until nearly midnight.

The sync crew will be working separately from me. I'll be concentrating, as I have been over the last couple of weeks, on specific bird behaviours and landscapes, while they will be filming Bruce as he paints landscapes and birdlife and delivers sync pieces to camera relating to the flood and its importance to the local people and wildlife. Just after dawn, Jamie drives Booba, Curanta and myself, along with all our gear, to the massive fishing camp at Tielde, where we load up a pirogue for the two-hour river trip to the little village of Dentaka, an area known for its large colonies of breeding herons, egrets and spoonbills; the breeding behavior that we hope to film here will be important to complete the water bird story. We set off at half past eight for a peaceful journey through the narrow channels in the *burgu*, a type of coarse grassland. We pass other pirogues, heavily laden with fish traps and families en route to other fishing camps, and the bird life – as always – is plentiful and varied, with marsh and Montagu's harriers and purple herons. Two hours later we arrive at Dentaka, a small, typical, dusty little village with animals and people everywhere. After transferring to our little straw hut our considerable amount of kit – film gear, bedding and food for two or three days – we head out to check the colony before it gets too hot. There are many species of waterbirds – spoonbills, night herons, open-billed storks, sacred ibis, black heron and great white egret – all nesting together in low, scrubby trees, mostly

Spoonbills with young at the nest

with large young, but some of the nests are frustratingly difficult to see through the dense foliage. After a meagre lunch of rice and sauce, I head back to the colony with the film gear and shoot from the roof of the Land Rover, which helps to give me some height, but I could do with a proper platform. Given that there just aren't the materials here to do that, though, I have to make the best of it.

Spoonbills feeding their large young are about all I get and by 4 p.m. I'm ready to pack in. The light has turned hazy and I feel rotten from a combination of diarrhoea and dehydration, so I head back to camp. I hear via the satellite phone that the Land Rover has to leave on Friday morning to get Curanta, the interpreter, back to Yuvarou for Friday night, meaning that I only get one more full day here, which just isn't enough to do justice to the colony. I feel a bit aggrieved, having come all this way.

My night in the hut is plagued with noise from radios blaring, donkeys 'hee-haw'-ing, jackals howling and cockerels crowing, not to mention rats hanging from the roof above my head. I'm glad when dawn comes at 6.30. It's a clear, sunny day for a change, with no wind, and the day turns out to be quite productive. I shoot open-billed storks and sacred ibis with large young at the nest, along with the odd black heron and great white egret, all from the Land Rover roof. I think there is enough for a small sequence to tell the story of this time of plenty, when all the waterbirds breed and the young grow quickly on the bonanza of fish from the delta.

Back at my hut, I cook up a supper on the little stove of potatoes and Vesta curry. Booba invites some of the village people in to drink tea and chat, but I can't join in, as they talk in French. They eat dates and spit the stones at high velocity around the hut. As I sit writing my diary, there are three young women and five children watching my every move. I think it's very rare that they see a white face. The people here have so little but are friendly and I feel completely safe in their company. The ladies are very attractive, with beautiful skin, lovely smiles and soft hypnotic voices. Fortunately, they leave by 9 p.m. and I'm in bed shortly after.

I have to endure another bad night, with the usual cacophony of sounds to disturb me. We're up just after dawn, I shoot a short sequence around the village to establish it within the harsh landscape, then pack everything into the pirogue. The whole village comes out to say goodbye as we slip silently away into the timeless waterways of the delta.

Loading our filming gear into the pirogue

Back in the chaos of the fishing camp at Tielde, bigger and noisier than ever, we meet up with David, Jamie and Bruce, who is just finishing a sketch of a kingfisher in the hand, rescued from one of the fish traps. We all head back to Youvarou for the evening, where it's great to catch up with what everyone else has been doing, have a shower, a cold beer and a decent meal.

Today is a day off for me and I luxuriate in reading a *Sunday Times* that the crew brought out, eagerly eating freshly baked bread and jam and drinking coffee. It's so peaceful here, now that the crew have all gone off with Bruce to film sequences at Toguere, Kombi and Serri. I work locally in the transition zone, the strip of land between the Sahara to the north and the lush delta to the south, trying to get shots of Egyptian vultures as they feed on dried-out scraps of fish around the old fish camps. There are Spanish wheatears and great grey shrikes, too, both of which prove to be rather elusive. Eventually, after much persistence, I manage a few shots, while a black-headed plover makes a bold establishing shot in amongst the dead stalks of millet. David Cobham, the producer, and Brian McDermott, a cameraman, have gone up to Timbuktu on the edge of the Sahara to recce locations, and now Bruce, Jo and the rest of their crew are going up to join them. I'm going with Booba, Sinai and our driver to a place called Cinni, near Dioura, where there are fields of millet now harvested and drying out in the ever-rising temperatures.

What a place. Bleak and desolate with isolated villages, starving cattle and a constant hot wind whipping up the dust. We head out into the millet fields and I find a woodchat shrike perched in the dried vegetation, but with a big lens it's impossible to film in the windy conditions. I spot a couple of bustards but they're off before I can get near them. I don't want to expose my equipment to this dust – it can ruin lenses if it gets into the focus mechanism. We decide to retire to the little clay hut on the edge of the village that we will use for the next couple of nights, if we don't pack in before then. Because of the dust and heat I feel continuously thirsty, but I wouldn't dare drink the local water – that way lies disaster. We have only a limited supply of bottled water which is strictly rationed.

The next couple of days are not productive. The wind and dust make life very difficult, and it's hotter than hell. I manage a few shots of the woodchat shrike

The barren landscape of the Sahel

in the millet fields and one catches a mouse, in typical fashion impaling the luckless little rodent on a thorn bush. I manage to get reasonably close and get a few shots of it pulling the mouse apart, but it's obscured by twigs and the light is milky from all the fine dust in the air. I suspect we will be leaving here tomorrow. I think our time will be spent more productively around Youvarou and the flood areas.

It's a bright morning, though, with little wind, so I get out early to the fields. Before we leave I manage a few good shots of the shrike perched in millet near to a big baobab tree, which sets the scene nicely. The wind is already picking up in strength so we head back to the village to pack for the four-hour journey back to Youvarou. Booba has been sick during the night and looks awful. A young boy is brought to us for first aid, as he's fallen onto a sharp stick and gashed his arm. We manage to patch him up with the help of our comprehensive first aid kit, for which the villagers are very grateful.

The journey back to Youvarou is uneventful and it's good to get back to the relative coolness of our courtyard by the river with its spacious rooms. My first job is to have a good shower, to get rid of the dust from myself, and then to give the equipment a thorough clean. David, Bruce and the crew arrive back from Timbuktu at around 4 p.m. having had a similarly hot and dusty experience. The evening is pleasant with an exchange of stories and a few cold beers from the paraffin fridge, which I'm glad to say is working well for a change.

The African fish eagle is an emblematic bird of the watercourses. I have made several attempts over the last few days to film them, with some success, mainly getting shots of birds perched on favourite trees and in flight, but still have no shots of a fish being caught. That was about to change. I was out early this morning in good light and the eagle was active, giving me great shots of it soaring, then skimming the water surface, when – bang! – it grabs a fish in its powerful talons and labours up into a big riverside tree with its catch.

Back for lunch with David, Bruce, Jo et al to discover that there's a catastrophic problem with the ancient Mercedes 4x4. The front suspension has collapsed, sending the shock absorber through the obviously rotten box chassis and leaving a gaping hole. The boys do a temporary repair with wire strapping but it doesn't bode well.

After lunch, I head back out to the old fish camp by the river, where many waders are feeding, mainly on the insects attracted by the decomposing fish. There are curlew sandpipers, ruff, marsh sandpipers and little stint and soon I've got a useful sequence of this interesting behavior, showing how adaptable birds are. This could be a great spot for the elusive garganey: there are many hundreds in the big channel and I think a hide here tomorrow could be very productive.

After breakfast I go up to the fish eagle site, dropping Bruce off on the way to do a big painting in watercolour of the river. There are no eagles about this morning, although I do get some nice shots of yellow wagtails feeding among goats, with a crested lark. I set up the hide for the garganey on the edge of the big channel. There

*Bruce Pearson
paints the river*

are lots of ducks around, the light is good and the wind has dropped, so I feel that it's going to be a productive afternoon. As I get settled into the hide I can see garganey and pintail edging closer and with my big 600 mm lens, I am beginning to see images grow larger in the viewfinder. They don't seem concerned by the hide so maybe, at last, I am going to get the elusive close-up shots that I have been trying for since I arrived. The closest birds are now just 30 metres away, closer than anything before. I can see the beautiful plumage of the male garganey as they feed at the edge of the flood, some settle down to preen and sleep while others feed ever closer until, eventually, they are only five metres away, bathed in the soft afternoon light. These are some of the most satisfying shots I have got of these very elusive birds, so persistence and a bit of good luck eventually do pay off. It's getting on for 6 p.m. when the light falls away and I head back to our base at Youvarou for the night.

A flock of garganey on the shoreline

*A drake garganey by
Bruce Pearson*

The next couple of days are spent tidying up loose ends. I film small waders feeding on the profusion of insects on the drying-out muddy margins of the flood, curlew sandpipers, marsh sandpipers, little stints and black-winged stilt and I manage a few shots of a chanting goshawk at the top of a big fig tree, which Bruce had painted earlier. My time here is coming to an end, I have just a few more days, culminating in meeting up with Bruce and the rest of the crew at Mopti in a couple of days' time to film the big cattle crossing of the Niger River. Now that the dry season is well underway, the waters are low enough to allow cattle, for the most part, to wade across. That should be quite a spectacle: thousands of cattle from the desert areas to the north being driven across the river to fresh pastures to the south, a noisy, colourful and extravagant event, with families reunited, music, dancing and feasting. It's an exciting prospect on which to finish a memorable trip.

PLANET EARTH AND DESERT LOCUSTS

I am standing on a red sand dune in North Africa, the milky sky filled with golden desert dust and unbelievable numbers of insects, so dense that they block out the sun, their wings clattering against each other as they fly just above my head, a continuously moving mass many kilometres wide. These are desert locusts, probably one of the most feared insects in Africa. Swarms of these voracious creatures have affected agricultural production in Africa for centuries and, although not entirely responsible, are a large contributory factor to famines. Because of the insect's life cycle these plagues do not occur every year, but their effects on national economies can be devastating.

It was in 2004 that I travelled to Mauritania to attempt to film the incredible phenomenon that I was watching. Because very particular conditions are needed before a swarm will form, trying to judge the best time to film is something of an inexact science. A BBC crew had been here in 2003 but failed to find any swarming behaviour; the desert locust can exist as a solitary insect, causing little damage.

The sequence we're trying to film is for the *Deserts* programme in the BBC *Planet Earth* series. We have flown from Paris to Nouakchott in Mauritania, a poor and arid country just south of the Sahara. We are using a local logistics company called Adrar Voyages, who are supplying vehicles, tents and generators, camp gear, a driver and an interpreter, camp hands and the like. Tom Hugh-Jones, the producer, and Pascale, a reporter for the BBC World Service, have to go into local offices to sort out permits and documentation, but by the time these are obtained it is late afternoon, too late to go any distance. We drive out of the shabby little town into a dune area where the lads soon have the vehicles unloaded and the camp set up. We have large, white, canvas tents with roll-up sides, great to let in what little breeze there is. It is incredibly hot, maybe 40° C by day and still quite hot at night. There are four of us in our tent: Tom and me, Pascale and a French photographer, Luc, who is travelling around Maurita-

nia. We have a good supper of potatoes, salad and fried chicken followed by a whisky or two, before turning in at 11 p.m, ready for a long travel day.

We're up at 7 a.m. and enjoy the coolest part of the day. After a coffee and bread and honey for breakfast, the team from Adrar soon have the camp stripped down and packed away into the two 4x4 Land Cruisers and we're on the road by half past eight. It's already

Our camp in the dunes

beginning to get very hot; the journey to Tarifa is about 400 km and my stomach is beginning to feel a little delicate. After about two hours' driving, we start to come across huge numbers of locusts along the road. We drive through great clouds of them, they're impossible to avoid, and the radiator grille gets clogged with the unfortunate insects. The engine soon begins to overheat and we have to make frequent stops to scrape away the corpses.

We stop in an open-sided tent nearby, which gives us some respite from the intense sun. The masses of locusts killed by traffic are attracting thousands more, which are feeding on the carcasses, a macabre site which we have to film. The passing traffic sends clouds of the voracious insects into the air, some are perched in nearby trees, and crops in the fields are already stripped bare to the stalks. These are really useful shots for a bonus sequence that was not envisaged back in Bristol.

My stomach pains are now serious and I have to rush into the scrub to relieve myself. Fortunately there aren't any flies or mosquitoes around, which is one blessing, but I do feel really debilitated and dehydrated from the heat. At about 3 p.m. we press on, still with 180 km to go. The sky ahead of us is ominously black with occasional bolts of lightning, a storm is brewing, and very soon we are travelling through heavy rain. It's almost dark when we get into Tarifa so we go straight to the airport to find the locust control officer, who should have the latest updates on where the big swarms are moving, but he's already finished for the day.

We head up to the dunes to make camp for the night. There's a lovely breeze and a good view, great expanses of red sand temporarily infused with green patches after the recent rains, and the donkeys, goats and camels are taking full advantage. We're all very tired after a long day travelling and filming in the relentless heat.

Loading up the spray planes

It's 7 a.m. and after a quick breakfast we head down to the airfield, where we see two locust spraying planes and a lot of activity. These specialist crop spraying aircraft, known as Ag (agricultural) planes, have been flown up from South Africa by highly experienced pilots, mostly from New Zealand. These guys are specialists in low-level agricultural flying and will be here for six weeks. The aircraft are being fueled up and the spray tanks loaded with a chemical to spray at low level, mostly over the hopper stage of the locust development. Locusts lay their eggs in the soft ground after rains and, depending on conditions, those eggs may remain in the soil for many months before they hatch. When they do hatch, the nymphs are solitary and flightless but, as numbers increase, their legs bump against each other, triggering various metabolic changes and initiating swarming behaviour in the hoppers. They roam the ground, devouring all in their path, and it is at this pre-flight stage that they are targeted by the spray teams. Once the locusts are airborne they are very mobile – they can fly hundreds of kilometres in a day – and are difficult to track down.

I set up my cameras. This is great stuff: bright yellow aircraft, fuel and chemical trucks buzzing around against a backdrop of barren, rocky landscape with little vegetation, the area already devastated by recent swarms of the marauding insects. Then the aircraft are up and away, providing a dramatic start to what I hope will be a detailed sequence on the spraying operation. The boss of the operation tells us there is a good location, for hoppers mostly, about 65 km away; armed with the GPS coordinates, we pack up the film gear and head off. It's a long drive, and a slow one, as it's mostly on sand tracks. We pass through small villages typical of the region, little clay rondaval-style houses with thatched roofs. The people who live in them are friendly – I doubt they see many westerners – and always come out to greet us, offering us goat's milk mixed with water. Out of courtesy, our Mauritanian colleagues always drink it, although we are advised not to. The water would almost certainly give us gut rot, to add to the one I have already had for several days.

We come across a big mass of hoppers at the side of the dusty track, some in a large bush, many on the ground and on the move. Quickly setting up the Arriflex camera with a wide- angle zoom lens, I take some establishing shots with the bush in the foreground. It is heaving, almost pulsing, with the bright green-and-yellow horde that is stripping the vegetation before our eyes. I get great close-ups of them feeding, packed together in this great mass. I switch my attention to the swarm on the ground. I take the camera off the tripod and put it in amongst the moving mass. Tom the producer and Chay, one of our guides, shake the bush to drop others down and add to the spectacle. These green-and-yellow hoppers are very different from the sub-adults and adults, which vary from brownish-pink to yellow.

While we are filming, one of the ag planes comes over very close to us, actively spraying. We cover our faces with clothing as we can smell the fine particles in the air, even though the spray is only at one litre per hectare. I manage to get some good stills as the plane banks and comes in for another low pass.

It's been a productive few hours and it's 4 p.m. We're starving, so we pack up and head back to camp, to tuck into a sardine salad with bread. Back near the airport there

An ag plane spraying

are some small swarms on the move which Tom is keen to film, though the area is not particularly filmable habitat. The evening air is full of dust, which blots out the low sun. It's a pity, but I film it anyway, suspecting that it may end up on the cutting room floor.

Back at our camp in the dunes, it's good to relax after another hot and dusty – but, above all, productive – day. The lads rustle up some soup and salad, while I spend time writing up my diary and making notes on what I've shot for the day. This is really useful when it comes to the edit. Sitting outside in the cool of the desert night, I'm using my headlamp torch, and a night-flying locust smacks into the side of my head. Pascale, the French correspondent working for the BBC World Service and travelling with us, is writing her dispatches and has the light on, attracting an array of bugs and beetles into the tent.

Another day dawns, clear and cool. After a quick coffee and bread, Tom and I, Chay and Jacob our driver set off to the dunes closest to town to check for any locust movement, and find nothing initially, but do see some fine birds – rollers, bee-eaters and various species of shrike. We drive back along the base of the dune system and I see some movement along the ridge – 'Locusts on the move!' We quickly park up in the shade of acacia trees and assemble the film gear. The light is good and it's still relatively cool (relative being the word: it's probably 25°C). I get some safety footage as the swarm passes, with the dunes in the background, but get the best shots from the top of the ridge after an exhausting scramble up through deep, fine sand. The breeze is blowing along the top of the dune and the swarm is flying low and straight towards the camera, the light is perfect and I manage various shot sizes and some slow motion as they pour past the lens. It's late morning so we head back to camp for an early lunch. There's another site for which we have GPS coordinates, about 25 km from camp, where large numbers of adult locusts have been seen.

Typical desert terain
Inset: A lorry's radiator plastered with locusts

It's gone 1 p.m. and is blisteringly hot as we head back into the desert. The route is entirely on sand and over dunes, so it's a good job we have experienced local drivers who know how to cope with this kind of terrain, as we probably wouldn't last five minutes before getting bogged down. It's a fabulous drive, with lots of camels wandering about, but when we get to the site the villagers tell us that the locusts have already moved on. There's nothing to be done but to head back to camp again for a quick change of T-shirt and to pick up some bottled water, before going to town to see if we can pick up any local intelligence on swarm sightings. Sure enough, we are told of a big mass just 15 km out of town. When we arrive, they're still there: a 200-metre stretch of road is covered with the bodies of locusts that have been struck by traffic, again offering us the rather unpleasant spectacle of other locusts flying in and feeding on the corpses at the roadside. Each time traffic passes, a great mass erupts into the air.

We film tracking shots from our vehicle at 100 fps, 4x slower than normal, following alongside the locusts as they fly parallel to the road. This is a great opportunity to get a unique 'flying with the locusts' shot and we are really starting to get some cracking material. The sun disappears into the hazy horizon, as usual, by 6.15, so it's back to camp. It's been a very productive day, and there's time for a relaxing shower behind an acacia bush – water from a jerry can heated by the desert sun is perfect to relax weary bones. We're changing our location tomorrow, so I do some pre-packing and get an early night.

We break camp in the dunes just after dawn, in preparation for a long drive to Tidijikja, the capital of the Tagent region of Central Mauritania. Leaving at half past eight, we call by the airfield to get the latest news from the spray teams. The aircraft are in so we get to chat with the pilots, though there's nothing that we can act upon locally.

The long drive is through stunning dune scenery, dotted with ancient villages. Fields devoid of any crops offer graphic evidence that big swarms have passed through here, and we feel for the poor farmers who have lost everything, although they seem resigned to the fact that it is God's will. We pass through an ancient city at the base of huge sandstone cliffs and from there up onto a plateau and on to Tidijikja. We set up camp beyond the town, high on the dunes as usual, the coolest place, and which gives a good overview if any locusts are on the move.

Tom, Chay, Jacob and I head off just after dawn to see what's happening locally and, just 15 km away, we find a swarm feeding. We need to show this in some detail so I get to work filming big close-ups of the heads of the adults as they munch on grasses close to the ground, followed by wide-angle shots with dunes and camels beyond. Back at camp, Pascale has been talking with the local locust control officer who knows of some hopper bands, to which he will take us. After a quick lunch we meet up with him in town. It's a drive of about 20 km on tarmac roads, followed by another 15 km through sand to the location, and it's incredibly hot, as it has been throughout the trip. We walk through cultivated areas and talk with the local farmers, then – after a

A mass of locusts strips a bush of its foliage

lot of searching – we find what we have been looking for: very small, black hoppers, just 12–15 mm long. They're really difficult to film as they don't keep still for more than two seconds, so I have to go to a wide shot. The farmers sweep them together into a dense group which I film, a seething mass that within weeks could have been on the wing and adding to the devastation. These won't be, though, as the farmers have other plans. They dig a trench 25 cm deep, sweep the whole lot into it and bury them, in a crude but effective control. It's a mere pinprick, though, in terms of the overall population. Some nearby fields hold quite big numbers of adults on the ground and, with the camera set at 100 fps, I run into the resting swarm and put them into the air. It could be an interesting 'point of view' shot to add to the sequence.

We only have a couple of days left but I think the sequence is virtually there. We have one more camp change, and by 3.15 in the afternoon, working on advice from the locust control teams, we've set up our tents in a new location. By choice it's close to the camp of the locust control group, which means we should get the latest info on any big swarms as soon as it's available. Apparently there was a massive swarm here yesterday which could return if the winds are favourable; locusts always fly into the wind towards low-pressure areas, where there is more chance of rain and – as a consequence – fresh growth to feed on. The men on the ground from the nearby control group suggest a few locations that we might check out but it's always the same story when we arrive and chat to the locals. 'Yes, there are many over there, lots!' but, by the time we get to wherever they have sent us, the swarm has already moved on. Second guessing the movements of locusts turns out to be a frustrating pastime.

A massive cloud of locusts darkens the sky

It's 29 September and, after an uneventful morning, we head back to camp for an early lunch. We sit around chatting and discussing our next moves when we get a report of a colossal swarm, 135 km to the south. We all decide to go for it, although it's 3.15 by the time we set off, so we need to go some to get there before we start to lose light. Fortunately the roads are good, and there's no sand to cross. As we approach the zone where the swarms were reported, we start to encounter larger and larger numbers along the road. Again we have to stop regularly to scrape them from the radiator and are now in amongst the most incredible density we've seen so far.

We pull off the main road and drive into an arid area of scrub. I quickly set up the gear but realise that I needn't worry too much: it's soon obvious that this swarm will be around for some time. The sky is black with locusts, an endless wave passing over us just seven metres from the ground, the hissing rattle of their wings blotting out any other sounds. I film them from all angles, against the sky, against distant dunes, in slow motion, wide-angles, close-ups in flight, from every conceivable angle, I need to take full advantage of this as we'll never see something on this scale again. I eventually shoot two rolls of film, 20 minutes of highly-usable footage, and we stay right up to sunset, when they are still flying west. This is one of the great spectacles of the natural world and one that I will never forget. We're in no doubt that we now have a very complete sequence on this amazing insect.

More than two hours later there is still no sign of the end of this swarm, and I start doing some calculations. The swarm is 40 km across and I reckon it's flying at speeds of 20 k.p.h., meaning that at least 40 km of locust have already passed us. That's 1,600 square kilometres of locusts, up to 2 metres deep. At up to 80 million per square km, I reckon that this, the mother of all swarms, could have held up to 200 billion locusts. 200 billion locusts weigh up to 256 tons in total, and – given that they each consume their own body weight in a day – that's 256 tons of vegetation being eaten daily by this one swarm. The cost of trying to combat this plague in 2004 was over US$400 million and harvest losses stood at US$2.5 billion.

Against the odds, I think we have filmed a sequence that really shows the life story of the locust and the devastating effects that this voracious insect has on the peoples of Africa and beyond. It really brings home how little these communities have and how entirely they are living – just four hours' flight from us – at the mercy of the climate.

Central African Republic

3,700 km to the south-east of Mauritania lies the Central African Republic, a land-locked nation of 384,000 square km, bordered by Chad to the north, Sudan to the north and east, the Democratic Republic of Congo to the south and Cameroon to the west. Though rich in natural resources such as uranium, crude oil, gold, diamonds, cobalt and lumber, it is the poorest country in the world. It is very rich in wildlife, with 3,600 species of plant, 663 species of bird, 209 mammal species, 187 reptile and 29 amphibian species; sadly, it also has the usual problems of poaching for ivory and bush meat, illegal felling of timber and subsequent forest clearance in favour of crop cultivation.

In the tropical southwest of the country is the Dzanga-Sangha National Park, haunt of forest elephants, lowland gorillas and African grey parrots, most familiar to people in the west as talking cagebirds. Here in the national park they occur in large flocks at a remote forest water hole where they gather, along with herds of dwarf forest elephants, to get important minerals essential to their diet.

Our arrival in the capital of Bangui is fraught with chaos at Immigration, where people are milling everywhere and there's no apparent system. We meet our African fixer Timothee, who seems switched on, and all our gear arrives, except – would you believe? – the cold box containing the film stock. We search every corner of the airport but it's just not there. We check in to the Sofitel, which to our surprise is quite a nice hotel, right by the river, looking across at Zaire on the opposite bank, and I stay to sort out some cash transactions while Paul Reddish, my producer on this trip, goes into town to meet various permit-issuing officials. I'm beginning to feel really lousy now, with flu-like symptoms. A chap from WWF (the World Wildlife Fund) is supposed to come with our vehicle and filming permits but doesn't show up, and isn't traceable by phone. So far, then, we have no film, no vehicle and no filming permits. It's not been a great start. Paul gives up trying to call the WWF and switches to phoning Bristol, to see if we can get more film stock sent out pronto.

After a poor night's sleep I still feel lousy, as though I have swallowed a mouthful of razor blades. My throat is so sore I can barely speak. Paul arrives back mid-morning, very stressed, from a trip into town: there is still no sign of the permit to film or of a vehicle and he is even talking about going home if it's not sorted in the next 24 hours. We decide to go to the WWF office to try and find the elusive Gustave Doungoumbe and come across him lurking in a dingy, fly-ridden office. He assures us that he has a vehicle, which we actually see, a somewhat tired-looking white Land Cruiser, and that he will have the permit by the next day. I go back to the hotel and flake out for the afternoon, while Paul goes chasing Customs, impressing on them the importance of getting hold of the film stock as soon as it arrives at 5.10 p.m. tomorrow. If we don't get it, we'll be up the creek.

By the next day, I feel slightly better and, although still achey and lifeless, have shaken off the sore throat and runny nose. Paul has spent the morning chasing Mr Doungoumbe and returns elated. We now have a vehicle, driver and filming permit, so things are happening at last. I go into town with the driver, Daniel, who speaks only French and virtually no English, to get provisions for a week's camping, while Paul goes with Timothee to the airport to await the arrival of the film stock. Food, especially luxury items like coffee, meat and cheese, is expensive and I quickly spend $240. I decide to buy fruit and vegetables from the street vendors, starting with just two and quickly creating an arguing throng of over a dozen, all trying to make me buy their produce. They are really persistent and won't take no for an answer, so I won't be doing that again.

I don't get back to the hotel until 7 p.m. and find Paul there with the film stock. We now have everything we need, so the plan is to leave at 6 o'clock the next morning. Mr Doungoumbe takes us to an outdoor African restaurant where we have a very tasty meal of barbecued chicken and fried plantains. Back at the hotel, we have hassle at the reception desk over a 15% discount which had previously been agreed but which the hotel is now trying to worm its way out of honouring, and we eventually get to bed at 10.45.

The driver is late and we're not on the road until 6.30 a.m. To start with, the roads are good but soon deteriorate into various grades of dirt track, crossing heavy tropical forest. We pass through tiny thatched villages, built by pygmies. We stop for some lunch in a forest clearing, to eat our standard fare of bread and tinned sardines, and see pygmies in tiny loincloths carrying huge bundles of split bamboo, and another with a very long spear. As we pass through another village we accidentally hit a wayward chicken, producing a cloud of feathers and cries of anguish and derision from a watching group of pygmy women.

After ten hours on difficult roads, we arrive at remote Bayanga at 4.30 p.m. The very helpful head of the National Park takes us down to the campground, which is amazingly good. We meet Andrea, the elephant researcher, and her helper Peter. She is very welcoming to us, although admits that she doesn't normally like visitors, and says that we are welcome to stay in her camp. We accept the invitation and set up our tents under thatched shelters in a forest clearing, hoping for protection from the tropical rains which we are bound to get. After an evening meal of pasta and meat sauce and convivial chat about what we hope to achieve, we turn in for what turns out to be a disturbed night, with elephants trumpeting, people snoring, mice scuttling and a hard sleeping mat. I lie awake, very excited about the next day.

The smell of elephant dung hangs on the cool morning mist as we wade through a clear, shallow river and into the dense tropical forest. The interior is a maze of corridors created by the dwarf elephants as they make their way to the mineral pool in a clearing some 30 minutes from here. There are four of us: I am with Paul, Peter and a pygmy helper making light of carrying the substantial amount of film gear. It's quite an odd experience to know that we could run in to these forest elephants at any time within this claustrophobic interior, and I hope they hear or smell us and keep their distance. Eventually, after 30 minutes of squeezing through these forest tunnels, we break out of the dense canopy into a large clearing. The weak sun is just rising over the biggest trees, and in the centre of a natural clearing we see a muddy pool. There are maybe 50 elephants, mothers and calves and some young and adult bulls, all sinking their trunks up to the hilt into little craters of mud which they have created. They are sucking up the mineral waters from below, and many of the animals are tinted a yellow colour where they have sprayed themselves with liquid mud to cool off in the intense tropical heat.

Right: The field camp in the forest
Below: The waterhole
with forest elephants

Nearby there is a substantial platform, maybe 20 feet off the ground, five metres square or so, with benches, open sides and a roof. It was built for research studies but will be perfect for filming, and so much more comfortable than being crushed up in a little canvas box with limited visibility. The light is wonderful now, soft and misty, bathing the elephants in a soft glow. There's so much going on: tiny babies trying to do as their parents do but finding that their trunks are too short, animals coming and going with some arguments over the best spots, all happening within 50 metres of the platform. In an action-packed half hour I've shot 130 m (400 feet – 10 mins) of good stuff. Then we start to see what we've really come for, the birds: African grey parrots, small groups of maybe ten or so, building up into bigger flocks wheeling around the clearing. It's a fabulous, colourful sight, grey birds with red tails showing up against the dark green of the forest. I get great shots of them in flight, some landing on the patches of little green plants on which they feed, and which contain the essential minerals they need for digestion. None of the ones on the ground are close enough to film but it's all very promising. From the platform we see some exciting new birds – Hartlaub's ducks, perched up in one of the big emergent trees, as well as the rare palm nut vulture and hamerkop – with, below, forest buffalo, red river hog, duikers and a sitatunga, a swamp-dwelling antelope.

By 10.30 all the parrots have dispersed so we head back through the forest to camp, to sort out the gear, charge batteries and reload film magazines, carefully taping up and storing away the exposed cans of film. At 2 p.m. we head back out to the

Two elephants, yellow with mud; notice the two Hartlaub's ducks nearby

platform, picking our way along the maze of pathways through the forest. There are six of us – Andrea and Peter, two pygmies, Paul and me – heading to the platform, as that is our best option. The sun is right on the elephants and they are beautifully lit: where they have been spraying themselves with yellow mud, they glow and stand out against the dark forest.

After a while we hear a big commotion and see a buffalo staggering, blood gushing from its chest. I didn't see it happen – my eye was on the camera viewfinder – but apparently, seconds before, a bull elephant had come across the buffalo lying down and failing to move out of the way. The elephant thrust its tusk right through the buffalo's chest. Staggering to its feet, it wanders about in a state of deep trauma before collapsing; other buffalos come to its aid, trying to get it up, prodding and pushing with their horns, but to no avail. Within ten minutes it is dead, right in front of us, dramatically proving just how dangerous these animals are at this time of musk when the bulls are highly charged for mating. We're really going to have to be on our guard once I start filming the parrots from a canvas hide on the edge of the forest. Apparently, on subsequent examination the next morning, it was found that the tusk went straight through a rib and crushed the liver. It's upsetting to learn that the buffalo was pregnant and just about to have its calf, which explains why it didn't get up when approached by the elephant.

We leave the platform at about 5 p.m. and have an uneventful walk back to camp. I cook up stir-fried vegetables with corned beef for supper. Andrea has made her place really comfortable, thatched, open sided and cool, with cane easy chairs and a table. We have a couple of very welcome rum and Cokes just before we eat, and I reflect on how much more civilized this is than I was led to believe.

Setting off at just after 6 o'clock on a misty morning, we cross the river in the usual place and cautiously make our way through the dark forest interior, the smell of elephants pervading the air. It gives me the creeps, as you never quite know what you may bump into. We arrive at the big observation platform where we are now leaving the gear overnight, safe in sealed metal cases, which makes life much easier. There are lots of elephants and some buffalo at the saline, with parrots wheeling around, eventually dropping at the left-hand side of the clearing. I get some establishing flight shots but no bird comes close enough to show the feeding behaviour. Eventually, the birds melt away, back into the forest, and we go back to camp for a midday break.

It's early afternoon and we are just about to head back to the forest when an army lorry full of French soldiers roars into the compound. We get ahead of them quickly, but they soon catch us up as we are putting our boots back on after the river crossing, so we all march through the forest together. They are very quiet and well-behaved, and turn out to be conscripts doing National Service, ten months in total, of which four are in Africa. We're at the platform by 3 p.m. and they stay only an hour, so we are free to get on with our work.

Down at ground level I do more elephant filming. This is rare footage and even if we only use a small amount in our programme, it will surely be used by the BBC in some later production or, indeed, form the basis of a whole story on forest elephants in the future. We film from near the buffalo carcass to get a different angle on the whole scene and we are told that the pygmies took a load of meat off it – too good to waste – this morning. We move to the left-hand side of the pool and do some filming from there, when a big bull elephant comes out of the forest just 20 metres behind us. Bulls look really threatening and their eyesight is not good, although they have an excellent sense of smell. He took us in quietly, stayed calm and carried on to the saline, leaving me with a pounding heart.

We finish off and take the gear to the platform to leave it there overnight. On the way out, we set up an old hide near to where the parrots were feeding this morning, to see if they accept it, assuming that the elephants don't demolish it overnight.

After the long walk back through the darkening forest we come to our usual river crossing point to find it blocked by two elephants. Our pygmy guide slaps the water with his *panga*, a large bush knife, but they won't move. We have to make a long detour through a deep part of the river and end up wading in waist-deep water. Darkness is falling as we get into camp – it's been an exciting day, one way and another. After a dinner of buffalo meat, we have another broken night's sleep, with tree hyraxes wailing in the forest and elephants moving about very close to camp. Sometimes you can hear them breathing, sniffing through their trunks or chewing, which is a very weird experience.

We're getting a lot of dull mornings, which is frustrating because, typically, the parrots are at their most active at that time of day. We get to the river by dawn, as usual, and go through the ritual of taking off our socks and boots, wading through the sludge of elephant dung into the river and out the other side, putting our socks and boots back on and setting off on the creepy 25-minute walk through the dark forest, passing steaming heaps of dung which tell us that an elephant has recently passed this way, which unsettles me even more. We retrieve the gear from the tower and set up a hide to the left of the saline, where the parrots have been feeding recently. I'm in and set up by 7 a.m. but it's dull and overcast. I don't feel very comfortable sitting here, as I can only see what's happening ahead of me and nothing to the sides or behind, with elephants liable to come out of the forest at any time and potentially trample the hide – with me inside it. I station my pygmy friend in the forest behind, with instructions to keep still and let me know if any elephants appear.

The parrots gradually build up in numbers, perched in the surrounding trees. Others fly in and I make some nice sound recordings of them screeching as they wheel around to land, elephants trumpeting in the background – a lovely atmosphere track – while a hadada ibis feeds quietly in front of the hide. The light is not improving and I fear that, yet again, we are not going to get any sunshine. Some parrots drop to the ground some distance away and start feeding on the little fleshy green plants, and although they're not very close and the light is poor, I run some footage anyway. By 9.30 a.m. they start to drift back into the forest. I had high hopes for this spot but it's just not happening, so I decide to pack in for the morning.

We have only a few days left and this sequence is proving to be a real struggle, with poor light in the early mornings – I'm always working at the extreme range of my biggest lens, the 500 mm. The parrots seem to have a favoured spot further around the pool, but it would be difficult and very dangerous to try and get closer because of the elephants, so there's nothing much to be done. We do have a sequence of sorts, establishing wide-angle shots of the parrots in their forest habitat, in flight and landing in the trees, with other inhabitants of the forest lagoon, parrots dropping down to feed and so on, but we are lacking the big close-ups in decent light which really make a sequence complete. Often, though, you're just resigning yourself to the fact that something's not going to happen when it all falls into place on the last day. We'll see.

MP filming from the platform hide

Today we're trying our luck from the big platform. It gives more flexibility, in that we can see everything that is going on. It's just 6.25 a.m. as a weak sun starts to burn through the gloom. I finish off a magazine of film on atmospheric misty scenics with ghostly images of elephants, and by half past eight parrots are starting to appear, some dropping into the trees opposite the platform. The sun is starting to break through and the whole forest clearing is bathed in soft light. Some parrots start to drop down and feed on the short mineral-containing plants; they are not close, but they do stand out well, side-lit against the dark forest. I get crisp slow-motion flight shots as they bank around before landing, their red tails flashing in the sunlight. I've shot 340 feet (about 8 mins), so I finish off the roll on a mother elephant with a tiny baby bathing beneath her in one of the pools. He's having a great time spraying himself with mud and trumpeting his delight.

Forest elephant with tiny baby

It's late morning by the time we pack up and leave the platform with all the gear for the last time, moving quietly along the dark forest trails, then breaking out into the brightness on the riverside. There are clouds of colourful butterflies sucking up moisture and minerals from the shoreline mud, so we decide to shoot a sequence on them. The camera is soon set up with a short zoom lens to do establishing shots along the riverside, using a low-angle with the camera on the ground and shooting at 100 fps to give a nice slow-motion effect; the shot is filled with massive blue swallowtails dancing in front of the lens and smaller, faster, yellow ones with the backdrop of the dark forest. I get macro shots of them drinking, too, and ultra-wides on a 5.9 mm lens at 150 fps as they rise up.

There is a price to pay for this beautiful action, though: the flies are horrendous. There are tsetse flies which inflict a painful bite but don't carry anything nasty here, although in the north they do carry sleeping sickness. There are various horseflies which pack quite a punch, and sweat bees cover our arms and legs, land on our faces and in our hair and sometimes get in our eyes. The flies are driving us demented so, having shot six minutes of film, we decide to pack in and get back to camp, so

Common swordtail butterflies

glad to escape that we barely give a second thought to the snake – about a metre long and with a small but venomous-looking head – which lives in the shallows of the river which we wade on our way home. I spend the afternoon cleaning and packing gear, ready to move on. The skies are very black, there is a big tropical storm brewing, but thankfully our work here is done.

KAZINGA AND ITS KINGFISHERS

The herd of hippos is so close that I can hear their loud grunting and smell the foul gases that they exude from both ends. The hippo is one of Africa's most dangerous animals and I must be on my guard. Buffalo and elephants coming to drink nearby add to the cocktail of potential hazards and my general feeling of unease.

I am sitting in my flimsy cotton filming hide on the banks of the Kazinga Channel, a kilometre-wide waterway in Uganda that connects Lake George and Lake Edward. It is brutally hot and sweat drips continuously from my arms as I stare through the viewfinder at the scene in front of me, a colony of pied kingfishers nesting in a sandbank just ten metres from the water's edge. There is a lot happening: birds coming in with fish to feed young already hatched, others still digging the tunnels which will end in a nest chamber 60 cm into the bank. Some birds are still courting, and using the backs of hippos to perch and display, even to mate on, but the hippos don't seem to mind. I constantly check my surroundings for approaching hazards through little spyholes in the side of my hide.

I am spending a week here to shoot sequences on pied kingfishers for a programme in the BBC *Wildlife on One* series, with producer Nigel Marvin. I have been dropped here by a ranger, Peter Mueller, who has left us alone for the afternoon, as he's had to go to sort out a snared water buffalo some distance away. It's been a great afternoon of filming, with all the elements you need to shoot great material: sunshine, lots of behaviour and a spot close to the action. I soon shoot 20 minutes of film, so we decide to pack in for the day – it's

Kingfisher hide on Kazinga channel

6 p.m. and the light has gone, but there's no sign of the boat. We're starting to get concerned as the light fades: we have 20 or more hippo and a couple of mean-looking buffalo just ten metres in front of us, looking like they may want to come out and feed soon. If an elephant or buffalo came down behind us, we could be in big trouble. I'm getting seriously worried. I wouldn't want to spend a night out here, as there are lions about.

As it passes 7 p.m. we hear the distant hum of an outboard, way off in the distance. It slowly draws closer, and we are relieved to see that it's Peter. We quickly load the boat and head off across the water to our hotel, the Mweya Lodge. It offers a rare touch of luxury for a wildlife cameraman, in a beautiful position overlooking the channel with a noisy colony of masked weavers just outside our rooms.

I have a few drinks after dinner with Peter Mueller and the head park ranger, Latiffe, and am told that we will have our own ranger/boatman to look after us. This is great news after the worrying time at the hide.

I don't have a great night's sleep. It's hot, as the air conditioning is malfunctioning, the bed is uncomfortable and I'm kept awake by lions roaring in the distance. There are strange noises outside, too, and peering through the curtain I see a hippo grazing contentedly on the lawn. They can travel up to a mile from water in search of good grazing so it's not wise to go wandering in the bush at night. Earlier I had been casually informed that a man-eating lion had killed fourteen people close to where we are filming the kingfisher colony. Fortunately, it was shot a couple of years ago, before it could make it fifteen.

A small herd of buffalo charge off in a cloud of dust as we approach the kingfisher colony and unload the gear from the battered aluminium boat. The hull is covered in small patches, and I casually enquire what caused the damage. 'Hippo tusks, where they have come up under the boat, bwana', replies the guard. There are lots of hippos in the shallows and three or four tiny ones, pink and chubby, with their mums.

I get the hide set up about five metres in front of the colony and my boatman stays nearby. I feel safer now, especially as he is armed with what looks like an AK47 automatic rifle. It's a hot afternoon and the sun is lighting up the sandstone face of the colony. It's busier than my last session and, as the temperature drops slightly, the birds become more active. There are four or five birds perched near the holes, their crisp black-and-white plumage and large dagger-like bills standing out against the warm colours of the cliff, while others are hovering before diving into their nest holes. I manage to get nice close-ups in slow motion. A male kingfisher passes a fish to his mate and others are calling from perches nearby. It's perfect, with lots of close-up action in lovely soft sunlight. Time flies and it's getting on for 6 p.m. when I decide to pack in and head back to the lodge.

Nigel has been checking out other locations where we may film different aspects of king-fisher behaviour. We really need

Right: Boatman at speed across channel
Below: Hippos watching nearby

to see into one of the nest chambers to watch the young being fed, which won't be easy. To try and excavate a nest in a colony could be disastrous, as the nests are so close together. Nigel has found a lone nest in a low bank along a quiet track which looks perfect, and I'll hope to get to this in the next day or two to start the delicate task of removing soil from behind to expose the nest chamber.

Kingfishers are expert fishers and we really need to show this behaviour in some detail. We brought out with us a small prefabricated aquarium which we have assembled and put in a location which the kingfishers regularly visit, along the edge of the channel. A strategically placed perch above – along with a few fish netted from the channel and placed into the tank – have already got the birds interested. This will give us the side-on shot as the bird hits the water and grabs the fish, while another angle we would like to achieve is from directly below, using a very simple set-up: a washing-up bowl with a three-inch hole cut in the bottom and a glass window sealed into place with silicone and mounted on a frame, three feet off the ground. Below this sits the camera, mounted on its tripod with a special periscope lens which looks vertically upwards through the glass port. Place a perch above the bowl with a few inches of water in it, and a few fish, and it's all set to go – all you need now is an obliging bird. This technique was first successfully used back in 1966 by the late Ron and Rose Eastman, an innovative couple who produced a superb film on kingfishers for the *Private Lives* series for the BBC. It was the first BBC natural history film to be produced in colour and was so successful that it has been shown eight times.

I have breakfast on my own apart from weaver birds for company – they love grains of sugar, scraps of butter and the skin off the hot milk. Nigel went early to Lake Mburo, where we hope to go next, to check on the prospects for striped kingfisher. It's a dull, overcast morning so there's no rush to get out. Peter Mueller comes over at 8 o'clock, as he's due to help me today, but we decide to delay starting until 8.45, as the light is too bad.

There's no sign of it brightening by then, so we decide that our time will be better spent in starting to excavate the kingfisher nest. Peter helps me for a while before he has to leave, and I continue alone, very cautiously. The soil is sandy and dry and I don't want to cause a collapse. I took careful measurements before starting to dig so I have a pretty good idea of where the back of the chamber is. Slowly a little hole appears and I can see the feathered forms of two well-grown chicks inside. Now I have to be really careful, as I don't want to spook them, so I give them time to get accustomed to the light. Then, when I am happy that the hole is where it should be, I block it with a heavy piece of plywood and stack rocks against it, as there are big monitor lizards about and they are very good diggers. That's the first and most difficult stage achieved; next we'll fit the glass panel, a hide, camera and lights.

The light is gradually improving so I think it's time to try with the periscope for hovering shots. The set-up is quite tricky but eventually I get it right. It's not long before a bird is hovering above the bowl, checking out the contents, and it's a fantastic viewpoint, with the bird just one metre above, then dropping vertically to snatch a fish. I run the camera at 150 frames per second to capture more of the action and it should look great as the bird climbs away with its catch. I get more shots as the light improves, the bird now lit from the side rather than from above, which produces just a silhouette.

It's a good start to the fishing sequence. It's been a productive day and Peter picks me up at 6.30 p.m. to head back to the lodge. Nigel arrives shortly afterwards and we have our now- customary pot of tea out on the verandah, discussing the day's events.

Tuesday 21 June starts with yet another cloudy morning, so we're going to put in a big effort at the nest site. We need a lot of gear– generator, lights, dimmer, hide, camera and tripod – and have the lot loaded into the van and down to the site by 8.30. The first job is to remove the rocks and board and replace it with a glass panel, covering that with a dark cloth, then placing the hide behind, from where I will operate the camera and lights remotely. The lamps are tiny, fibre-optic flexible rods which produce no heat at all, so minimising stress for the chicks. The light can be directed exactly where it's needed, right into the nest chamber.

Camera set up at nest *Pied kingfisher chicks in nest*

The little generator is set up a distance away so there's no noise, and the camera viewfinder is replaced with a video assist so that I can see the action on a little screen in the hide. I need to see the reaction of the chicks to know that the adults have arrived in the tunnel and get the camera running in advance. Everything is in position, so I get settled into the hide and Nigel fires up the generator; we have light and I start to build up the intensity using the dimmer. The chicks don't seem bothered and, with the lights at full power, I'm able to get the first shots of them in the nest. I turn the lights back down and await events. They spend quite a lot of time sleeping, then suddenly become very alert – there's an adult in the tunnel. I rack up the lights to full power but, as I suspected, the adult is reluctant to come into the brightly lit chamber. I turn the lights right down and within a minute the adult is in, feeding the chick. The youngsters are very mobile now, with eyes open, so tend to go down the tunnel to meet the adult coming in, which is something we'll have to work on. I decide we have pushed things as far as we dare for today, so we pack everything away, replace the glass with the board and rocks and head back to the hotel. A shower is the first priority, as I am covered in sweat and sand after grovelling around in the ditch behind the nest site. We then take our traditional tea and scones on the verandah before dinner at 8 p.m.

Over the next two days, with the weather still overcast, we gather more material on the nest chamber. The adults are becoming used to the lights and will come and feed the chicks with them on. We get close-ups of the chicks swallowing fish, and this should make a great sequence once it is intercut with birds in the colony flying into the tunnels with fish.

By 10 a.m. the weather is improving, bringing clear skies, so we switch our priority to getting tracking shots from the boat, passing the hippos and buffalo with the kingfisher colony in the background. I do this with the boatman William, and we pass uncomfortably close – about three metres, in fact – to the large number of hippos in the water. One hits the bottom of the boat with a thud, but we do get the shot we want to establish the colony. After going back to the jetty for a break and a change of boatman, we head back out to the point accompanied by our ranger with the AK47.

Most of the hippos are now in shallow water, sleeping, while some are on land quite close by. I manage to get the gear out of the boat and set up on the tripod without disturbing them, and the shots I get are all backlit and very atmospheric. Adding to that atmosphere was the large amount of gas produced by the hippos' vegetable diet, producing a sound like a depth charge exploding underwater.

*Buffalos close to the bank
keep an eye on me*

There are a couple of buffalo not far from our landing spot, so extreme caution is called for. Some kingfishers are perched on hippos' backs, one with a fish, which makes a great image.

With blue skies more frequent now, the tank shots are beginning to pay off. The periscope shot with the bowl – a bird hovering nicely above, then plunging into the water and back out with a small fish – could, in particular, be great in slow motion. The deep tank is trickier – the little fish are all hiding in the corners at the bottom, until one comes up to within five inches of the surface. The kingfisher on the perch above spots it immediately and plunges down to take it, I run the camera at 150 fps as soon as it leaves the perch and keep it running until the bird flies away with the fish, making what could be another great shot. Of course, we won't see the results of our hard work for a week or so until the film is back in Bristol, processed and shown on a screen in the viewing theatre. This is nerve-racking stuff.

The last and most difficult shot is an ultra-slow-motion one of a kingfisher hovering. This entails using a camera called a Locam, which shoots at 500 fps, 20x slower than normal. At this speed it gets through 400 feet of film in 20 seconds. It sounds like a malfunctioning coffee grinder and is infuriatingly difficult to load, the film having to be threaded through a maze of sprocketed rollers in the dark, in a changing bag. If this is not done properly, the results are disastrous: the film will be torn to shreds when the camera is run, scattering powdered film emulsion all over the internal optical system. Needless to say, a sensitive pair of hands is required to perform this delicate operation. The viewfinder on this camera is also very dark, so critical focusing can be difficult, though it's not so bad on a locked-off shot such as this. To muffle the noise level at this close range, I wind a sweater around the camera.

There is hardly any wind, which makes it difficult for the bird to hover for more than a second or so, although a second of action at 500 frames translates to 20 seconds on the screen. The bird duly obliges, though, and I manage a couple of shots – thank goodness I don't have to reload. The rest of the afternoon is spent packing the gear away and loading the vehicle, ready for the tortuous three-hour drive to Lake Mburu and our next sequence, on the striped kingfisher.

6 CAPE YORK AND BOWERBIRDS

Our camp in the rainforest seemed to attract all sorts of rodents during the night, especially large forest rats, so it was just as well that the food was locked away in the vehicles. Lying awake, watching the lightening sky from my camp bed, I hear the dawn chorus kick in.

We are in the Iron Range National Park on the Cape York peninsula, a remote and largely unspoiled tropical wilderness in the far north of Australia. It has a huge diversity of plants and animals, partly because of its proximity to New Guinea, just 160 km to the north. To the west is the Gulf of Carpentaria and to the east the Coral Sea. We are fortunate to have with us John Young, one of Australia's finest bird finders, and David Hollands, a well-known Australian wildlife photographer, both of whom are very familiar with this region.

It's still dark as John and I head off through the forest to a hide that he has built, well in advance, for a nesting eclectus parrot. The hide is just 20 metres up, in a substantial rainforest tree, and ten metres from the nest hole. John climbs up first – he can quite easily scale a tree bare-handed – then, with ropes and pulleys, hauls up the filming gear and drops down the caving ladder for us lesser mortals to climb up. John and the producer, Paul Reddish, leave me to it, as it's now 7.30 a.m. I'm nicely settled into my office up in the canopy, where I will be spending a lot of my time in the next ten days or so. This is where I love to be, completely alone in the treetops, surrounded by the sounds and smells of the forest.

The eclectus parrot is one of the most beautiful members of the parrot family. The male is bright green with a yellow-orange bill, the female is red and blue with a black bill. I am hoping to get shots of the adults coming to the nest to feed the chick, and as we may be here for two weeks or so, the youngster might be big enough to be poking its head out by then. We also want to film the most charismatic of all the parrot family, the palm cockatoo, both sequences for a film on parrots called *Look Who's Calling*.

I have brought my sound recording gear, which is all set up with a microphone outside the hide. It's vital to get good recordings of all the atmospheric noises of the forest at this time of day, as they play a big part in creating the mood of a film. We are miles from any roads, towns or air routes so I shouldn't have to suffer the frustration of unwanted background noise.

At just after 11 a.m. I hear a piercing scream echo through the forest close by: it is the female eclectus returning to the nest. They are timid birds so it's essential to be absolutely still in the hide and not move the lens until she's settled. She flies to the nest hole and pauses momentarily before popping in to feed the chick. I can hear it calling and it sounds well-grown. Several times she hops in and back out again before flying off; it's very satisfying to have made a start, using the 300 mm zoom lens to get a range of shot sizes around the nest hole. Over the coming days I will need to build the sequence with a variety of behaviours: birds feeding in the forest, the pair together, then one taking off and landing back at the nest, big close-ups of the birds around the nest hole and the chick putting its head out.

Over the next few hours I film some useful material of the birds away from the nest, the female perched up in the forest canopy, the male dropping down and feeding her on an open branch. I have just the 300 mm zoom lens on so it's not a big close-up, but a useful establishing shot of them in their forest habitat. Hopefully over the coming days I will get the close-ups on the 600 mm lens to cut into it.

The sky becomes menacingly heavy, thunder rumbles in the distance and the light levels plunge. Even with high-speed film stock, I fear there will be no more filming today. The hide is secure, and despite being 20 metres off the ground I feel safe. My remaining time is spent making sound recordings and taking notes before John comes to let me out of the hide at 4.45 p.m., after nine hours in my little canvas box.

Paul is away checking the nest site of a recently discovered palm cockatoo, which has created great excitement. This is one of the most charismatic of all the cockatoos, a huge, intelligent bird, found only in the remote and pristine forests of Cape York, in New Guinea and the Aru Islands, and one of the few species that uses tools: the male cuts a branch into a drumstick about 15 cm long by 2.5 cm thick and beats it against a tree or dead branch. No one knows the precise reason for this behavior – it is probably to attract females, but it's possible that the birds are able to discern from this beating the quality and suitability of a potential nest chamber, or use the drumming as a declaration to other males that this is his territory. Palm cockatoos are prized by aviculturists and have been known to live up to 56 years in captivity, though little is known about their lifespan in the wild. They only lay one egg every second year and have a very low breeding success rate.

After supper we are all shattered. It's been a long but successful day in the forest and I'm looking forward to more time with the eclectus and palms tomorrow.

Disappointingly, it's cloudy at 6.15 a.m. as I head off with John through the darkness of the forest to the eclectus nest. All the gear is quickly and quietly hauled up into the hide and I'm settled in by 7 o'clock. I start off with the big 600 mm lens, hoping for the close-ups to match yesterday's shots. The female comes at 8.20 a.m. but

*A female eclectus parrot peering from her nest cavity
(photo by, copyright and courtesy of Clifford and Dawn Frith)*

doesn't stay – I think she may not like the big lens which protrudes slightly more from the hide than does the 300 zoom. I get a few shots, even if rather distant, of her away from the nest and carrying out some mutual grooming with her mate. Frustratingly, there's no action at the nest, which is very disappointing and makes, I feel, for a wasted morning. I really should stay in the hide all day. John comes at half past eleven to let me out but, to make matters worse, I hear the female calling and the chick responding just as we are leaving, and I suspect that she is just on her way in. We head back to camp for lunch before heading off to set up the palm cockatoo hide.

The good thing about this site is that it is filmable from the ground, so there's no need for platform hides or to haul gear up and down each day. We set the canvas hide about 20 metres back from the hollow stump where the birds were displaying yesterday and camouflage it well with leafy branches. I suspect they are very aware of anything different within their territory, as they are hugely intelligent birds. John leaves and by 3 p.m. I am settled in to await events.

It's very hot in the hide and soon I'm pouring with sweat, but it's exciting to be waiting for my first view of this stunning cockatoo. Watching the clouds build up is depressing, though, as I know that the light levels will crash and, even if the birds do come, that will lead to more frustration as I won't be able to film them. By 5 p.m. it's hopeless, with the cloud, as I thought it would, blocking any light from falling on the nest stump. It's very frustrating. John comes to help me back with the gear and it'll be more of the same tomorrow.

It's an even earlier start than usual – 4.30 a.m. – and I've had a rotten night's sleep with mosquitoes, noisy fruit bats squabbling in the trees above and an assortment of forest rodents hurtling through the leaf litter. After the customary breakfast of cereal, we trudge reluctantly through the darkness to the cockatoo hide. By 5.30 I'm settled into my damp, dark, canvas box. This is a tough start, but we need to try different times of day to see when we might get visits to the nest.

Dawn comes and goes and I'm staring in vain at the nest cavity. There's no sign of the birds and no calling, so that's been another few unproductive hours. This is par for the course, though: I achieve nothing for days, then suddenly it all happens and I can shoot five minutes of usable footage. Not this morning, though.

John comes at 8 o'clock to take me out. We head back to camp for a rest and a proper breakfast, and the good news is that he has found another nest site just 200 yards from the first one, so we'll go to that this afternoon. The weather really is against us at the moment – it's difficult enough to film in dense forest, even when it's sunny, but it's virtually impossible when it's overcast. We just have to keep on plugging away and hope for a break.

We build the hide for the new nest site from heavy green cotton material wrapped around stout saplings to form a box about 1.5 metres square, the whole thing then heavily camouflaged with leafy branches. It's with great anticipation that I get settled in by 3 p.m., although the weather doesn't look good and the sky already has an evil look about it. Unfortunately , and unbeknown to us, the branches we used for the hide housed several nests of vicious green ants, which are now seething around the inside of the hide, attacking with their impressively powerful jaws any bit of exposed skin they can find. Sadly, I have to resort to insect spray to deter further attacks, having tried all other means to get rid of them.

Soon after this unpleasant episode, the wind picks up, the heavens open and I get soaked in the hide. I'm feeling generally miserable. Any filming or sound recording is out of the question now. Of course, at 5.30 p.m. when the meter reading is minus two and a half stops and beyond any chance of an exposure, the female palm cockatoo appears on the nest stump. She is holding a piece of stick with her foot and begins to drum it against the hollow stump. What an amazing-looking bird, with her intelligent eye, bright red facial patch and huge, powerful bill. It's amazing to see this behaviour at close range and she appears to have accepted the hide, so all we need now are some bright days on which to film it. John picks me up at 6.30 p.m. and we're back in camp by 7 o'clock. It has been another frustrating day, but has left me feeling more optimistic.

A palm cockatoo at its nest cavity (photo by, copyright and courtesy of Clifford and Dawn Frith)

We have our evening dip down at the creek, taking care to scan for crocodiles that may have travelled overland and taken up residence.

We discuss the day's events over coffee, before an early bed at 9 p.m. I'm determined to get a decent night's sleep, so I rig up a mosquito net and light a mosquito coil under my camp bed to deter the irritating insects. I'm already itching from dozens of green ant bites – the last thing I need is mosquito bites, too.

After the now-routine early morning hike through the forest with all the gear, I'm set up in the palm cockatoo hide by 5.30 a.m. Just as we are getting some usable light, there is a thud on the nest stump and there she is! I catch her popping inside, then coming back out onto the stump. She does her 'aah-wo' call a few times.

Palms have a very complex range of vocalisations and even have a surprisingly human 'Hello!' call, which is quite disconcerting when you are all alone in a remote forest. The male doesn't appear, but it's fantastic to get shots of this stunning bird at last. What a difference a day makes – just picking up a few shots here and there all adds to the sequence. I walk out at 8.15 and John picks me up to take me back to camp.

After breakfast I take a short stroll into the forest to check out the nest site of a yellow-billed kingfisher. It typically burrows into a termite mound, building a nest chamber about 45 cm along the tunnel. I also find the huge nest mound of a jungle hen, also known as the incubator bird, the most colossal I have ever seen, standing about six metres high and ten metres across at the base. The top of the cone is filled with decaying vegetation which heats up like a compost heap, ready for the hen to lay her eggs. To judge by the size, this must be a very old mound indeed: it could have been here for 20 years or more, probably being added to by successive generations of these birds, compulsive builders who continually add more material. I find it fascinating and walk around the base looking at this amazing work until, suddenly, I realise that I'm not quite sure which way is back to camp. It's impossible to see the sun properly through the dense canopy to get a bearing. I call out to see if anyone replies, thinking that I might get a sense of where the camp is, but there's no reply and I realise that everyone is out checking other sites. I think I recognise certain trees, but I'm not really sure. Heading off, I quickly realize that I'm completely lost. One thing I do know is that the main coast road is about six km away, so if I follow streams which I know are running to the sea, I should eventually hit that road. The streams are dry but the way in which debris are piled up against logs shows the direction of flow. I set off, trying to keep a straight line, but it's not easy, with fallen trees, dense thickets of vine and deep gullies to negotiate. I jump over a rotting log and am terrified by a huge wild boar which explodes from beneath it, careering off at great speed. I press on, cautiously. It's getting very hot now, it's mid-morning and I'm in a potentially dire situation. I am sweating profusely, losing a lot of fluid, but have no water. Insects are making a meal of me and I'm lacerated by the vicious hanging rattan vines. I am reminded of a recent story from Cape York, about a helicopter search for people lost for four days. They were found – not in great condition – walking west towards the Gulf of Carpentaria, a distance of over 150 km. I am, at least, pretty certain that I am heading east for the coast.

I really am getting very tired now, having been walking for more than two hours. Eventually I hit a road, but not the main road: it's on the West Claudie River. I follow this for some distance in the baking sun, still not knowing where I am, until I come to a junction with signs for 'Rainforest Campgrounds 4 km'. At last, signs of civilisation. I carry on along the road and hear a vehicle coming in my direction, which turns out to be that of a park ranger. Slightly shamefaced, I explain my predicament and he gives me a lift back to camp. It's 2 p.m. by the time we get back, I've been walking for four hours in withering heat and humidity, and all I want is to drink gallons of fluid.

Paul has spent a few hours in the eclectus hide to see what stage the chick is at, and he has good news: the youngster is starting to crawl out onto the edge of the nest hole. It will make a pleasant change to spend time with the eclectus after the frustration of plugging away at the cockatoos every day. It's now December 4, with only a few more days to go here. I must say I will be glad to move on to the next location.

I get into the hide at about 7 a.m. and Paul helps me to haul the gear 20 metres up to the platform in the lower part of the canopy. Half an hour later, we're all set up and ready to go. It's a breezy morning so the hide is swaying a little, and it's also rather overcast, although sometimes a degree of brightness is better than bright sunshine, which can create hard shadows and too much contrast. The birds seem nervous and are screaming continuously, almost as if they know I'm in there. Did they see Paul leaving? I hope that's all it is. Eventually it quietens down and I get useful shots of the youngster coming out onto the rim of the nest, calling to be fed. The male is nearby, giving me my first chance to get shots of him, so it's all very useful.

It's now nearly midday and there's not a lot of action, so I set up the sound recording gear. The conditions are good, with no wind, and I'm picking up the strange chimes and clangs of the eclectus. This is all very important to build up the sequence. Shortly after 2 o'clock, Paul comes to the hide and helps me with the heavy gear down the rope system, to go across to the palm cockatoo site. I'm in and settled by 3.30 p.m. but, annoyingly, although the male comes back quite quickly, he takes me by surprise and is into the hole before I can run the camera. I'm feeling very tired after seven hours in hides and my reactions are not quite as sharp as they should be. The light, as usual, is not good, with heavy cloud making it impossible to film by 5.30 p.m.

Over the last few days the sequence on the eclectus has really started to come together, with a great shot of the chick crawling out onto the rim of its nest cavity. Because of the heat and humidity I have been sitting in the hide in shorts, sweating profusely, the salty fluid dribbling down my legs and attracting plagues of horseflies, which I have been swatting. As I look through the camera's viewfinder I feel a sensation at the top of my thigh, and assume it's another irritating horsefly. On the verge of smacking it, I turn to look and see that it is not a fly at all, but a very nasty-looking little black scorpion, just about to disappear into my shorts to a very important area of my anatomy. This not being an appealing proposition, I flick it off in the nick of time and it falls through the floor of the hide. That was rather too close for comfort, and I'm glad I didn't get to find out how poisonous that particular scorpion was.

My persistent and determined visits to the cockatoo hide have gradually produced more material from which I think we can produce a reasonable sequence, a key shot being the male with his enormously powerful bill, cutting his drumsticks from branches up to 2.5 cm thick. The weather has not been kind to us, and a lot of behaviour has been impossible to film because of the dull conditions, but even so, over the 13 days we've been here, I've managed to get enough shots to produce two sequences on parrots and cockatoos that have rarely been filmed before. It's been fascinating for me to live and work in these little-known forests with two of Australia's most charismatic birds.

THE BOWERBIRDS

As we've seen, the birds of paradise of New Guinea attract partners with extravagant displays of extraordinary plumage, but there is another family, the bowerbirds, which use a quite different strategy to attract a mate. They build bowers, in their simplest form a twin avenue of twigs pushed into the ground maybe 10 cm apart and 30 cm long, and decorated with items such as colourful fruits, stones, bleached bones, and even – in urban situations –bits of glass and coloured plastic. Some bowers can be very large, made up of vines or suspended limbs of trees decorated with moss and other items such as birds' feathers, beetle wing cases and small, bright flowers. The most extravagantly decorated bowers with the rarest treasures attract the females into the avenue, where mating takes place.

Having made a very successful film on the birds of paradise in New Guinea, filmed between 1994 and 1996, the producer Paul Reddish thought a programme on bowerbirds would be make a fascinating contrast. It would be aptly entitled *The Art of Seduction*. Sir David Attenborough agreed to appear as presenter and narrator and the budget was agreed. We had the assistance in the field of Dr Cliff Frith and Dr Dawn Frith, world authorities on bowerbirds, both of whom had been our advisors in New Guinea on *Attenborough in Paradise*.

Satin bowerbird at its bower on the forest edge

Most of the filming was to be in Queensland and in Ormiston Gorge, to the west of Uluru, or Ayers Rock. There are eight species of bowerbird in Australia and we hoped to film most of them. Cliff and Dawn, our partners in the field, live in a wonderful part of Queensland, over 700 metres up on the Atherton Tablelands, where it is much cooler than down on the coast. Their property is located in a large tract of rainforest where for many years they have studied numerous bowerbird species, including the tooth-billed and satin, both of which will make important sequences in our film.

Cape York and Bowerbirds

It was in October 1998 that we made our first trip to Australia to begin filming, October and November being the main display season for bowerbirds. We were staying in an old property called 'the dairy', a basic old wooden building with a tin roof. The surrounding forest had a healthy population of cane toads, snakes and monitor lizards, some of which were clearly living in our roof and walls. After a couple of hours of sorting gear and generally getting the place organised, we were invited down to Cliff and Dawn's house for drinks and supper at 6 p.m. It's a wonderful property, set in a clearing within 25 hectares of rainforest, and it was that special time of day when the birds of the forest are calling and flying to their roost sites. This is the area in which I will be working for the next two weeks. After a very relaxing evening, jet lag kicks in and at half past eight we make our way back to our accommodation.

After a good night's sleep we walk down the forest track to Cliff's house. We are going to check out the most promising tooth-billed and satin bowers. The tooth-billed's is a bare court on the ground, carefully cleared of any falling or existing debris, upon which are placed specially selected types of leaf. By contrast, the satin is an avenue builder, placing two lines of twigs about 15 cm apart and decorating them with numerous treasures, skulls of small rodents, coloured fruits and flowers. Male bowerbirds spend most of the year building, improving, defending and, most importantly, displaying from a well-decorated bower. Female bowerbirds nest inconspicuously, and the male plays no part in incubation or raising the young, leaving those solely to the female.

As is normal with 50-minute films, we are shooting over two seasons. It's not unusual not to get all of the required material you need at the first attempt, usually because of the weather – if it's too dry, the birds breed earlier or later than usual, if it's too wet, it's just too dark to film in the forests. Apart from anything else, continuous rain affects behaviour, and not just of the birds. For anyone filming, it's just downright miserable. There is also the real risk of damaged equipment, especially digital cameras, and raindrops on the lenses protruding from a hide can ruin a sequence. These birds are generally extremely timid and will not tolerate lenses being pulled in and out to be cleaned.

Cliff has already set temporary hides on the bowers, allowing the birds to get accustomed to them before my arrival. We first look at the two tooth-billed sites, both of which are active. They are in good positions but in dark areas of the forest, so we may have to use additional lighting if the natural light levels are too low. The hides are set close to the display area, only about three metres away, which means I can use shorter focal length lenses which are faster, with more light-gathering power. We exchange these temporary hides for my full size ones, 1.5 metres square, as I need a bit more space for my large tripod and all the other associated camera and sound gear.

There is also a satin bower in a lovely situation, more open than the tooth-billed site and just down the hill. In fact, the great thing about all of these sites is that none of them is more than 300 metres from Cliff's house. It all looks promising, but time will tell. Around 2 p.m. we head back to base for a sandwich. Jet lag is still hanging over me and I am beginning to feel shattered again. Working in these humid forests means you are continuously wet and, changing my T-shirt, I discover a huge, bloated leech which falls to the ground. It's disgusting but will soon, no doubt, be a daily occurrence.

It's 6.30 a.m. as I walk through the dripping, humid forest full of sound, the distinctive calls of catbirds, whipbirds and riflebirds ricocheting through the trees as I pick my way down the track to Cliff's house. We're going to try the tooth-billed hide this morning, to see if the bird has accepted it. Cliff sees me in with all the gear, then walks away, and I'm set up by 7.30. Amazingly, within minutes, the male returns and starts to sing continuously from a horizontal perch just two metres in front of me, but the light is marginal, even with 500 ASA film and fast lenses, and I'm struggling for an exposure. After a few shots, taken more in frustration than anything else, I decide it's going to have to be a lighting job; I stay in the damp, dismal hide until 11.30 a.m. then signal Cliff on the radio to come and let me out. We try a couple of hours in the hide during the late afternoon but, as Cliff suspected, there is no action.

The rest of the day is spent checking out the small generator that we shipped from the UK. It could be a very handy piece of kit in these dark forest situations. Although it only needs 250 watts from the generator, the high-tech lamphead produces the equivalent of 800 watts of daylight balanced light. It needs to be on a dimmer switch so that we can accustom the bird to the light over a period of several minutes, and a considerable length of cable allows us to position the generator far enough from the display area for the bird not to hear it. We're all set to go for tomorrow.

It's another early start. I'm down at cliffs for 7 a.m. and we load all the gear – there's a lot of it – into the Land Rover and run it up the track through the forest. We are loaded down with 100 metres of cable, the generator, lamphead and stand, tripod, camera and lenses, plus a pack with spare batteries, film stock, and drinks and snacks for a few hours. I'm all set up by half past seven and await developments. It's an anxious wait: will the bird freak out with the big, shiny lamphead three metres away? It seems not. Apparently unconcerned, the male tooth-billed drops silently onto his song perch, but I don't dare to turn the lamp on to full power. The dimmer switch allows me to start off with just a trickle of light and build it up slowly. He starts to sing and doesn't seem concerned as the lamp reaches full power, although it looks so bright in the dark forest. Thankfully he stays and sings above his meticulously cleaned display court, on which he has laid out the leaves selected to attract interested females. Today, sadly, there are none, and he continues to sing in vain. Cliff lets me out after four hours and we take the gear back to his house, ready for another try tomorrow.

This afternoon I am going to have a session in the satin bowerbird hide, to see how the light levels are, how the bird behaves with me in the hide, how often it visits the bower and what behaviour is taking place. The first visit by the male is at 3.10 p.m. What a stunning bird it is: quite big, about the size of a jackdaw, a stunning iridescent deep-blue colour with a purple iris to its eye and a horn-coloured bill. It stays for eight minutes, 'painting' the inside of the bower with a substance made from masticated vegetable matter, and also spends time rearranging its treasures –small, brightly-coloured fruits, snail shells, leaves and a bleached mammal skull. It comes back again for five minutes at half past three, and does a little dance around the bower, warbling a very quiet sub-song, as though he is just singing to himself and no one else. It then goes very quiet until half past four, when a strange thing happens. Another male comes to the bower and starts to pull it apart while the bemused owner looks on from just half a metre away. He makes no attempt to stop the destruction of his finely crafted construction. This is apparently a dominant male from a nearby bower, who's not too happy about having competition for the local females. Frustratingly, it was far too dark to film this amazing behavior, but I could well see it again, as it's a regular occurrence in the competitive bower bird world. I pack in at 4.45 p.m. and take all the gear back to Cliff's, ready for another try at the tooth-billed in the morning.

I head back to the dairy for 5.30, walking through the failing light. We have our landlord Mike and Marianne coming round for drinks, and sit out on the back patio watching the darkness fall over the forest, sipping a fine glass of Houghton White Burgundy, now a firm Aussie favourite. Birds come to drink and feed and the forest is full of the intriguing sounds of birds and insects, followed – as they fall silent – by hundreds of hidden frogs starting a chorus of their own.

My hide, set up with lights, at the satin bower

The next few days are devoted to the tooth-billed in the mornings and the satin bower in the afternoons. Both situations need to be lit, so the generator, cables and lamp have to be moved from one site to the other each day. This effort is starting to pay dividends on the satin bower, and I'm getting a good sequence on general maintenance behaviour. This includes the male removing unwanted bits of forest debris that might have blown in, adding fresh moss to the base of the bower, repainting the twigs inside the avenue and adding newly acquired treasures, perhaps fresh fruit or shells.

During one hide session I had the camera on the ground, picking up remote shots of the bower with the male bringing in moss and incorporating it into the walls. I decided by 11.30 that the bird had finished his duties for the morning and that I would get out of the hide and just finish off the roll of film, shooting some close-up shots of the 'treasures' in front of the bower. As I bent over to frame up the shot, I felt a presence nearby. Looking up, I was confronted by the colourful head and horn of an impressive male cassowary with, behind him, two downy, striped youngsters. He was peering straight at me and looking very curious. Cassowaries are very large birds, standing 1.5 metres high, and quite capable of inflicting a very nasty injury with their powerful kick and sharp claws, especially if they or their young feel threatened. They also have a reputation for chasing people, so I felt particularly vulnerable and glad there was a large fallen log between us. Slowly, the chicks start to move off, the male following them, and I'm glad that the encounter – although memorable – was also brief. It's a fascinating bird, though: the male is responsible for the incubation and

The male cassowary checks me out

rearing of the young, and the female may have several nests, with males incubating between three and eight eggs for 50 days.

The time spent at the tooth-billed court has produced some useful footage towards the display sequence. We have used a dummy female on a stick, moved with a piece of fishing line from the hide in the hope of initiating some response from the male. It's effective and, I have to admit, hilarious. We set up the camera on the ground, activated with a remote switch, with the dummy behind it. The male sings from his horizontal perch then, spotting the movement of the female, drops down onto the court and hides behind the base of a tree, singing and starting his display, wings outspread, throat expanded, peering out then hiding again, making strange buzzing sounds, all the time becoming more and more wound up. He then suddenly explodes out onto the court and fires himself at the dummy and copulates with it. Not satisfied, he flies back up onto his display perch and starts again, sidling up and down with outstretched wings, singing loudly then dropping down onto the court, hiding behind the tree, peeking out, buzzing and erupting onto the court. I manage to get a few closer shots, especially peering from behind the tree, to intercut with the remote wide-angle shots on the ground, which isn't easy, as his movements are fast and erratic.

We don't want to over-stress the bird so I call Cliff up and he comes back to the hide, we take away the dummy and put the camera back on the tripod. We now need a copulation with a real female to follow on from the male going out of frame, which again won't be easy, but we're getting there.

The male tooth-billed bowerbird at its display court (photo by, copyright and courtesy of Clifford and Dawn Frith)

A career filming wildlife is full of frustration and disappointments. One morning at the satin I had elected to put the camera on the ground, close to the bower, for a remote wide-angle shot. Such angles are really valuable to editing the sequence, to cut in with close shots from the hide. This, of course, locks the camera into a fixed point, so if something happens to either side of – or, as in this case, inside – the bower, you miss the action. Here, Murphy's Law comes into play: what can go wrong, will go wrong. A female appears from nowhere and drops into the bower, followed by the male, who postures in front of the avenue. I do get shots of the male but I can't see the female, which is frustrating in the extreme. I do get them flying away, which may come in useful. I bring the camera into the hide and set up with the big zoom lens on the tripod, in the hope that they may return and repeat the same behaviour, but by half past one, there's been nothing, so I take a break for lunch, returning an hour later. It's quiet initially, as it usually is in the early afternoon, then a male comes in and starts to scatter the treasures at the bower entrance: it's the trasher from the nearby bower. I run the film and within seconds there is the sickening, unmistakable sound of the camera grinding to a halt – the battery has gone flat. I grab another, take off the flat one and snap on the replacement, but the sensitive hearing of the bird picks up the sound and it's off in a flash. This is definitely not my day. I doggedly sit it out until half past five, but there are no more visits.

Missed opportunities are difficult to cope with but it's important to dwell on the great shots you did get, not the ones you missed, as no one ever sees those ones. I think we do have two sequences with the satin and toothed-bill, including bower building, destruction by other males, some females around the bowers and a little display. It would have been nice to get a mating, but that would have been the icing on the cake and we still have several more species to film.

ORMISTON GORGE AND THE WESTERN BOWERBIRD

The towering walls of Ormiston Gorge, which lies 135 km west of Alice Springs, were created millions of years ago by huge geological forces. Having driven from Alice Springs, we can't wait to explore the gorge; it's stunning, with the huge, white trunks of ghost gums contrasting with the awe-inspiring red walls of the narrow canyon. There is a deep waterhole used by a tantalising variety of wildlife, including dingoes and wallabies, and it offers good opportunities for pieces to camera – known as sync pieces – with Sir David. The surrounding area of bush is prime real estate for the western bowerbird. Cliff has been here for a few days, checking out locations and putting up hides at suitable bowers, and I can't wait to get filming on this little-known species. We are staying at Glen Helen Lodge, a motel and campground up on a ridge with fantastic views of the West MacDonnell Ranges.

It's 8 a.m. and I'm settled into my hide just a few metres from a western bower. Within 30 minutes the bird comes, and what a stunning little creature it is, with rich buff under-parts, darker above, covered with buff-coloured spots and with a lilac patch on its nape.

The western bowerbird has great powers of mimicry, imitating dogs barking, cats meowing and humans coughing. Its bower is massive, the twigs beautifully woven into a curved, basket-like shape with, at both ends of the avenue, loose platforms of twigs covered in the treasures amassed over weeks and months, some no doubt pilfered from neighbours' bowers, others painstakingly collected from the bush or from the nearby campsite. It has a definite love of white or bleached items – white plastic bottle tops, bleached white bones, a silver clothes peg and what I think is the most prized of all, judging by the amount of time he spends moving them around: children's glass marbles, no doubt collected from the local school playground.

The first couple of hours in the hide are quite productive, giving me good establishing shots of the bird in its bower, tidying up sticks in the avenue, arranging his finest decorations, keeping everything in order lest a female should visit. Suddenly another male drops down and sparks off a terrific display sequence. Weird contortions ensue, the birds

Male western bowerbird

Male western bowerbird with marble

Male western bowerbird in its bower

Western bowerbird's bower with various decorations

stretching out one wing and twisting their heads to one side, flashing their purple nape colours and making strange buzzing sounds, running through and around the bower. It's very exciting to see this unusual behaviour, which has probably never been filmed before. There's great potential here for remote cameras, big close-ups on the 600 mm lens and for the sync piece with Sir David.

We have a week to construct the behavioural sequence before Sir David arrives but, annoyingly, we are again dogged over the next few days by overcast and windy weather. Bowerbirds do not like windy conditions and my productivity at the bower drops. These elaborate constructions are usually built underneath the overhanging bushes of rock figs, which offer the bower some cover, with the fruit forming an important part of the birds' diet. Their food items are extremely varied, including fruits, buds, flowers, seeds, beetles, moths and grasshoppers, and the birds will adapt to taking unusual foods from gardens and campsites.

Gradually, though, the sequence takes shape. I gather lots of the essential establishing shots with the male bird, interactions with other males, stealing of treasures and some trashing of the bower by other males.

It's 8 August and Sir David arrived this afternoon. I must say I'm looking forward to filming with him again after working together on birds of paradise in New Guinea. We have beers in what is simply a magical setting, talking of recent exploits in the field as we sit around the outdoor fire pit at Glen Helen, the sun setting over the bush, until the desert evening cools and we go inside for dinner. I'm having an early night as

DA and MP set up for filming a piece to camera, Ormiston Gorge, Central Australia

tomorrow is a big day with the sync pieces. I want to be on the ball, and check through all my equipment, charge batteries and load up film magazines.

At dawn, Paul and I, Dickie and Cliff go down to the bower with all the gear – my film equipment, Dickie's sound gear and the mini-jib for doing crane shots. All is in position when Sir David, Nancy, the production assistant, and Dawn come to the bower at just after 8 a.m. The camera is mounted on the mini-jib for the first shot, starting with the camera at full height of two metres. Sir David enters frame and, as he settles down beside the bower, the camera follows him to his position and he delivers the sync piece. That done, I change to a reverse angle of him standing up and exiting frame, get a few close-up shots of Sir David picking up some of the decorations as cutaways and that's it. The more complicated shots with the crane are yet to come.

The approach to the canyon is on a narrow, rutted, sandy track and the driver of the crane does well to get it into position at the narrow entrance. We have the assistance of the rangers from the National Park as we have to stop the traffic on a nearby road for the sake of the soundtrack, and also need to control anyone walking through the canyon. Everyone has radios so that we know what's happening. The crane shot starts at the top of a group of ghost gums, 15 metres high, and the camera moves slowly down to reveal Sir David walking through the canyon, delivering his piece to camera. After several takes we are happy that the shot has worked and we bring everything down to ground level. Now we get another shot of David walking through the canyon delivering the same sync piece to camera, which will cut with the crane shot. It all seems to have worked well.

After the excitement and pressure of the sync shooting, it's back to the relative routine of picking up the behaviour from the hide, although I'm not sure I should describe sitting in a hide in the Australian bush, filming one of the world's rarest birds, as routine. The next few days consist of many hours with little to show for them, always waiting for the big moment, then 'Wham!' With a dull thud a male bird drops into the bower. It's the trasher and he immediately starts to pull the bower to pieces, grabbing hold of the sticks and scattering them about. I soon shoot 60 metres of film (five mins) in good light. I need him to go out of frame, so I smack the canvas of the hide and he flies off, but within seconds he's back and continuing the destruction. This is terrific stuff. We've been trying to get this important behaviour for weeks and it could be worth a minute-and-a-half in the programme. The bird slips away and I get out of the hide to do a low-angle shot of the bower in disarray before the soft sunlight fades, as it's surprising how quickly they can reconstruct the bower. Cliff comes just after 5 p.m. and helps me with the gear. He is amazed – and quite disappointed – by the destruction of the bower, but it is all part of the natural scheme of things and no doubt has its purpose.

GREAT BOWERBIRDS

Bowerbirds, especially the great bowerbird, can be quite urban in their choice of bower site. This is the largest species of the family, although males still only weigh a maximum of 225 grams, and the bower can be up to a metre long. We are filming them around Townsville, a coastal town in North Queensland, where Cliff knows of a variety of sites, all in very different situations. Several males have bowers in the local cemetery, one is in the local army camp and another in a children's playground. Permission has been sought and granted, so we can go ahead with watching the birds' behaviour and putting up hides.

Probably the easiest one is in the cemetery, where the birds are quite tame, as they see people on a regular basis. The male that we choose to follow has a liking for white marble chips from the graves and small chunks of broken glass, but they have to be green, it seems. The pre-school bower is in a lovely, open site in the corner of the playground, just behind a white picket fence, so we get permission to remove one panel and get an unobstructed view of the bower for the camera. The army camp bower is on the edge of some bushes, but accessible, and the choice of adornments for this bower reflect its location: spent brass cartridge cases, little green plastic bottles that once contained foot powder and various brass buckles from belts.

The decorations in the pre-school bower were also amazing. The local electricity board had been replacing some poles and wires, and large nuts and bolts were being used to secure the metal arms carrying the cable. These must have been at least an inch in diameter, beautifully galvanised and shiny, and obviously an irresistible treasure to

Great bowerbird bower in a schoolyard

A male great bowerbird in its bower

a great bowerbird. The site of these works was at least ten yards from the bower so – as with the buckles and cartridge cases at the army camp – the bird must have spotted what he wanted and dragged the prize items, probably equivalent to his own body weight, into the bower.

This playground bower is really fun to work – the birds are quite confiding so I don't need a hide, I just sit on my camera box. The bird has a huge choice of items to pilfer from the school children: toys left behind, such as a little green rubber elephant and a green plastic dagger. The things they really like, though, are the coloured chalks that the children use at the schoolyard desks. As soon as the children go in for a break, the boxes of chalks are tipped over and scattered, the birds then selecting the best colours – usually green or white – for their bowers.

It's 7 a.m. when Paul, the producer, Dickie Bird, the sound man, and I go down to the cemetery. We have a big day ahead of us doing two sync sound pieces on great bowerbirds with Sir David. The first, an ambitious crane shot, involves a cherry picker and it needs to be right, so we have to do several rehearsals of the moves before Sir David arrives. For the main, crucial shot, I will be with the camera in the bucket in the specially dug-out 'grave' at ground level, before elevating right up over the bushes to reveal the cemetery stretching into the distance and Sir David walking away.

We do several trial runs which look very dramatic through the camera, but although I'm relatively confident that it will work, it's nerve-racking when it's all down to me. I'm having to hand-hold the camera, as there's no room in the bucket for a tripod, so I need to steady my nerves. David, Nancy, Cliff and Dawn come down for 8 a.m. and we're ready to go. We start off with the shots under the bushes next to the bower, with Sir David lying next to it, talking about the three bachelor males that are honing their building and display skills here. A real bonus is a two-shot of David with a male displaying in front of the bower, something we wouldn't have dared script for. The light is tricky, with some shadow on David's face, but we manage to bounce in some extra light with a reflector.

Now for the difficult one. I get into the bucket, making sure my film magazine is fully loaded and that there's a charged battery on the camera. I'm right down at ground level looking across to the bower. Paul calls 'Action!' and I run the camera for ten seconds before the action starts, then – as David stands up and begins to walk away – the crane operator starts to raise the bucket, ever so slowly, out of the ground. As it clears the trees, the extent of the cemetery becomes clear as David walks into the maze of headstones and pathways. It all seems to have worked remarkably well.

We take a break for lunch then go over to the army barracks for the second piece to camera. This is a straightforward sequence in which David walks into frame, lies down by the bower and picks up various items that the birds have collected: snail shells, green plastic foot powder containers and bits of green glass. They certainly love green. David talks about various behaviours of the young males, then stands up and walks out of frame, job done. Sir David is amazing to work with and he rarely makes a mistake with his delivery. If more than one take is needed, it's more than likely down to the soundman or – dare I say it – the cameraman.

MP in crane bucket in the cemetery in Townsville

7 CUBA – NATURE'S TREASURE ISLAND

It's April, and the ground is coming alive with a hissing, crackling sound. The limestone floor of the swamp forest is honeycombed with holes and crevices from which emerge brightly- coloured crabs – land crabs – of every conceivable hue, from yellow to deep red. Thousands turn into millions and the forest floor becomes a moving carpet as they head to the sea to spawn. This is Zapata Swamp in the southwest of Cuba, on the famous Bay of Pigs, site of the failed American invasion back in 1961. The forests in Cuba are home to more than 20 endemic species of birds, including the world's smallest, the bee hummingbird.

Cuba is best known for its old cars, cigars, rum and Havana, its magnificent, if crumbling, capital. But few people know of its staggering array of wildlife. Huge colonies of Caribbean flamingoes live in the northern barrier islands, while off the south coast lie unspoiled coral reefs.

We are making several visits to this remarkable island to make a 50-minute documentary for ORF TV in Austria. It's an exciting prospect, filming somewhere that hasn't really been covered in any depth before, although we don't expect it to be easy. There are many bureaucratic hoops to jump through, though we are lucky to have good people on the ground to help us.

An old Cuban car in a side street of Havana

A view of the Old City of Havana

179

Having eventually got all the permissions we need, we head down to Zapata for the great migration of the crabs. We are staying at a hotel on the beach called the Hotel Girón. Cuban hotels are not the best in the world and this one is no exception to that rule. The food is poor, sandwiches are always jamon e queso, the ham and cheese served on dry, white bread, and the meals are usually rice, salad and chicken. It's so poor, in fact, that we decide to check out and move 20 miles down the coast road to Hotel Playa Larga, in a nicer location with slightly better food.

There is lots of crab movement to film, as those that have already been to the sea to spawn are heading back to the forest. I get my camera low down, on the kerbside, as the crabs spill off the pavement onto the road; this is where the carnage starts. Crabs have absolutely no road sense and react to approaching traffic as they would to any predator, by stopping and waving their claws in the air. The consequences are predictably catastrophic for the poor crustaceans. Huge Russian lorries rattle down this road at high speed, killing thousands of crabs each time. The crabs have probably been using this route from the forest to the sea for thousands of years, of course, and have no way of dealing with this strip of tarmac blocking their route. It will get worse with increasing traffic; some people, mainly tourists, will slow down to let the crabs cross, but something needs to be done. Tunnels could be built under the road at the busiest crossing points, but that would cost money, and crabs are probably not high on the government's list of spending priorities.

Large numbers of land crabs crossing the road, heading to the sea to spawn

One of Cuba's endemic species, the Cuban tody

*A female bee hummingbird on
its nest, incubating two eggs*

This is all, of course, very dramatic from the filming point of view: low-angle shots of hundreds of crabs passing right in front of the lens as they march like great armies back into the safety of the forest. Those that are hit I film in slow motion, their little coloured bodies thrown high into the air after their futile attempts to defend themselves. Even though the road is covered in the crushed carcasses, the vast majority of the colourful crustaceans do make it back to the forest, having shaken their precious cargos of eggs into the sea to secure the next generation.

The crab movement is sporadic and seems to occur in waves, some at night when there is less traffic, so in between these periods of activity we work on other sequences.

The Zapata swamp forest is full of colourful, unusual birds: Cuban trogon, Cuban green woodpecker, Cuban tody and Cuban emerald hummingbird. Cuba has 26 endemic species of bird, but the one we really want to film is the world's smallest, the bee hummingbird, found only in Cuba. We are working with an amazing local naturalist called Chino who has an in-depth knowledge of the resident birds and who has found us the nest of this tiny hummer. The minute structure, constructed meticulously from lichens and spider silk and smaller than a 50-pence coin, is glued to a horizontal limb of a swamp forest tree about three metres from the ground. The female lays two miniscule eggs, around 6 mm in length, which need 22 days of incubation, long for a bird this small. The fledging period – 18 days – is also unusually long for such a tiny bird. The female, who does all the incubation, visits the nest while we are just two metres away, quite unconcerned by our presence.

We're grateful that we don't need a hide, as the discomfort of sitting in a canvas bag at 35°C, being eaten by mosquitoes, would be too much to bear. We do need a small platform, though, to raise me to nest height, so bring in some timber, cut saplings from the forest and soon have it in place. When I stand on the two-metre-high platform, my lens is in the perfect position, just level with the nest. The bird leaves the nest every 20–30 minutes to feed and is away for between three and five minutes, so I have plenty of chances to get the bird arriving at and leaving the nest. As is often the case, though, the afternoon clouds over and we have an early finish to filming for the day, giving us a chance for a well-earned mojito at the hotel beach bar.

There has been a big storm overnight, with torrential rain and high winds, and when we meet Chino he warns us to prepare for the worst – the tiny nest may have been destroyed. As we enter the dense, dripping forest, fresh clouds of newly-hatched mosquitoes around us, we can see that there has been some storm damage, with trees left shattered. Approaching the nest site with some trepidation, we see – remarkably – the little hummer sat tight in its tiny lichen-decorated cup. It's survived the storm.

At this stage, once she is settled on the nest, there is not a lot of behaviour to be seen, apart from the odd turning of the eggs. Getting the departure from the nest is not easy, of course, although with experience come the little signs: a glance around and a little shuffle before – with a whirr of tiny wings at 80 beats a second – she goes. Everything with this smallest of creatures has to be filmed in slow motion to extend the time for which the bird is in frame.

The biggest challenge is to try to get bee hummingbirds feeding. The male bird will quite often sing from a high perch, maybe ten metres from the forest floor, then will suddenly plunge into the dense undergrowth, feed for ten seconds and return to its perch. At this point we try to get to the spot where we think it fed, maybe a patch of favourite flowers, so that we can set up, ready for the next feed, but it's not that easy. Often the ground cover of vines and thorny shrubs makes it impossible to get access, and many times we find that the bird, for whatever reason, doesn't use the same patch twice. Bee hummingbirds weigh only two grams and need to consume half their body mass in nectar each day, visiting up to 1,500 flowers in the process.

Over several days, in between surges of crab-spawning activity, we return to the areas where the bee hummingbirds are feeding. Chino has been keeping an eye on the best locations but we are having little success. We see the same pattern of behavior: the male singing, the plunge into the dense undergrowth and the return to the perch

A male bee humming-bird on its song perch

seconds later, the bill coated in pollen, a tell-tale feeding sign. The female is even more difficult to spot: she doesn't perch high, like the singing male, but just buzzes through the forest, feeding at random, so it will be difficult to pin her down. Then, one morning, when we are beginning to lose faith in our chances of ever getting a feeding shot, the little male does his usual plunge into the undergrowth and we do our usual fruitless pursuit, to find in a little clearing quite a big patch of tiny red flowers. Surely he could return to these? I set up my camera with the 50–300 zoom lens and watch intently. The tiny iridescent male has returned to his singing perch less than 20 metres away – will he come down again? I wait, my finger poised on the release button, the speed set at 150 frames a second. I only need the bird in frame for a single second to give me six seconds on the screen. I wait, heart pounding. I have a good feeling about this spot, but he may just fly off to another perch and another feeding area. He carries on singing then, suddenly, plunges to the flowers in front of me. There is so little nectar in each tiny flower that he stays at each one for only a split second. I set the zoom to wide-angle as he buzzes between flower heads, giving me my establishing shot, then in a flash he is back up to his perch. Now I have to wait for another five minutes or so to see if he will come down again. It's all very stressful. This may be the only shot I get. Then, a little fluorescent flash of crimson, and he's back feeding. This time I go for the mid-shots on the zoom, trying to follow the bird from flower to flower – not easy – all the time having to adjust the lens as this smallest of all birds, with a total wingspan of ten centimetres, drifts in and out of the plane of focus. Then, in a blur, he is gone. The whole event took less than ten seconds.

I now have a big decision to make. I would dearly like a close-up, meaning putting on the 600 mm lens with a very small angle of view. I am going to be on minimum focus distance of five metres, and at this range such a tiny bird – especially one that spends a fraction of a second at each flower – will be difficult to find. I opt to pre-focus on one flower to get the bird entering and leaving the frame, as it would be impossible to follow the bird and keep it in focus. This is a risky strategy, of course, as the bird could visit many other flowers and ignore the one that I have focused on.

It's a risk I have to take and it seems that the bird has an affinity to this group of flowers, so I may get more than one chance. The male drops from his perch and starts to feed. He is close to my flower so I set the camera running, film burning through the camera at over a metre a second, my eye pressed to the viewfinder waiting for the flash of colour, then he's there, feeds for a split second and is gone again. I can't believe it, I have the close-up. This will be vital to intercut with the wider shots to make a proper feeding sequence. Over the next half hour I get several more shots and feel I have a great sequence, even if that's all I end up getting.

The crabs are still moving in huge numbers to the sea. What we need now are shots of the crabs cautiously entering the water to release the packages of fertilised eggs which they carry beneath their body. Paul has a small Sony camera which he puts

*Land crabs with eggs, preparing to shed them
into the warm waters of the Bay of Pigs*

*Crabs with eggs on rocks,
preparing to enter the water*

into a special underwater housing and, very carefully, we move to the jagged rocky outcrop where the brightly-coloured crustaceans are entering the sea. This is a critical time for them: they cannot completely immerse themselves in the water or they would drown, and we have to be careful not to panic them or the whole group could rush back into cover. I get set up, with the camera on short legs to get as low to the subject as possible, giving a more dramatic viewpoint, and fitted with the 50–300 mm lens it should get cracking close-ups. Crabs in ultra-close-up are amazingly complex, weird and beautifully coloured, a mixture of red, orange and crimson. Paul has worked his way around the rocks and is up to his armpits in the sea, at crab level.

The first crabs tentatively slip into the water, hanging on all the time to the rock, then start to shake their little armoured bodies rhythmically to release the precious eggs.

*An average female can
carry 85,000 eggs*

Each crab of 10–15 cm in size probably carries up to 85,000 eggs and, very soon, as more crabs enter the water, the sea becomes cloudy with millions of eggs, which immediately hatch into little swimming larvae called *Naupilae*. I am getting amazing close-ups of the huge claws, the strange mouth parts and the packages of tiny eggs as the females slip into the water. Paul is getting all the action just below the surface as the eggs are released, which will make editing the sequence much easier, and showing all the action both above and below water will help to tell the story. It doesn't take long before shoals of little fish are attracted to the scene and are very soon enjoying a feast of crab eggs.

TAKING TO THE AIR

For most of the sequences we are shooting, it's useful to have aerial shots to show the habitat and to put it into context in terms of area and location: rainforests, offshore reefs, flamingo lagoons, the Bay of Pigs and the Zapata swamp forest at its fringes. Paul and Juan Carlos, our naturalists and fixers, have spent many tiring hours negotiating with Aerogaviota for the rental of a helicopter. Under normal circumstances, this would be quite straightforward: pay the rental fee and off you go. But this is Cuba, and there are many hurdles to cross, with permits and licences for this and that from various departments. It makes me glad that I'm not a producer. In the end, all is in order and on the morning of 1 April we head down to the airport to see what is in store for us. Rather than a modern Bell JetRanger or the like, we find an ancient Russian Mi8, and are peering at it through the chain-link airport perimeter fence when a very shifty young policeman comes up. 'You can't stand there looking at that helicopter!' he says (in Spanish, of course) which acted like a red rag to the proverbial bull. We tell him (in English, of course) to b....r off as we're paying $1,000 an hour for that helicopter and we'll look at it as much as we like. Things get tense and we ask our fixer, Juan Carlos, to explain who we are, in case the policeman pulls his gun out. There's an army guard inside the fence who confirms that we are, in fact, bona fide passengers for the helicopter and, after clearing security, we head over to the helicopter to meet the pilot and engineer, get on board and check out the best positions for filming. There's a little jump seat right by the sliding door which we will have open for filming. (We set up the safety harnesses to the correct length so that I can't fall out, which wouldn't go down well on the insurance claim.) It really is a very ancient machine and we just hope that it keeps flying for the next three days. It's so big that we have to taxi out to the main runway, but it does manage a vertical take-off.

We head east, out over the sea, with Havana on our port side. Sadly it's rather hazy so it's not worth filming yet. Below us we see mostly oil wells – so-called nodding donkeys – which give way to the Northern Cayes, with mangroves and lagoons with Caribbean flamingoes. We head for Cayo Coco where we land to refuel. We take off again at 5 p.m., hoping that the light is better, to film the strip of hotel development along the fabulous beaches. We fly west at a height of 100 metres, 200 metres offshore. I am sitting in the doorway and conditions are not ideal: we're flying towards the sun, it's hazy and a little bumpy from the stiff sea breeze so we decide to call it off – it's pointless to spend $1,000 an hour for something we won't use. It's been a good dummy run and we'll be better prepared for tomorrow.

We head back to the airport and the hotel Tryp Cayo Coco, one that we've used before, for the night. It's actually very nice, right on the beach and all-inclusive, which means that the drinks are free. We quickly drop off the gear in our rooms and head up to the bar for mojitos. Very soon we're on our fourth. We crash out after dinner, ready for what we hope will be a better day tomorrow.

We meet up at 6.30 a.m. for a quick coffee before heading off to the airport. We meet the pilots and the weatherman, who produces the latest weather maps of the areas we'll be flying over today. They don't look good, showing a cold front right over us from Pinar del Rio to Camagüey. It's Murphy's Law again: this is probably the cloudiest weather we have had for weeks. It looks as though it will remain cloudy all day but clearing this evening, so tomorrow should be good. After much discussion we decide to go back to the hotel and wait it out until morning, so we get a rare day off on a filming trip.

I make the most of it, getting up-to-date with my diary entries and walking the humid tropical shoreline beyond the hotel. There are, of course, birds to be seen, and I reflect on the fact that, wherever you go in the world, there they are, living their daily lives. Some, like turnstones, far from their Arctic breeding grounds, are familiar faces: others, like the brown pelican and royal tern, are a little more exotic. The day passes quickly and I am excited about tomorrow's planned helicopter trip to the south of the island. Paul and Juan Carlos come to my room at about half past six and drag me off for more free drinks at the bar. Today, it's rum and cokes.

An early call comes at 5.45 a.m. and – thank goodness – it's a clear morning. We're down to the airport by 7 o'clock and the flight crew arrives shortly after. Security takes a while, which is frustrating, and it's getting on for 8 o'clock by the time the engines are fired up. We lift off to the west and do some initial filming of the hotels to show the development of this part of the coast, then swing south toward the Jardines de la Reina, a huge expanse of coral reef. I am sitting at the front of the helicopter, near the open door and well strapped in with harnesses; this isn't the best machine for filming aerials, as it's big, old and vibrates quite a lot, but it was all that was available. All I can do is hold the camera firmly and use a higher frame rate to smooth out the bumps, and I'm glad that, so far, the morning is calm.

We stop at Ciego de Avila to refuel and carry on south. We cross the coast at around 11 o'clock and in the distance see tropical islands set in shallow seas, with mangroves, sandy cays, golden beaches and tiny islands. The waters go from pale green to almost black, out in the deep ocean beyond the unexplored reefs. Who knows what treasures lie in these waters? We film at various altitudes from 150–400 metres, setting the scene for the underwater sequences which will be shot later by a specialist cameraman. This is a unique experience and a rare opportunity to see this region – the Jardines de la Reina – from the air.

We land at Trinidad, a charming old colonial town with narrow, cobbled streets and brightly coloured houses. We refuel the helicopter and have lunch before taking off once more, flying over Cienfuegos and glimpsing the eastern edge of the Zapata swamp in the distant haze. Continuing on to the airport southwest of Havana, we unload the gear and head for our hotel, the Triton, where we will spend the night. Tomorrow we head west towards Viñales, the tobacco capital of Cuba. The evening is a pleasant interlude from being shaken around in an ancient Russian helicopter, and a couple of rum and Cokes and a fine Havana cigar settle the nerves.

We have another early start, at 4.45 a.m., to get down to the airport and do all the paperwork, have our permits checked, our equipment x-rayed and so on, in time for a 7 a.m. take-off. Just a few minutes can make all the difference when shooting aerials – the light is better first thing and the air is more stable before the day warms up – so we need to be ahead of the game. The flight crew are very punctual and we are away right on time, flying in clear, sunny conditions as we head west over Saroa towards Viñales. This is a stunning area of Cuba: the fertile valleys are the centre of the tobacco-growing region. The land is studded with huge limestone pinnacles called *mogotes* and beneath the surface run huge cave systems, some of the biggest in the world and home to tens of millions of bats. We do high circuits at 300 metres to establish this unique landscape, then at 100 metres fly up and over ridges to reveal misty, mysterious valleys beyond the jagged limestone pinnacles. It's all looking very good in this soft, early morning light when the radio spits out what sounds like an urgent message in Spanish. Juan Carlos tells us we have been ordered back to the airfield immediately, with no explanation, so now there is great speculation as to what the problem may be. Have we strayed out of our permitted filming area? Or been reported by the army for flying too low? All is revealed when we get back to the airfield at 9.15 a.m. We should, apparently, have taken an army security person with us, who was supposed to have been at the airport for 6 a.m. As he hadn't shown up, Thelmo – one of our fixers – had decided we should go without him. Poor Thelmo blames himself for the interruption to our day but all is now resolved, as long as we pick up another security chap before proceeding south to Zapata Swamp. This means a detour north to Varadero, miles out of our way, but there is nothing we can do about it. We land, quickly pick up the security man and head south to Zapata, half an hour away.

As we approach this huge area of rivers, lakes and forest we can see that it is very dry, not like swamp at all. We manage to pick out a large, meandering river, and go higher to show it broadening and emptying into the Bay of Pigs. We find some small lakes with carpets of water lilies to establish the habitat for the Cuban crocodile sequence which we will be filming later. At lower altitudes we can see cenotes, deep holes in the limestone that connect the forest to the sea with tunnels. These cenotes are full of tropical fish which have moved in from the Bay of Pigs. Our specialist dive team will be going into these mysterious depths in the forest to film this unique habitat. The pilot takes me low along the main road between forest and sea, where the tropical blue water is accentuated by the rich greens of the forest. Our hour of filming is up and we land in a cloud of dust and stones at the disused strip at Hotel Playa Girón, saying our goodbyes to the flight crew for a job well done. Juan Carlos is going back to Havana in the helicopter, meeting up with our driver Blanco and coming back out to the hotel later. In the meantime, an irate farmer has arrived and is lambasting the crew for terrifying his horse or not having a *permiso* to land or some such thing, maybe going for a little compensation payment. We make ourselves scarce and head for the hotel with rucksacks on our backs and briefcases in hand, looking like some sort of travelling tropical insurance outfit.

Almost within sight of the north coast tourist resorts is one of the world's biggest colonies of Caribbean flamingoes (although they're now, in fact, called American flamingoes – why do they have to keep changing bird names?) This flamingo is the deepest red of the seven species and at this colony, at Rio Maximo, there are over 40,000 pairs. It's a seven-hour drive from Playa Largo through uninspiring, poor agricultural land where subsistence farmers scratch a living, but I'm really excited about the flamingoes. They should be quite a spectacle.

Once we're in the town of Camagüey, we have to find the home of Mr Fefou, the head of the reserve at Rio Maximo. It's not easy to track down, and we have to ask several times before we eventually find it, down a little back street. After various discussions he comes out with a 'daily cost fee', a bombshell for Paul as all payments should have been made by the Ministry of Tourism (Mintur), which Mr Fefou knows nothing about. A few phone calls seems to sort it out, but it's been a huge waste of time. We are beginning to realise that this is typical of Cuba. We're all starving, as we've not eaten all day, but thankfully we find a surprisingly good pizza place in the local hotel and soon we're back on the road again, following Mr Fefou in his Toyota pick-up to the colony, still nearly two hours away on poor roads. It's 9.30 p.m. and dark when we arrive, I feel really tired and just want to drop into bed, but first we have to unpack all the gear and set up the tents. Putting up tents in the dark with a strong, humid wind and clouds of hungry mosquitoes is not for the faint-hearted. I get increasingly frustrated and Paul and Juan Carlos, seeing my growing rage, give me a hand to get finished. Finally I crash onto my sleeping mat and fall into a deep sleep.

I awake at 6.30 a.m. with clouds of mosquitoes buzzing at the fly screen, trying to get at me. I get dressed quickly and put repellant on any exposed parts. Unzipping the tent, I launch myself through the fly screen, closing it up quickly behind me. After a basic breakfast of some coffee and cereal, we are going out for our first look at the colony of 40,000–45,000 pairs. Travelling in the back of a pick-up truck and driving through the dense, dry woodlands that surround the massive tidal lagoon, we are subjected to the most horrendous onslaught by mosquitoes, and repellant has little effect. As we drive down the narrow tracks, brushing against overhanging branches, we disturb the ravenous insects which fall upon us by the thousands, and are just glad that they don't carry any infectious diseases.

We park the vehicle at the muddy edge of the lagoon and, in the distance, about a kilometre away, we see the pink haze which is the colony. We start the trek towards the flamingoes, crossing thick, hot mud and wading in water up to a metre deep, enough to conceal fallen branches and old tree stumps. It's going to be a nightmare when we have to walk through this with all the camera gear. The mosquitoes are much less of a problem here, though, as there is a breeze which keeps them down and cools the air somewhat, although it is still very hot and humid. On the exposed mud we see least- and semi-palmated sandpipers, roseate spoonbills and black-winged stilts, but the highlight for me is a West Indian whistling duck, perched high in a dead tree.

The flamingoes are only just laying eggs so it's a very sensitive time and we decide not to go any closer. We know now what the problems are going to be and the plan is to return in two weeks' time, when the birds will be well into their incubation and less

The colony of Caribbean flamingoes at Rio Maximo

likely to be disturbed. Nelson, one of our guides, says he knows a better route to the birds, going through the forest by tractor and coming out onto a dry shoreline with only a 300-metre walk to the site, where we will set up a platform on the mud to film the closest nests, maybe 20 metres away. It will be a case of seeing how the birds react to us and taking it very slowly and carefully.

We're going to spend the next two weeks in the east and southeast of Cuba, close to the infamous Guantanamo Bay, where it is hot and dry. The coast here is rugged and very scenic with many cactus plants: one that dominates the dry coastal region is called the Turk's head. Other taller, denser species of cactus make good, safe nesting habitat for the endemic Cuban gnatcatcher. This is a small and very confiding bird, about the size of a wren, with a long tail. It is busy feeding small young, so we make a start shooting a sequence on this little-known bird. Nearby there are flowering cactus which are attracting another Cuban endemic, the Cuban emerald hummingbird.

Leaving the Guantanamo region we head into the forested mountains en route to Baracoa, the most easterly town in Cuba. This gives us great opportunities for forest scenics along mountain ridges, showing Cuba's spectacular and unspoilt flora. Coming out of the mountains, we drop down into Baracoa where Columbus landed on 27 Nov 1492, and where there's an old fort which dates back to that era. The town, founded by a Spanish *conquistador* Diego Velázquez de Cuéllar on 15 Aug 1511, is the oldest Spanish settlement in Cuba and was its first capital, giving rise to its nickname, Ciudad Primada, or 'first city'. We stay for just one night in an old colonial hotel, the El Castillo, perched on top of a hill overlooking the historic harbour and town, before heading back via Guantanamo to finish off the gnatcatcher sequence.

We spent last night in Santiago, our final stop before heading back to the flamingo colony at Rio Maximo. After a relaxing morning we have a hectic hour packing the van and shopping for basics – drinking water, rum, Coke, cereals, milk, coffee, tinned meats, biscuits, sugar and bread – and hope to pick up good, fresh veggies and fruit from roadside stalls on the way. We're OK for time and even offer a frail old lady a lift. After that, though, the day takes a sudden turn for the worse. We hear a loud bang, and find that the rear off-side tyre has exploded, completely stripping the tread. Blanco changes the wheel to the spare, which in itself isn't brilliant, and we head for Camerguay where Transtur, the hire company, has a base. It's 6.30 p.m. by the time we get there, too late for anything to be done, so we refuel and resign ourselves to a trip back here for Blanco tomorrow. As this is likely to be our last decent meal for five days, we eat, and then drive on for two more hours, eventually arriving at Rio Maximo at 11.15 p.m. I'd forgotten how unpleasant it is: the mosquitoes are still horrendous and it's unbearably hot and humid.

It's 6.20 a.m. and the sun is trying to squeeze through the cloud cover. I get dressed quickly and dive out of the tent through the waiting clouds of persistent mosquitoes. I go over to the observation tower, which gives a great view of the freshwater stream that flows through the mangrove and out onto the mudflats. The flamingoes love to come here to bathe and preen and I'm hopeful of getting some exciting shots of groups of them as they fly in from the colony. The tower is around ten metres high with a good, solid platform, there's a cool breeze here off the water and, best of all, no mosquitoes. It looks as if it's brightening up so I rush back and put together the camera, with the biggest lenses and tripod. As I work, I hear Paul cursing the mosquitoes as he emerges from his tent. Back at the tower, I set up quickly: this is the best time, when the low sunlight is striking the birds and accentuating their pinkness. The birds are rather distant – between 200 and 300 metres away – which is not ideal, but they still look very impressive because of their large numbers. In the early morning sun the deep pink of their feathers looks spectacular. I start to get great shots in slow motion, mostly at 75 fps (3x slower than normal), of groups of ten or fifteen birds, flying in and landing, and big numbers at the edge of the mangrove bathing in the freshwater stream. Conditions are not perfect – it's quite breezy and the sky is milky – but I've shot 130 metres (ten mins) of safety footage to get the sequence rolling. It can always be reshot if conditions and time permit. I head back to the camp for toast and coffee and to change a film magazine. Mosquitoes in the film magazines would be a disaster, so I have to turn on the air con and do this in the van, the only place of respite from the pesky insects.

We can't do any filming at the colony until Mr Fefou arrives later in the morning to confirm that all documents and fees are in place. When he arrives, though, just before midday, we find that all is not well. He hasn't been paid his money by Mintur (the Ministry of Tourism) which means we cannot film. After much discussion it is decided that Paul will leave a deposit of two days' filming fees which, at $465 a day, is an outrageous sum – even the African national parks don't charge that much. If Mintur pay up, Paul will get his money back, and if – as is quite possible – they don't, he won't. Paul, Juan Carlos and Blanco go into Camerguay to sort out Mintur and get the tyre fixed, and won't be back until tomorrow. I load up the camera with high-speed film, 250 ASA, as I want to do slow-motion of the flamingoes in the evening light.

I go to the tower at just after 5 p.m. as the best conditions are from 6 o'clock onwards, so I'm set up in good time. Big groups of between 15 and 20 birds start to fly in, looking glorious in the evening light, their deep pink plumage glowing in the low evening sun. A feeding group comes closer than the rest and I get some quite respectable close-ups of their amazing technique as they trawl the mud with their oddly shaped bills. There are six species of flamingo: lesser and greater, James's, Andean, Chilean and Caribbean (or American). The lesser, James's and Andean have a deep-keeled bill adapted to feeding on algae, whereas the greater, Chilean and Caribbean have a shallow-keeled bill more suited to feeding on insects, invertebrates and small fish. More particularly, the Caribbean feeds on the larval and pupal forms of flies, brine shrimp and small fish. The usual group is bathing at the edge of the mangrove and provide some additional shots as the sun drops even lower. It's been a very productive hour so I pack up and head back to camp. In the kitchen area I cook up a satisfying supper, chorizo chopped and cooked in tinned tomato with –surprise, surprise – beans and rice, all washed down with a relaxing rum and Coke, or two.

It's 5 a.m. and pitch black as we get the gear together for our first attempt at filming the colony. Everything is packed into the back of a trailer, towed by an ancient, Russian tractor – in fact, those two adjectives apply to most pieces of machinery here. Nelson and another assistant are helping me and we pick up two other guys from the pig farm. The access to the colony would, I think, deter any but the most determined. Forty minutes of bumping and lurching down dusty, rutted tracks through sugar-cane fields, then 20 minutes through dense, dry woodland and mangrove, the haunt of the most vicious and voracious of mosquitoes.

Alfred Russel Wallace summed them up very well in his famous book of 1856, *The Malay Archipelago*: 'In the plantations where my daily walks led me, the day biting mosquitoes swarmed, and seemed especially to delight in attacking my poor feet. After a month's incessant punishment those useful members rebelled against such treatment and broke into open insurrection, throwing out numerous inflamed ulcers, which were very painful, and stopped me from walking. So I found myself confined to the house, and with no immediate prospect of leaving it. Wounds or sores in the feet are especially difficult to heal in hot climates and I therefore dreaded them more than any other illness... The stings and bites and ceaseless irritation caused by these pests of the tropical forests would be borne uncomplainingly; but to be kept prisoner by them in such a rich and unexplored country where rare and beautiful creatures are to be met with in every forest ramble, a country reached by such a long and tedious voyage, and which might not in the present century be again visited for the same purpose, is a punishment too severe for a naturalist to pass over in silence.'

Finally our torture is over, as we break out from the woodland onto the edge of the lagoon where, mercifully, there is a breeze off the water which downs many of the insects. We can see that the nearest part of the colony is less than 400 metres away and between us we get together the camera, the sound gear and the makeshift platform, which is in fact a discarded pallet on which I will, I hope, be able to keep myself and the gear relatively mud-free. It is not an easy walk. It is already 30° C and very humid, and at every step there is some hidden obstacle – a mangrove root, a dead branch – in the mire, which is sometimes knee-deep. Step by step, though, we near our target, the edge of the colony of 45,000 breeding pairs of the most colourful of all flamingoes. When we are 40 metres from the nearest group, we stop to take stock of the situation and see how the birds are reacting. The last thing we want is for birds to start leaving their nests. All seems calm so, slowly, quietly, we edge a little closer. Now the nearest birds are just 30 metres away and I decide that this is close enough. We can always edge a little nearer tomorrow.

We put down the platform and find a submerged root that stops it from sinking into the mire. I erect the tripod and carefully set up the camera, placing all the gear within easy reach on the platform, where it won't get coated in mud. We decide that a hide is unnecessary: it would be incredibly hot and restrictive, in that it would prevent us from filming the birds flying in. A flapping canvas could easily disturb them, too – they seem quite content with three of us here and I'm sure that when the boys leave they will be completely settled.

It's now almost 7.30 a.m. so the Cubans slip away quietly. They will come back for me in four hours, which should be enough time to make a start and see what behaviour presents itself. The flamingoes are constantly chattering and calling as they fly in and out from feeding and bathing areas and, as the wind has dropped a little, I decide to record some sound. I take just eight minutes of background track, but it's really useful to have it in the bag – all too often, sound is overlooked and grabbed in a rush at the last moment. Carefully packing the sensitive gear into its waterproof box, I set up the camera with the 50-300 zoom lens, which will give me the ability to get a variety of shot sizes without changing lens. I need to establish the colony as a whole and then move in to medium shots of groups of nests with sitting birds.

The birds' nests, constructed of mud, form a pedestal which may be 50 cm above the surface of

Inset: MP on pallet with camera and two Cuban field assistants
Below: Flamingoes on their nests with eggs

the lagoon. This becomes baked by the sun and provides a relatively dry nest cup for the chick when it hatches after 28 days of incubation. Just ahead of me are a group of eight nests, all with recently-laid eggs, so I concentrate on the action there. There is a lot of activity, especially when there is a changeover at the nest, when a partner that has been away feeding or bathing returns to take its shift at incubation. I get great slow-motion shots as birds fly in to land and then walk delicately over to their pedestal nests, where they are greeted with great enthusiasm by the sitting bird who is, no doubt, ready to go and take a bath. They seem to get very mucky at the nest as they are constantly picking up mud and adding it to the structure. The birds are really used to me now and some have walked past within five metres. I change to the 600 mm lens to get big close-ups of the birds, watching their long, pink, spindly legs fold neatly beneath them as they settle down onto the two large white eggs

It's beginning to cloud over, but I have shot almost two rolls: 20 valuable minutes of behaviour rarely filmed before, so it's a great start. It would be so easy to overshoot in a situation like this, surrounded by thousands of some of the most fascinating and colourful birds in the world. This is one of many situations in which I have found myself where I am almost overwhelmed by the spectacle and the wildness of the place. So few people get to witness this and yet I am being paid to be here, so the poor food, lack of sleep, the heat and constant onslaught from mosquitoes are a small price to pay. I seize the opportunity to take a few production stills and a few images on my Fuji 617 panoramic camera, before the lads come to pick me up at 11.45 and we make the unpleasant journey back through the mud and mosquitoes to our camp.

Paul, Juan Carlos and Blanco return from Camerguay in the early afternoon. They have had a meeting with Flora and Fauna (an organization similar to Natural England, that has control of National Parks, reserves, visits, permits etc.). It did not go well, Paul will not get his money back and our film budget won't stand us paying for more days at $450 a shot. This means we will be limited to two days' filming at the flamingo colony although, as it happens, I think this may be enough, as the behaviour with incubation is quite limited. In the evening we pick up shots – birds flying in and out to bathe, feeding and so on – from the tower next to the mangrove, all useful for telling the nesting story.

The final, violent journey through the cane fields and the dry forest and the endless onslaught of the mosquitoes are now behind me. As we break out onto the muddy lagoon, I can see the haze of deep-pink flamingoes ahead. Even the trudge through the ankle-ripping, root-infested mud doesn't seem quite as bad today, probably because I know this will be my last trip. Settled onto the rudimentary platform in the hot mud, I soon have the camera set up, the lads leave me and I can concentrate on getting the shots I need to complete the sequence: flamingoes perched on their nests, shuffling onto eggs, preening, squabbling with their neighbours, taking off and landing. I need to get the biggest close-ups possible of birds turning their eggs and settling down to

incubate, which will cut into the wider shots taken yesterday. The birds are even more used to me being here now and are passing by very close to my position, allowing me great shots of their delicate, pink legs as they move effortlessly through the ooze.

As usual, I've got four hours here before the boys come to pick me up at midday, by which time it will be very hot and the sun will be too high and severe for filming. The time passes quickly, as there is always something happening: great flights of birds passing overhead en route to feeding or bathing areas, making a stunning sight against a deep blue tropical sky. I get my close-up egg-turning shots and changeovers – always noisy affairs – as one of the pair arrives to relieve its muddy, hot partner, who's ready for their feed and bath.

It's approaching midday and in the hazy distance I can see two shimmering figures moving slowly. It's my relief party and I quietly – so as not to disturb the closest birds – pack my gear into its waterproof boxes. We trudge back in the intense heat and humidity to the waiting tractor to make the final journey through the forest and hordes of biting insects to our camp. On the drive back, the tractor shudders to a stop. What now? The boys from camp swarm around the engine looking for the cause of the problem, which turns out to be a small scrap of cotton jammed in the fuel pipe. We are soon up and running again. Back at camp, I have a tepid shower and at last get out of my muddy clothes, before one last visit to the tower in the evening. It's windy and overcast, not ideal conditions for using telephoto lenses, but I have to, as the birds are never that close. We have a good sequence from the two days at the nests and the other shots from the tower, so I'm ready to move on to another challenge.

It's a 4 a.m. start from our hotel in Havana and we are heading for Isla de Juventud to film Cuban parrots and endemic palms. The downside is that we are going by ferry. After picking up our fixer Juan Carlos, we head for the terminal, just over an

195

hour's drive away, arriving at the port gates at just after 5.30 a.m. to find they won't be opening until 7. We could have had another hour in bed, and with the afternoon we'd just had, we could have done with it.

It had been one of those typically stressful Cuban days: we had left our passports at the grandly named Press Accreditation Centre for our visas to be extended, and had been told to 'Return mid-afternoon!' We duly did, to find that the passports had not come back. 'Try after 4!' was the best we could get. In the meantime we went over to the Cubatur office (a quite efficient organization, compared with some) as I needed to drop off exposed film to be stored in an air-conditioned room, while Paul and Juan Carlos made phone calls relating to our next three-week trip in June and July. Returning at 4.15, we were told that the passports had still not come back. Paul was beginning to lose patience and, after several heated phone calls, we went over to the immigration office to collect them in person. We had them in the nick of time – in another few days we would have been illegal.

I mooch idly around the dockside watching the comings and goings while Paul goes into the grotty little town to find some fresh bread. It's approaching 7 a.m., lorries and cars are beginning to arrive but the whole place is chaotic with no apparent system. It's going to be a long day. The ferry boat comes in from Isla de Juventud at 7.20 and things – slowly – start to happen. The ancient Russian lorries trundle through the guarded gate, blasting out clouds of filthy diesel fumes, the harbour itself is very polluted, with sewage, by the smell of it. After presenting our papers, our driver Blanco takes the van, packed with all our gear, onto the ship and below deck. We sail at 11.45 a.m. It's slow, we reckon maybe 10 knots, and there's a fresh breeze with a few white caps. There's a little room with a few filthy benches and some old cardboard to lie on. The lorry drivers that do it regularly bring their own camp beds, which they erect in the shade under their lorries, a highly dangerous idea considering that the lorries are not chained down. Some of the more safety-conscious among them have a rock or chunk of timber jammed under the wheel. Most of the tyres on most of the lorries are bald through to the canvas, but apparently it's not illegal. This is going to be a long, noisy, hot and smoky journey. In anticipation of a total lack of refreshment on the ship we have a brought a small supply of rum and Coke in our rucksack, and we soon feel a bit less stressed.

Over seven hours later, we are passing through a channel in the mangroves on the approach to the port of Gerona. By the time we dock, it's gone 7 p.m. and just getting dark. The lorries are off first and it's nearly an hour before we have cleared security. As we're all starving, we dive into the first restaurant we see, a so-called Chinese, but what is called a 'peso' restaurant so very cheap. For A$2.5 we get four portions of a supposed pork and cabbage chow mein, a slop of a sauce with some spam-like meat, served with fried rice. I carefully remove the 'meat' and eat just the rice. It is without doubt the worst meal we have had in Cuba and there are quite a few competing for that title.

We are heading for a reserve called Los Indios, part of the Flora and Fauna organisation with which we had so much trouble at the flamingo colony. We were supposed to be sleeping there tonight, but apparently they are not ready for us so, after a few frantic phone calls, we manage to get in at the Colony Hotel. This is a blessing in disguise – I'm sure the Los Indios rooms would have been shared, with camp beds and their attendant mosquitoes. The hotel rooms are large, cool and comfortable, which is bliss after a shattering 19-hour day.

After a rejuvenating sleep and satisfying breakfast, we pack the vehicle to head off to the Ecological Centre, though yesterday's traumas mean that we are all a bit slow. It takes a while to find the right turning: we know it's by a derelict school but there are several of those crumbling Communist institutions and they all look the same. Apparently their purpose was to straighten out people's way of thinking –to indoctrinate them, in other words, if they weren't towing the line – and they are scary-looking places.

We find our way onto the right track and eventually to the small wooden building that is the Ecological Centre, a very grand name for a shack about ten metres square. Los Indios is largely made up of sand dunes with low scrubby woodland and fantastic specimens of the endemic palm for which Cuba is famous. These palms are used for nesting by the endemic Cuban parrot, part of the Amazon parrot group, and our main focus whilst here is to document the feeding and nesting behavior of these very rare birds.

There is a manager here and a warden called Pauol, but I can't film until the usual fees have been paid. Paul is fuming with all this petty bureaucracy, wasting so much valuable time, and is heading for a red mist. He and Juan Carlos have to go into town to sort out the fees with the local director and I stay behind with Pauol to check out the parrot nests. At least, that's what the manager had agreed to while Paul was here, but now he's changed his mind and says I can't even do that. I spend the next couple of hours sitting about in the heat, birdwatching from the little area of wooden decking. I find a shady spot to write up my diary and the guard that has been assigned to look after me – called El Chino, or The Chinaman – brings me a refreshing coconut. He is Cuban, despite the nickname, and speaks quite passable English. Nearby is a mango tree in which, he tells me, the parrots have been feeding a lot, though I've not seen them in it today, as it's quite windy. It should provide some good opportunities for big close-ups of them feeding, and as they're used to seeing the wardens about, I won't need a hide.

A cloud of dust rising through the scrub shows that Paul is heading back and I dread to see how he will take the news of my wasted day. They've had a load of headaches with payments, politics and permissions. When I tell Paul that I'd not even been able to go and look at the nests until the payments had been made, it was the last straw. He went ballistic. I've seen Paul in bad moods before but never quite this bad, shouting that he'd just about had enough of Cuba and everyone in it. He's now determined to find this two-faced manager and tell him what he thinks of him. Now, at least, though, I can go to look at the nests with Pauol. He takes me to three, all with eggs, but just one is suitable in terms of height, allowing me to use a hide on the ground rather than build a platform, which would be time-consuming for us and potentially disturbing for the birds.

There is also a Cuban green woodpecker excavating a nest hole in a termite mound on the side of a tree not more than eight metres off the ground, so things are looking up. I'll be back in the morning to try working on the parrots from a hide, although from past experience in Australia I know they are not easy subjects, very wary of anything new near the nest site. We shall see soon enough. I meet up with Paul back at the Eco Centre and we head back to the oasis of calm that is the Colony Hotel for our routine rum and Coke, or two.

It's a 5.30 a.m. start. I set to, sorting my film gear, and everything is packed into the van in half an hour. We grab a quick breakfast, make up some ham rolls for lunch and we're away by 6.30 a.m. On the way we pick up a couple of our rangers from the village of Victoria and give them a lift to Los Indios, less than an hour from the hotel. I get my gear prepared and we set off for the nest tree of the parrots, a walk of just a few hundred metres through the palms from the Eco Centre. I set up the hide at a safe distance, maybe 30 metres away, until I know how the birds will behave, as I can always move closer if they are relaxed. I get settled into the hide just as the sun has risen through the palms and Paul and the others walk off, leaving me to await developments.

The parrots are nearby and very soon one flies to the nest hole and peers in, seeming relaxed enough. If they are still laying, it may not yet have started incubation. It flies off without warning and is replaced at the hole by a West Indian woodpecker which peers into the nest hole and then pops in; within seconds, it's out again and flies off. I have my 500 mm lens on which gives a reasonable close-up at 30 metres, and set the frame speed to 100 (4x slow motion) in anticipation of a return visit. Sure enough, within minutes the woodpecker is back, goes straight into the hole and comes out with an egg. It pauses on the lip of the nest hole for two or three seconds and I hit the run button, just managing a shot of it before it's away with its prize. This is amazing behavior and probably never before seen or recorded in these species, although European woodpeckers are known to steal the eggs and chicks of other birds. One of the parrots flies straight to the nest hole – it was probably watching from nearby, although it was strange that it didn't try to chase the woodpecker away before it stole the egg. I get close-ups of it but it doesn't go in. It's 10.15 when I hear the rangers coming through the bush to let me out of the hide and it's been a good start – the birds have accepted the hide and I have a variety of shots with which to start the sequence. We head back to the Centre where I set up by the mango tree, in the hope of getting the parrots feeding. Nothing appears, and I think it's too hot. If time permits it will

A Cuban green woodpecker at its nest hole in a termite nest

A pair of Cuban parrots

A Cuban parrot on its eggs in a palm trunk

have to be an early morning session. Over the next couple of days I spend quite a few sweltering hours in the hide at the parrot nest, getting more shots of the birds flying to the hole, both in wide-angle and close-up, perched in trees nearby and taking off, and in open flight in slow motion, all of which will cut together nicely.

We were taken to another nest in a broken-off palm where, using a ladder, it was possible to peer into the nest from above. The bird was very settled and would not move off the eggs so, using the camera hand-held, we got good shots of her incubating, a vital part of the sequence. Sadly the mango tree didn't produce anything usable, as the birds were too high in the branches, partially obscured and in poor, hazy backlight.

Paul, Juan Carlos and Blanco, our driver, have been into town to get the ferry tickets for our return journey and it's gone 3 p.m. by the time they get back. We load up all my gear, say our goodbyes to Los Indios and head to the Colony Hotel for a shower and a final pack. The ferry doesn't leave till 1 a.m. so there's time for an evening meal in Gerona. Paul and Juan Carlos know a place, a 'pork restaurant', where we actually have very good pork medallions with rice and beans. We head down to the filthy little port of Gerona at just after 9 o'clock. It's in a mangrove area so the mosquitoes are prolific and ferocious, the place stinks of urine, mixed with diesel fumes from the decrepit Russian trucks, it's dimly lit with nowhere to sit in comfort, and we know we're in for two or three hellish hours waiting around in this stinking hole. Paul and Juan Carlos wander off and return with large sheets of cardboard – actually packaging from freezers – which will be our beds on the deck of the ferry. Eventually we board at around half past midnight, half-choked by a combination of diesel fumes, Blanco and Paul's cigars and cheap Cuban cigarettes. We select our spots to bed down: Paul goes under a lorry and I manage to find a spot in the bows. We have a rum and Coke nightcap from our rucksack 'kit' and settle down as the ferry pulls out through the mangrove channel. After two hours of sleep I wake up, hammered by mosquitoes on my face and hands, and eventually, at 6.30, give up trying to sleep and go to the starboard side of the ship, where there is a sea breeze and some respite from the insect life. We dock at 8.15 and unloading starts straight away, so we're soon off. The next thing I know, I'm waking up in Havana.

Cuba has some of the most extensive limestone cave systems in the world and many millions of bats within them, 26 species, of which seven are endemic. We will be working in the Caguanes National Park in the north of Cuba and world bat expert Gilberto Silva will be helping us to film and featuring in the sequences. We are staying at an old but pleasant hotel called San Jose del Lago, set up as a spa for rich Americans in the late 1920s, pre-Revolution, with beautiful, established gardens. Gilberto used to stay here over 50 years ago: he's well into his 70s but still spritely and enjoys his Cuban cigars. We are being assisted by four guys from the Flora and Fauna department who arrive with their pick-up truck just after breakfast. It's going to be quite a crush, with four of us inside and four in the pick-up with all the filming gear, plus batteries for the lights and ladders to access the cave entrances. It's an hour's drive through hot and dusty cane fields, then across dry cattle-ranching country and finally along a very rough track through mangroves to a massive rock outcrop right on the coast. The whole thing is hollow, with 32 separate caves.

It's now gone 9 a.m. and beginning to get hot, so it's time to go underground. The cave entrances are semi-concealed by the dense forest and very photogenic. We set up establishing shots of Gilberto walking through with a ladder and disappearing into the cave system, which will help to establish the habitat of the bats and the work that Gilberto has been doing on them for 50 years. To get into the first cave system we have to use the ladders; a sinkhole 20 feet deep drops down into the darkness. All the filming gear, cameras, tripods, lenses, car batteries and lights have to be carefully lowered into the chamber below. Here we find some people's idea of hell. The ground is covered with six inches of bat guano – the consistency of thick custard and smelling very strongly of ammonia – which in turn is covered with a heaving mass of giant cockroaches. The walls of the cavern are plastered in cave crickets and, as if that weren't enough, we were to discover that bats flying out at night send a continuous spray of urine falling from above, and that snakes lurk on ledges in the darkness, ready to strike at any little creatures that stray too close.

It takes a while to assemble the infrared-sensitive camera and lighting and, to minimize disturbance, all of our torches have infrared filters. There are many millions of bats of four different species in this cave system. When all is prepared, Gilberto walks into the huge cavern shining his dragon torch (powerful flashlight) to reveal the unbelievable number of bats hanging from the walls, then swarming through the air.

This is going to make a very dramatic sequence. As we move back towards the cave exit, I pick off close-up shots of bats hanging on the walls and in flight, to cut with the dramatic numbers in the big cavern. It's now getting on for 4 p.m. and time for our afternoon tea break and a sandwich before preparing for the main event of the evening, the emergence of the butterfly bats. Again we have to use ladders to go down a sinkhole to the cave entrance, which is far more difficult to access. I assemble the infrared camera and pack it into a case for protection. We have to wriggle through a very narrow passage, not more than a metre high, with sharp stalactites above, dragging the gear behind us, including 12-volt batteries to power the infrared lamps. This is certainly not the place to be if you suffer from claustrophobia. This tunnel goes on for about 20 metres before opening into a big chamber where we have space to assemble and test all the gear. These are known as 'hot caves', as they have only one entrance – caves with multiple entrances get through-draughts and so stay much cooler.

The side cave where the butterfly bats are to be found is very hot indeed and even though this tiny creature is the world's smallest warm-blooded animal, millions of their tiny bodies still produce a lot of heat. The temperature in the chamber must be over 25° C. We are set up in a side passage that leads to the cave and is the only exit so, come evening, the bats will pour past us on their way out to the forest, where they will feed on billions of insects. Gilberto reckons it will be at about 6.30, but it's actually an hour later than that when the first bats take wing. Paul is doing sound as the little creatures take to the air, I switch on the infrared lights and start running the camera, and they look like fluttering bow ties, thousands of them now filling the air. Gilberto is sitting near the chamber entrance so I get nice shots of him as he watches the bats leaving, and get lots of different camera angles, wide-angle and close-up shots, always keeping in mind the needs of the film editor. With a little net, Gilberto catches some of the closest bats for weighing and examination, giving me a good opportunity to get close-ups in the hand and adding another angle to the sequence. All the bats are gone by 8 p.m. so we decide to pack in.

The Flora and Fauna guys think it will be easier to get most of the gear up the ladders – 25m or so – through the cave roof. Paul, Gilberto and I are left to crawl out of the cave down the tortuous low passageways, dragging and pushing the heavy car batteries through the dried-out guano of centuries. Bats carry a serious lung infection called histoplasmosis, transmitted by inhaling the spores of a fungus which is found in the dust, the air and the soil of these bat caves, as well as on droppings. We did wear masks but I was very aware of the risks of this potentially serious disease. When I returned home just five days later I noticed a dry cough, one of the flu-like symptoms of the disease. Samples were taken and sent to Bristol, where they have experience of the disease, and it was confirmed some days later that I did indeed have a mild case of histoplasmosis. Fortunately for me, it was diagnosed at an early stage and the antibiotic treatment was effective.

Having left the cave we still have to haul the batteries seven metres up a ladder to our base camp in the forest. Then came the final back-wrenching journey through the cane fields to our hotel. All the gear is unpacked and stored, ready for a thorough wash-down in the morning. Blanco, our driver, has thoughtfully arranged supper in our rooms, but I cannot eat until I have had a shower – I am filthy and smelly. It's been a long, hard day but very productive, and we find time for the usual nightcap.

We have a bit of a lie-in the next day, all shattered after yesterday's exertions. Breakfast is at 9 a.m. then we set to, cleaning all the gear, which is covered with dust and guano from the caves, and leaving it in the sun to dry. We still have one more sequence to do, on flat-headed bats which roost in palm trees, and we hope to film this over two nights. Our time in Cuba is coming to a close for the moment, but we return in July to go to the Alexandra von Humboldt National Park, not widely known but a treasure chest of amazing creatures. It's a truly exciting prospect.

8 DRAGON ISLANDS

A cloud of flies and a foul stench indicate a corpse nearby. The heat is overwhelming and the tinder-dry leaves crunch under my feet. Parting the dense scrub, I see what I suspected would be there: the rotting carcass of a decomposing deer that has been attacked by a large predator. This is the remote island of Komodo in Indonesia which has only one dangerous carnivore – only the Komodo dragon could have inflicted the fatal bites.

The dragons hunt by ambush, lying in a shallow hole or dense scrub, then charging out at high speed and grabbing the prey by the throat. There was a common belief that komodos killed prey with a serious tearing bite and that toxic bacteria in the saliva of the dragon was the ultimate cause of death, but recent research has shown this not to be the case. Multiple ducts between the teeth deliver a venom as powerful as that of the most poisonous of snakes, which lowers blood pressure, increases blood loss by preventing clotting and induces shock. Smaller prey such as wild pigs and deer die quickly. Water buffalo, a species introduced to the islands, also fall victim to the dragons, but they are too big to be killed outright and will escape into the bush. They are killed by infection to the initial wound caused by water-borne bacteria in the stagnant pools frequented by the buffalo.

Most people are familiar with the name Komodo dragon from David Attenborough's *Zoo Quest* programmes, and remember the black-and-white images of these massive monitor lizards, actually the largest in the world, which grow up to nine feet in length and weigh up to 200 lbs. There are two main islands where they survive in good numbers: Rinca, with about 1,300, and Komodo itself, with approximately 1,700. Sometimes the dragons will hunt in groups, but here on Komodo they tend to hang out in dried-out river beds, waiting for prey that may come down to drink in small pools. They may, though, be found anywhere in this rocky, dry, savannah-type landscape, even patrolling the beaches where they will feed on any carrion washed in by the tide.

We are focusing our initial filming attention around the massive nest mounds of a megapode, the orange-footed scrub-fowl, a small chicken-like bird sometimes called the incubator bird. It is a compulsive mound builder, its impressive volcano-like structures often reaching up to 5 metres in height and up to 10 metres in diameter at the base. The top of the mound is filled with decomposing vegetation which creates the heat to incubate the eggs, laid deep in the mound, though occasionally the dragons will dig them out with their powerful claws. The dragons will lay their own eggs either in the mound or in a shallow underground tunnel. They usually lay around 20 eggs which can take up to seven

A Komodo dragon walks down the dry river bed

months to hatch, usually in April, when the insect prey for the young dragons is most plentiful. The youngsters quickly take to the trees as they are very vulnerable and subject to cannibalism from their own species and other ground predators.

We are going to try and document as much of this fascinating behaviour as we can in our ten-day stay here. Komodo is now a national park and a world heritage site, not only for the dragons but for its extensive offshore marine life. Although the islands of Komodo and Rinca are the stronghold of the dragons, populations on the smaller islands of Gili Motang and Gili Dasami are falling, due to habitat loss and disturbance, with only around 100 left on each.

Our accommodation is basic: rustic rooms at the back of park headquarters with the usual resident wildlife in the walls. The walk up to the dry riverbed where the big dragons hang out is around half an hour, through forest, with all the filming gear. It's quite exhausting in the heat: we are only 600 miles from the equator and the temperatures now, at the beginning of the dry season, are up to 40° C. This is a place where the dragons are fed by park rangers as a bit of a spectacle for the tourists. Although we don't film much of this, it does give us the opportunity to see the dragons at close quarters, interacting over a carcass – usually a pig or goat – provided for them. To begin with there is nothing to be seen but then, one by one, they appear from the forest, sliding down the dry bank in a cloud of dust into the riverbed. Cautiously they analyse the still, tropical air with their ultra-sensitive forked tongues: they can detect a carcass up to six miles away. Slowly they heave their massive bodies on short powerful legs to the carcass. I carry a big stick, although I'm not quite sure how effective that would be at repelling a 200-pound (almost 100 kg) reptile. Very soon, six of the huge beasts are tearing into the goat, hissing, squabbling and snapping at each other. There is something primeval about them. I get some great shots, big close-ups of their powerful jaws as they tear at the flesh, then suddenly a three-metre dragon grabs the goat and swallows it whole, the flexible skull and articulated jaws, along with the

Komodo dragons gather in the dry riverbed

expandable stomach, making this possible. Having eaten such a large meal the reptile has to drag itself into a sunny position to speed up the normally slow metabolism. If large prey is not digested quickly enough, it could rot in the stomach and kill the dragon.

As the dragons move along the riverbed, I can get tracking shots from a low angle, which makes them look even bigger and more impressive.

After a break for lunch and to shelter from the intense sun, we go up to the scrub-fowl nest mound, and find the birds there doing their compulsive scratching behavior. I film them but it's turned quite overcast so the footage is not brilliant. I hope to get better shots but can never be sure I will, so it's always wise to get some safety footage.

The forestry boat is here for a day or two so, as there is not much happening on the filming front, and we get a lift out to a beautiful, sandy bay. On route we recce a fruit bat roost which looks fantastic. It's in a small and very accessible mangrove forest, so we'll come back with the filming gear tomorrow. On the way across the bay, the water crystal-clear and stunning, we are followed by a small group of dolphins. We land on a perfect little beach, its white coral sand tinged with pink coral dust, on which the water is gently lapping. There is a little group of us, including a few visitors to the park from around the world, and we swim quietly out in just two metres of water. After just a short distance we find ourselves over the most incredibly pristine coral garden. The water is gin clear, and there's not a trace of damage to the stunning variety of fish and corals. I almost feel that I shouldn't be here, in case I damage this most beautiful, perfect organism, and sense that everyone feels the same. After several failed attempts, I master the art of paddling a dugout canoe – not easy, as they are only 70 cm or so wide – and we head back across the bay at sunset after a memorable afternoon.

The chances of filming a Komodo dragon digging out the nest of a megapode are very slim indeed and, as fortune would have it, we find an old megapode mound which appears not to be in use. I'm wondering whether or not I should share this secret, but we get a few hens' eggs, which look remarkably like those of the megapode, smear them with a little fish essence to give the dragon something to home in on, bury them in the mound and sit back to wait for some action. It isn't long before a crashing in the bushes alerts me to the arrival of a massive dragon, his head appearing first, tongue flashing, tasting the air and looking very excited, a full nine feet (3 m) of prehistoric, scaly reptile emerging and lumbering towards the mound.

I start the camera running to get the approach. He is definitely going to the buried eggs and very soon is digging with his powerful claws to expose them. Breaking them on the spot, he eagerly licks out the contents. I take the camera off the tripod and

A Komodo dragon comes close to the camera

move in for a low wide-angle, the real 'killer' shot, but the dragon takes exception and lunges at my foot. I just manage to jump aside but get whacked by a broadside on my arm from his huge, armoured tail. I jump back to give him space, really not wanting to get bitten as the nearest hospital is two days away. He tucks into the remaining eggs which gives me a few more shots before he slowly moves back to the forest. My arm is swollen and red with a perfect impression of the tail, almost like a tattoo. I'm sure that if it had struck across the arm, it would have been broken.

It's mid-afternoon and time to get the film gear over to the roost of the fruit bats. We're going to film these large, furry mammals – sometimes called 'flying foxes' because of their facial features – as this all helps to set the scene of this remote island. There are huge numbers, all hanging upside down in the mangrove trees, squawking and squabbling over the best branches. I'm also recording high-quality stereo sound, which gives us a powerful addition to the filmed sequence. They look amazing, backlit with the sun shining through their transparent wings. At dusk, they will fly out in great squadrons to the forests, seeking out a variety of fruits on which they will feed before returning to the relative safety of their treetop roost.

The nearby stilted village of Komodo is beautifully situated at the water's edge and as we pass by, scores of excited children, all laughing and shouting and crowding around, run out to see what's going on. Back at camp for 6.15, I feel shattered after a long, hot day, have a basic supper of an omelette and noodles and am in bed by half past eight.

Just after dawn we're at the scrub-fowl mound. The sun is streaming through the canopy, illuminating the birds digging, tossing soil and leaves onto their enormous volcano-like structure and scratching for food. Using my big zoom lens, I soon have a variety of shot sizes, which will help to build the mound sequence involving the komodo.

Up at the dried-out riverbed the dragons are hanging about in the long grass. This is serious snake country and you have to be very careful where you're putting your feet. I get good tracking shots alongside a large komodo as it lumbers along, its sensitive tongue flicking in and out, tasting the air. These are great build-up and approach shots for finding a carcass. I hold the camera down at ground level, trying to hold it steady as I walk slowly alongside, only a metre from the dragon, keeping a very close eye on its demeanour, as they can turn nasty very quickly. The cold eye gives no indication of its mood. Nigel walks close to me to fend it off with a big stick if required. We get more shots of dragons coming down the steep slide from the forest into the riverbed: now that it's dry, the dust kicks up and looks great in slow motion.

Nigel has an idea for a sequence to show how humans can be attacked by komodos. Choco, one of our Indonesian helpers, runs through the grass while I film close-ups of his legs and feet from the knee down. I then do the same with a komodo running through the grass, and hope that the two, intercut, will give the impression of a chase, as an illustration of the facts as they are narrated. Human deaths from komodos are not common but there have been fatalities, both in the wild and in captivity. According to Komodo National Park, there were 24 reported attacks on humans, five of them deadly, between 1974 and 2012. An eight-year-old boy was killed on Komodo in 2007, in 2009 a 31-year-old man fell from a tree where he was picking sugar apples and was killed by two dragons, then – in 2017 – a 50-year-old Singaporean tourist survived an attack but was left with a damaged leg. Perhaps the most bizarre attack was on Rinca Island, where a dragon walked into a ranger guide's office, lay under his desk and ambushed him, giving him a serious bite when he returned to his seat.

Rinca is where we're heading tomorrow.

The village of Komodo from the hillside   *A view of the islands from the mountain top*

It's our last day on Komodo and we have a very early start – 5.15 a.m. – as we are going to climb Mount Ara. It's over 600 metres high and will give us some amazing views of the outlying islands. The forestry boat takes us on the 20-minute ride across the bay to Komodo village. Apart from myself, there is Nigel Marvin, the producer, Choco, our field assistant, two Indonesian guides and two American tourists. At 6.30 we start walking. The terrain is rocky and dry and the grasses are parched, and we want to do the worst part before it gets too hot. It's a really steep climb but we're fortunate to have plenty of willing hands to share the camera gear and the huge quantity of water that we are carrying. Around half way up, the ground levels out somewhat and the going becomes easier. The views are stunning and, from the top of the mountain, we get the panning shots that we came for, to establish the mass of little islands, bathed in golden light, that surround Komodo.

Generally speaking, when walking, it's wise to be at the back of the group. That way, any snakes on the trail get moved away by the lead walker. On this occasion, though, I was away from the main party, taking pictures. I just managed to stop myself from taking the next step, as there on a stony track, just a metre ahead of me, was a Russell's viper, one of the deadliest snakes in the world. I took a step back and the snake slid silently into the grass.

By 10 a.m. it was getting too hot so we headed back down to the delightful-looking village of Komodo. Looking from the slopes of the mountain it is an idyll: the stilted houses jut out into the bay and outrigger canoes bob contentedly in the blue tropical waters. This distant view, though, is deceptive. The people are poor, with most eking out a living from fishing. Being one of the driest areas in Indonesia, with less than 1,000 mm of rainfall, fresh water is a scarcity and some of the smaller islands have to rely on jerry cans brought in by boat. Local health is not good, especially in the dry season, and malaria is rife.

We are back at our base at National Park headquarters at around midday and it is intensely hot. Nothing much – including us – moves in these temperatures. I take the opportunity to do some washing (laid out on the grass, it's dry in half an hour) and all the gear is packed up, ready for the long boat trip across to Rinca Island. The people we have worked with from the park come down to the beach to see us off. The local pirogue with its outsize outboard soon leaves Komodo in its wake and, after a noisy couple of hours, we pull in to the even more remote island of Rinca at 5.15 p.m. We unload all the gear, carrying it the considerable distance through mangroves alive with fiddler crabs to our small wooden stilted house on a rocky hillside. It is already getting dark so we go up to the warden's house nearby to discuss plans over a beer. I remember to check carefully under the desk.

It's a clear morning and I'm up at 6 a.m., full of anticipation for a new location. After our usual basic breakfast with the warden, we head off to try and film monkeys that are nearby, but they are extremely timid and we get nothing. Back at camp I do some general atmosphere sound recording before taking the sound gear down to the mangrove. While recording and watching the antics of the colourful crustaceans, I am really excited to see a large komodo moving purposefully through the dry grass. I explore further into the dry, grassy areas, and that's how I end up following that foul stench in the air, leading me to the partially eaten remains of that deer carcass. This is just what we had come for.

I tuck myself into some scrub to give a little concealment, feeling sure that the big komodo that I have just seen must come and feed on it. Sure enough, 20 minutes later, the large beast appears through the scrub and plunges its head into the rotting carcass, releasing clouds of flies into the air.

I rush back to camp to tell Nigel and the ranger about the exciting discovery and we quickly grab the film gear and head back to the carcass. Concealing myself in the same spot, camera at the ready, I wait with bated breath for the return of the big komodo. Time seems to drag but then, from the bushes, a mid-sized dragon

A Komodo dragon feeding on a deer carcass on the island of Rinca

approaches the carcass, apparently totally oblivious of my presence, and goes straight in to feed on the rotting flesh.

A brahminy kite is perched nearby and although I get shots of it circling, it won't come down to the carcass. I 'm determined to stay here for the rest of the day, as this is a unique opportunity and anything could turn up. By late afternoon a wild dog comes to feed and then, just before sundown, a wild boar, but there's no sign of the big komodo from this morning. Monkeys are calling in the trees but we don't see them, and a little hide is constructed from branches which may help to get shots of the kite tomorrow. The lads haul the stinking carcass up into a tree so that it doesn't get eaten during the night. We are back at camp just on dusk.

It's pitch dark outside. I'm sitting writing up my diary by oil lamp, with large ants crawling over the table and up my legs. The Indonesians are lounging on their communal bed, smoking and chatting, fireflies are twinkling outside, geckos calling from the walls and crickets chorusing, I catch the smell of wood smoke from the little fire that has just cooked fresh fish. I have another shandy, warm but refreshing, music plays on Radio Australia, the Indonesians play cards by the light of an oil lamp and it's all very relaxing. Tomorrow may be our last day in the Land of the Dragons.

It's 7.30 a.m. and we're back at the area where we left the carcass. The lads drop the foul mass to the ground and drag it into the open, near the hide we built last night. I get settled in, camera fully loaded, ready to go. After a short while, two small komodos are feeding at the carcass, then a brahminy kite comes to the tree but won't drop down. I set out the camera, fitted with a wide-angle lens, on the ground next to the carcass, as from the hide I am able to operate the camera remotely. I do get some shots of the smaller dragons feeding, which will help with constructing the sequence: the low angle from a different viewpoint is always a valuable shot. By 1 p.m. it's blazingly hot and there's no action, so I pack up and head back to camp. I spend the afternoon filming fiddler crabs in the mangrove before starting to pack, ready for our early departure tomorrow.

I have a disturbed night's sleep with rats scrabbling about in the roof and an early start at 5 a.m. The gear is all down to the boat by 5.45 and we're away by 6 a.m. It's a clear, calm morning, fortunately, for the four-hour boat trip to Labuan Bajo on the big island of Flores.

It's the end of Ramadan so there are thousands of people on the quayside. We are jostled and hassled while waiting for our taxi, it's roasting hot and we get very agitated when it fails to turn up on time. By the time the taxi does come, it's gone 11 a.m. and our chances of getting to Jakarta that night are receding rapidly. It takes two hours to drive to the airport, rather than the one hour that we were told, and by the time we get there, at 1 p.m., everything is locked up until the next day. We pile back into the little van – six people and 16 cases – cramped and stinking hot. The roads are chaotic, thousands of people, all in their best gear, travelling by pony and trap with traffic jams all over the place. It's very disappointing: we were looking forward to a spot of luxury at the Mandarin Oriental, instead of which we're in the grotty £7-a-night hotel in Labuan Baja.

In the end, we're there for two nights, thanks to overbooked flights, cancellations and the general chaos. Eventually, on the morning of Tuesday, 9 May, we get a flight to Bali in a Fokker F27, but the flight to Jakarta later that day has only two seats left. After some discussion and persuasion, Choco and Whyon agree – very reluctantly – to let us have the seats and we pay for them to stay in Bali for the night, hoping that they'll get a flight in the morning. We take off at 3.40 p.m. in a Garuda DC10, finally arriving into Jakarta at 4 p.m. local time. The cool calm of the Mandarin Oriental hotel is bliss after the chaos and drama of the last few days. Tomorrow is a day off and we can do a little sightseeing before flying to Malaysia to film at the Snake Temple in Penang. The Land of the Dragons already seems a world away though the dragons and their remote island homes will remain vivid in my memory for many years to come.

9 BLUE DUCKS, DALMATIAN PELICANS AND BALD EAGLES

After a brief sighting of a blue duck while on holiday in New Zealand some years ago, I resolved to go back some day to spend time getting to know and photograph this rare and elusive bird. After extensive enquiries, I decided that the Retaruke River on North Island was my best option and that I should spend up to ten days there to be in with a chance of getting good images.

At the time of my visit, there were fewer than 600 pairs of blue duck in the wild and the reasons for this are well understood. Over the last 800 years, two major blows have been struck to these highly specialised inhabitants of New Zealand. The first was the arrival of the Maori over 700 years ago, while the second was the influx of European settlers in the late 1700s. Both set about the mass felling of important forest habitats and also introduced alien mammals such as pigs, brown rats and stoats, which continue to have a catastrophic effect on the native fauna. Continued habitat loss from agricultural expansion and the use of dangerous agro-chemicals, with associated runoff into rivers, has further contributed to the blue duck's decline.

A blue duck on the alert for predators

My visit was timed, I hoped, to coincide with the arrival of blue duck young. My base was to be the aptly named Blue Duck Lodge, part of a large sheep farm with several thousand acres of native forest and bush and the essential pristine rivers. The owner and self-confessed blue duck addict, Dan Steele, had kept me informed by email of the birds' nesting progress. The last message – 'A pair sighted with four young' – was the one I had been waiting for. I was in Perth at the time, so within 24 hours had flown to Auckland and driven the three hours to the lodge, just west of Lake Toupo. It was 30 October and on my arrival, I was told that the brood of four were still on the river, about two hours' walk upstream.

I have had a lifelong interest in wildfowl since my teenage years, when I worked at Peter Scott's Wildfowl Trust (from 1988 the Wildfowl and Wetlands Trust). I have photographed them all over the world and this trip promised to be one of the most exciting.

I was up before dawn the next day, full of the anticipation of seeing and photographing one of the rarest of waterfowl. The walk up the stony track through some of New Zealand's most pristine native forest, the chiming of bellbirds ringing in my ears, was memorable in itself, but when I came onto the river, flowing swift and clean through a forest of tree ferns, I saw that this was a very special place indeed.

Dan had told me to check out several places in their one-kilometre territory. The birds are not always easy to find, and can be hidden under overhanging banks or in steep and inaccessible river gorges. After walking virtually the whole riverbank, I'm disappointed not to get a single sighting. Slightly dejected, I walk back down to the spot where I had started, which gave good views up and down the river, as I knew they move up and down the territory to feed. After what seemed like an age, I saw a faint movement on the far bank about 20 metres away: a blue duck slowly emerging from a cave in the bank, followed by four blue-grey downy ducklings. I couldn't quite believe my eyes.

The Retaruke River: a typical wild river habitat of the blue duck

A pair of blue duck with young, feeding at the river's edge

Blue ducks pair for life and defend their territories aggressively. They nest in caves and under fallen logs along the riverbanks. The female incubates between four and six eggs which take about 35 days to hatch, while the male will watch for predators nearby. These tiny ducklings are already capable of diving in the turbulent waters for the invertebrates on which they depend – caddis fly, stonefly and mayfly – but they will face many threats in the next weeks before they become independent. Sudden rises in water levels can wash out nests and separate the ducklings from their parents, giant eels in the river will snap them up and the voracious stoat – probably the biggest threat of all, and a catastrophic introduction by the Europeans – will take both adults and young. Add rats, wild pigs and possums to this list, and the odds are stacked heavily against the survival of any young. Dan Steele is fully aware of all these threats and is doing a terrific job at keeping the predator numbers down, with hundreds of traps set for stoats and rats, poison bait-drops using helicopters for possums and regular pig hunts by experienced marksmen help to keep predation in check.

Over the next week I grew to know the duck family very well as they accepted my presence more each day. This gave me wonderful opportunities to photograph them at close range, as they would often feed within five metres of my position on the bank. Both parents were always in close attendance, keeping an eye out for predators above and below, whether stoats, giant eels or hawks. The youngsters were always adventurous, diving to the river bottom in search of their invertebrate prey and chasing winged insects over the mossy boulders, their little bills already showing the characteristic shape of the adults', with the fleshy tips to the mandibles. They had favourite logs where they would haul out to preen and dry their feathers in the spring sunshine. This made for memorable moments, sitting so close to these very special birds.

I have wonderful pictures from my time there, more than I could have hoped for, but my time spent with the blue duck has made me realise what very special

A blue duck and young hauled out on a log, preening

needs they have: swift-flowing, pristine rivers to support their invertebrate prey and predator-free banks in which to nest. If they are to survive into the future they will need constant help from the many conservation agencies and committed individuals working on their behalf. The future does give cause for optimism: some captive-bred birds have been reintroduced to areas which they formally occupied and the commitment to eradicating the most serious introduced predators continues.

DALMATIAN PELICANS

It's hot and humid as we strain to heave the heavily laden lodkas (traditional wooden boats of the Danube Delta) through narrow channels in the reeds. The water is up to our chests in parts and unseen holes threaten to plunge us in over our heads. The murky water is full of huge leeches and we are constantly bitten by plagues of horseflies and mosquitoes. Where are we going and why are we submitting ourselves to this torture? We are in Europe's largest natural wetland, the Danube Delta Biosphere Reserve, and we are aiming to see a colony of rare Dalmatian pelicans which are breeding on a tiny lake in a colossal reedbed. We made one abortive attempt yesterday, thinking – foolishly – that we could make it there and back in one day. After just one hour, we realized how wrong we were. It's going to take at least five hours of sweat and toil to get there, and we will have to stay overnight.

We push on through the dense forest of reeds, four metres high. It's impossible to see where we are heading and we are fortunate to have an experienced boatman who has made the journey before, as it would be easy to get lost in this watery maze and never be seen again. Also guiding us are the flights of pelicans overhead, as they head to and from the colony. It's very hot, we are pouring with sweat and exhausted from pushing the heavy boats through the dense vegetation, the broken

Pushing the lodka through dense reeds

reed stems concealed underwater ripping at our flesh, which is breaking out in rashes caused by dust from the dry reed stems. This is suffering for your art. After 4.5 hours we know we are getting close, as ahead of us we hear the heavy, flapping wing beats of pelicans starting to thermal in a huge spiraling wheel above us. They ascend rapidly until they are just specks in the deep blue sky. As we break out of the reeds, we see ahead of us the dark little lake, its perimeter studded with the nests of hundreds of these huge white birds.

Now we have a difficult juggling act to perform. The second lodka is returning to the jet boat based on the main channel, so we need to get everything into our craft for a 24-hour stay. We have with us strips of timber, 2 cm thick, to make the filming platform, as well as the canvas hide, cases of film equipment, a tripod, sleeping mats, food and water. The empty lodka slips quietly away into the dense reedbed and James and I now have this amazing place to ourselves.

The lake deep within the reedbeds where the Dalmatian pelicans breed

We cautiously edge into the lake, but the wind is getting up, creating wavelets on the surface of the black water. I fear we are somewhat overloaded and to capsize would be a total disaster – we don't want to cause a panic in the nesting birds and must allow them time to get used to this intrusion into their crowded colony. Our biggest problem soon becomes apparent, though: where can we put a platform on which I can sleep and, at dawn, erect a hide from which I can film? Every inch of the floating crust of dead reed stems and sun-baked guano appears to be taken. It would be very easy to break through this fragile surface and end up in the black, foul waters below, which is not a pleasant thought, and we realise that we have a major headache.

The first essential is to try and find a clear patch where we can establish a base camp and get all of the gear unloaded. After several failed attempts we find a spot that has a good, thick crust which we think is capable of supporting us. We manage to dock the lodka in against it and carefully unload all our precious equipment. It's big enough for us to sleep on and to build the four-feet-square platform on which I will be sitting at dawn tomorrow.

After some initial disturbance the birds are all settling down, so it's time to take stock and have some food; bread, paté, some molten chocolate and lots of bottled water. We construct the pre-drilled platform for the hide, set it carefully in the lodka and need to find the best location for it. A thorough reconnaissance of the lake is needed to get the best out of our limited time here: the special permit from the DDBRA (Danube Delta Biosphere Reserve Authority) only covers us for 24 hours. Carefully loading a minimal filming kit back into the boat, we paddle cautiously away from our tiny base, the lake too deep for us to use the traditional long pole. I need to do some establishing shots of the lake and after much searching we find a small floating island with a thick crust, but there are nests on it with eggs and small, black, naked young pelicans. I have to be quick erecting the tripod and setting up the camera, being really careful not to tread on anything. I set myself a time limit of ten minutes to get the shots and be away to allow the parents to return. It's a warm evening and the chicks will be safe without being brooded for 20 minutes or so – I wouldn't dream of trying to get any of these shots if it were cool and breezy.

Birds are arriving and departing on fishing trips, so I manage a few shots on my big zoom lens before we have to get away. The lake is home to many species, great crested and red-necked grebes with young, garganey, tufted ducks and coots. Now we face the difficult task of finding an area on which I can put my platform, not less than 1.5 metres square and no closer than 15 metres to the chosen nests, as the adults are very wary and may not return if put off. The position of the sun is a major consideration, too. I have to be facing west, and must also take into consideration any nests behind or to the side of me. Eventually, after much searching, we find a tiny solid area with no nests that I think is suitable for the platform, far enough away from the nesting birds for me not to disturb them.

We set the platform in position so that in the morning I can erect the hide in minutes with a minimum of disturbance. Most of the birds fly off as expected, but some stay, enabling me to get a few establishing shots of the adults and young together. The older chicks have already banded into groups, forming crèches, surrounded by the parent birds, which presumably gives a greater degree of safety from predators. Otters might take the smaller young, although the parents have a fairly formidable bill with a serious hook at the end of it. Finally, I get some nice close-ups of groups of pelicans flying back into the colony in the soft evening sunshine.

As we paddle slowly back to our little base I feel optimistic about tomorrow. It's going to be another sunny day and the birds don't seem too concerned about the platform. We erect the mosquito nets on our tiny island, put down foam mats to sleep on, have some bread and pate and demolish a fine bottle of Romanian red wine. It should help us sleep.

During the night I wake up feeling cold and have to wrap the canvas of the hide around me. I am just a metre from the dark water as the moon sets over the lake, the calls of roosting greylag geese and pelicans echoing in the starry night. It is wonderful.

We crawl out of our mosquito-net tents at 6.15 a.m. to a glorious sunny morning. Pelicans are starting to depart for feeding grounds further out in the delta and I quickly set up the camera, getting great flight shots as little groups of four or five birds take off. They are heavy birds and it's an effort for them, with no wind, to get airborne. I can plainly hear the sound of their creaking flight feathers as they skim the dark mirror-like surface of the lake, the small parties joining up with others to form long, meandering lines as they climb into the clear sky.

The Dalmatian pelican is a charismatic but vulnerable species and its numbers are falling, due in part to the fact that it needs over a kilo of fish a day, which brings it into conflict with local fishermen. Poaching and power cables also play their part, but conservation measures are being put in place, now that the threats facing them have been recognized. In some areas, for example, power cables have been rerouted to reduce fatalities, artificial islands have been constructed on lakes to encourage breeding and consultations are being held with fishermen and fish farms to reduce conflict and illegal killing.

Weighing up 15 kg, this is one of the world's heaviest flying birds, on a par with the great albatrosses, Andean condor and great bustard. The wingspan can exceed 3.5 metres, equal to that of the wandering albatross and the longest of any flying bird.

It's now 9.30 a.m. and time to load up the lodka and paddle quietly over to the filming platform to get the hide up. In quick time the green canvas box, just over a metre square and 1.5 metres high, is erected on the wooden platform and I manage to squeeze myself in alongside the camera on its sturdy tripod. This could be the climax of the trip: I need to get close-ups of the feeding behavior to make the sequence work.

In the darkness of my hide, peering through the viewfinder of my Arriflex film camera, I can see groups of featherless, black, prehistoric-looking chicks huddled together about 20 yards away. At this range I should get reasonable close-ups on my biggest lens, a 600 mm with approximately 24x magnification. It's already hot and the youngsters are flapping their gular pouches to keep cool, just as dogs pant to reduce their body heat. Some of the adults flew off when I put the hide up but many stayed with their young and are now shading them with their huge bodies. There is quite a variety of size among the chicks and I get good shots of wing-flapping and preening. Now, around midday, adults are flying back from their early morning fishing expeditions, cruising in at low level over the reeds. I'm able to pick off some lovely flight shots in slow motion, before they land rather clumsily onto their nests. Some have come in near my group and, amid much begging and clamour from all the youngsters nearby, they make their way through the crowd to find their own chicks. There's so much activity, it's a job to know where to look. With such a narrow field of view through the lens it's easy to miss something happening to the side, but because I'm at a reasonable distance from the birds, I'm able to change lenses without causing any upset.

Now the adults are starting to feed the young, the youngsters thrusting their bills right inside the adult's throat to receive the regurgitated fish. This is great behavior and it makes all the pain of getting here worthwhile. Even though we've had such a

Pelicans feeding young

short spell of time in the colony, under difficult circumstances, I feel that we've got a reasonable sequence: lots of flight shots, eggs and young at the nest with adults and a variety of feeding shots. All we need now is to get them fishing on the lakes, which could be the most difficult of all, although we can try other lakes.

We must pack up, as the relief boat is coming back for us at 1 p.m., when our 24-hour permit expires, and we have to be ready to go. The platform will stay here and will no doubt have a nest built on it next year. James has packed up everything that was on the base island, I roll up the hide and pack away the camera gear, and the lodka is looking slightly less dangerous than it did yesterday as we paddle cautiously back over the lake to our rendezvous in the reeds.

The other lodka is there and we balance up the loads between the two boats for the return journey, which I'm not looking forward to. It is very hot as we start the long haul back through the forest of reeds, though the fact that the boats have been through several times has opened up a kind of channel and it's possible to use the long poles to propel the craft through. It's no less unpleasant, though - we still have the

Poling the lodka through dense reedsink beds

A bald eagle in the Chilkat Valley, southeast Alaska

mosquitoes and horseflies, and when we have to wade to get through a dense patch of reeds, the giant leeches are waiting for us. It takes three hours before we break out of the reedbed into the lake. We use the little outboard on one lodka to tow the other, so I put my feet up during the rather choppy crossing over the open water. It's 6.45 p.m. when we reach the cabana belonging to the DDBRA, just off one of the main delta channels. The gear is all unloaded, I throw off my filthy clothes, including the odd leech, and dive in for a wonderful, cold shower. After what we've just been through, I think the next sequence should be something less strenuous: maybe standing on a riverbank filming nesting penduline tits is the kind of contrast I need.

BALD EAGLES IN THE CHILKAT VALLEY

Some years ago, the BBC produced a series of programs called Wild, each programme just ten minutes long and featuring a place or single species of animal. They were shot in just ten days and low-budget, so the costs of travel and baggage limited the locations somewhat. They were filmed and directed by the cameraman, who was often the author too, based on experience gleaned whilst on other projects. I filmed several of these programmes on very diverse subjects: Bardsey Island and its wildlife, seaweed-eating sheep on North Ronaldsay in the Orkney Islands and Lake Hornborga in southern Sweden, famous as a stopping-off point for migrating common cranes on their spring migration.

The series producer, Wendy Dark, was very approachable and up for new ideas to push the limits of the series. Many years before, I had done some filming of the mass gathering of the bald eagles in the Chilkat Valley in Alaska, for the series Land Of The Eagle. This, I thought, would make a fantastic Wild; the amazing spectacle of many hundreds of bald eagles hauling out huge salmon with the backdrop of stunning mountain scenery would surely be a winning combination. The main problem was trying to stretch the budget to accommodate the extra expense of flights to Alaska and the excess baggage involved, but by trimming the equipment to a bare minimum and making a few other savings, it was just possible, and everyone agreed that it was a great subject. For my part, I was so keen to go back there that I was willing to put in a few extra days without pay to get the material we needed.

So it was on 17 November 2006, the day after my 60th birthday, that I set off for Alaska, a place I had been to many times before and which still excites me like nowhere else in the world. The Chilkat Valley is not the easiest place to get to: first there's a flight to Seattle, then another to Juneau in southeast Alaska, and there the fun begins. I need to get to Haines, a town at the seaward end of the Chilkat Valley, but because it's November the ferries are few and far between. I elect to fly the 100 or so miles by light aircraft. At Juneau airport, the check-in for the bags is done in no time. A young lady in boots and an anorak appears and carries the gear to the plane, a four-seater Piper Cherokee, which is parked nearby. 'I assume the pilot will be here shortly?' I say. 'I am the pilot', she replies.

She allows me to board the plane anyway, despite that awkward start, and off we go. We head up and away into a strong headwind blowing straight down the Lynn Canal, a huge waterway that runs from Haines right down to Juneau and named after Kings Lynn in the east of England by Captain George Vancouver (who also gave his name to Vancouver in Canada). It has snowed heavily in the last few days and the conditions are now perfect, with clear blue skies. My confidence in the very young pilot increases as we chat. Her previous job involved piloting a tourist plane over the Grand Canyon and she is now spending time in Alaska to get her flying hours up and progress to greater things. We land smoothly on a snow-packed runway and I pile my gear into a waiting taxi that whisks me the 10-minute ride into the beautifully situated little waterside town of Haines, my base for the next eight days. The timing for this trip was critical: I wanted the birds in snow, so didn't want to be here too early, but had I come later the days would have been much shorter, with fewer eagles around. Even now, the sun doesn't rise until gone 8 a.m. and has slipped behind the mountains by 2 p.m., allowing for a frustratingly short filming day. I'm staying in a B & B in the centre of town, an old traditional clapboard house called the Summer Inn. It's very warm and friendly, which is just as well because the weather takes a turn for the worse, with a blizzard raging for the first 36 hours. I now have my hire car which is equipped with studded tyres, and the snow ploughs have been busy keeping the roads open, so I'm hopeful for tomorrow.

I wake at 6.30 a.m. and am delighted to see a clear blue sky. I make a flask and sandwiches and have a hearty breakfast of coffee, pancakes and sausages. My camera gear is all ready to load but I need to de-ice the car, as it is pipe-cracklingly cold, about −7 °F, which equates to −25 °C. I am wearing most of what I brought and soon have the heater going. It's a drive of about 30 km up the valley to the best viewing site and I arrive there at just on 8 o'clock. The sun is forcing its weak rays through the thick mist which cloaks the valley and the water vapour has condensed onto every surface, including the eagles, coating all with a frosty glaze. Ghostly images of the great birds come and go as the mist swirls then burns away to reveal dozens of them on the gravel bar not 50 yards from where I stand. When other rivers are frozen solid, the Chilkat continues to flow, enabling the salmon to spawn into December. After spawning, the fish die and their carcasses are preserved by the bitter cold, ensuring a food supply for the eagles well into February. So why doesn't five miles of the Chilkat freeze when temperatures drop so low? The answer is an alluvial fan reservoir, a fan-shaped accumulation of gravel, sand, rock and glacial debris. In the spring and summer, water from melted snow and glacial ice flows into the alluvial fan faster than it can escape,

Bald eagles roosting in cottonwood trees, Chilkat Valley, southeast Alaska

creating a huge reservoir. This water stays 10–20 degrees warmer than surrounding water temperatures and slowly percolates out during the autumn, keeping this section of the river ice-free.

All the elements for a great sequence are here: stunning morning light, fantastic scenery and dramatic behaviour. There's so much happening that I have to work as fast as I can to capture all the action – wide-angle shots of the eagles perched in the cottonwood trees along the river's edge, the sun burning off the mist, then mid-shots and close-ups as the eagles swoop from their overnight perches to join others already heaving the hefty carcasses onto the bank. Earlier in the season brown bears would have been here too, but they have had their fill and are already in hibernation. That's good for me as it's one less large obstacle to worry about.

Most of the salmon spawn in the little side streams with gravel bottoms; there is just such a stream at the base of a tree-lined bank, and the remains of carcasses all along the water's edge indicate that it has been heavily used by eagles. I know from talking to other photographers here that the birds are extremely tolerant of people, and it's not unknown for the great birds to come within five metres of you. I think it may be possible to get down the steep bank to the stream edge, so I pack as much as possible into a rucksack, use my tripod as a third leg and make a completely out-of-control descent through knee-high snow, ending up in a heap on the bank. Getting back up could be a problem, but I'll worry about that later. Fortunately there are no eagles nearby which gives me time to find a semi- concealed position, set up the tripod and put on the Arriflex film camera with a 50–300 mm zoom lens. It should be perfect for any birds within a range of five to 20 metres, enabling me to do a whole range of shots from medium wide-angle to close-ups.

The stream is shallow, less than half a metre deep, with many carcasses already pulled out onto the bank in various stages of being eaten. There are many fish in the stream, some actively spawning while others are moribund and close to death. These are the ones preferred by the eagles as they are easy to catch, fresh and soft. Once out of the water they will freeze solid within 30 minutes, providing a continuous supply of perfectly-preserved food for many weeks to come, not just for the eagles but for magpies and ravens too.

Though many of the adult and immature eagles perched in the trees above me are Alaskan birds, a high proportion will have flown some distance from neighbouring British Columbia in Canada. They sit patiently scanning the water below, waiting for the chance to drop down onto the feast beneath them, and frequent scuffles break out as the birds jostle for positions around the best concentrations of fish. Sometimes an eagle will fly in unseen, fast and at low level, talons outstretched to try to displace a feeding bird, which in turn will roll onto its back, with talons erect, to meet the incoming attacker. This is a very dramatic piece of behaviour to film in slow motion, the two birds locked for a second in a flurry of flying snow, talons and wings. The

A bald eagle feeding on salmon, with a raven and magpies waiting for scraps

Arriflex film camera can run at 150 frames per second (the normal speed is 25 fps), so one second of dramatic action becomes six seconds on the screen.

The eagles are gradually getting closer, the nearest ones less than 50 metres away, and it's just a matter of time before they come really close. Where the salmon have laid their eggs in the gravel bed of the stream, some trickle out and are quickly snapped up by a plump American dipper. A magnificent adult eagle lands just 20 metres away and wades purposefully through 20 cm of snow to a freshly dead salmon, lying in shallow water just a few metres from where I sit. I'm sure it sees me but it's not concerned. It drags the five-kg salmon up onto the bank with one huge talon, then starts to tear into the soft flesh. I can't believe how close this bird is. I can see every detail, the piercing eye, the massive hooked bill and the powerful talons. I focus the camera precisely and set it to run, and it purrs reassuringly as the action is recorded to film.

A bald eagle eating a salmon

Though I have only been here for four days I have already filmed more than I could realistically have hoped for. After 30 years as a natural history cameraman, I have come to expect regular doses of disappointment, so it's all the sweeter when everything falls into place. The freezing weather has been perfect for filming, producing atmospheric dawns and a low sun throughout the day to bathe these powerful birds in soft winter light. The short day ends as the sun dips behind the St. Elias Mountains and the first eagles begin to fly to their roosts in the cottonwood trees, their piercing calls echoing through the icy valley, temperatures plummeting as darkness falls.

For the next few days the weather stays crisp and cold and I get lots more footage of this amazing spectacle. It's been a memorable experience and has left me feeling that this won't be my last visit to Alaska.

This is a good point for an update on Sunshine, the tundra swan from the Yukon Delta that went to a collection in Juneau. He survived to be a full adult and quite a character. I have seen him in Jim's collection, with the emperor geese and other waterfowl, and while I was there he strode into Jim's kitchen and gave me a hefty nibble on the leg. It was quite moving to see him as a fully mature and magnificent swan. He lived for twelve contented years in Jim's collection until, sadly, he was killed one night by a great horned owl.

10 'HUMMINGBIRDS – THE ULTIMATE POLLINATORS'

I am staring at a patch of heliconias – bright, showy flowers in the darkness of a South American rainforest. There's a slight movement in the shadow behind the blooms. Is it what I am waiting for? No, not this time, it's just some other little brown bird. As the available light begins to fail, I start to lose hope of seeing one of the world's strangest birds, then catch sight of another movement in among the strange blooms. Suddenly, there it is, just visible, though brilliantly camouflaged – the sickle-billed hummingbird. Superbly adapted to feeding on these strange flowers, its deeply-curved bill mirrors the shape of the bloom, fitting like a key in a lock, meaning that only the Sickle bill can access the nectar.

Many years ago, in 1986, I spent several weeks in Ecuador filming some of the world's smallest and most stunning creatures, the hummingbirds. It was a 25-minute film for a popular series called *Wildlife on One* and although the producer Paul Reddish and I were pleased with the result, we had always had a yearning to go back to South America some day to make a longer, more detailed programme of 50 minutes, really doing justice to these amazing little gems. Hummingbirds, of course, live an extremely fast lifestyle and to have any chance of catching shots long enough to use, most behaviour had to be filmed in slow motion. Looking back on it, the means of recording slow motion was rather primitive. The camera, called a Locam, ran up to

Long-tailed sylph

227

500 frames per second (20x slower than normal) so one second of action became 20 seconds on screen. As my trip to Ecuador had demonstrated, the camera was difficult to load, in total darkness in the confines of a changing bag; it sounded like a coffee grinder gone wrong, it had a dismal viewfinder system and ran through 120 metres of film in 20 seconds. If there was any error in loading the complex maze of sprockets and rollers the film would be shredded and the emulsion scattered over the entire prism system, entailing a massive and time-consuming cleaning job.

For most of my 25-odd-year career up to this point, I had used film cameras, but from 2005 onwards digital camera systems became the norm and huge advances had been made, especially in the development of high-speed, slow-motion high-definition cameras. These were the ideal tool for making a stunning film on hummingbirds and we knew that Terra Mata Austria had at least one. They run silently at up to 2,000 frames per second and have up to 30 minutes recording time on their hard drives. Now, surely, was the time to make an approach to them with the hummingbird film idea; Paul put together a script for the story which was submitted for consideration to the commissioning editors at Terra Mata. These ideas are rarely accepted at first go, and there is generally much to-ing and fro-ing of ideas, meeting after meeting, rewrites of potential stories and, further down the line, what is usually the biggest stumbling block of all, the budget. To cut the proverbial long story short, I got a phone call from Paul one evening, when I had in fact given up hope of it ever happening, to say that 'It's going ahead!'. It was exciting news and I could hardly believe it.

The shooting period was to be between September 2011 and January 2012 and would take us to Texas, California, Ecuador and Brazil. This would give us many of the species that were important to the story; Ecuador, in particular, has a very diverse range of habitats from sea level to 5,000 metres, each region with its own very special hummingbirds, and this was where the bulk of the filming would take place. Before this, though, we needed to visit Rockport on the Gulf of Mexico. Every September, the town hosts the Hummingbird Festival, a celebration of the huge numbers of ruby-throated hummingbirds that pass through here in September on their migration across the Gulf of Mexico to Mexico and beyond. Many of the town's residents put out feeders for the birds in their gardens, attracting hundreds of the hummers as they need to double their weight from three grams to six grams to sustain their flight of over 500 miles across the sea.

This attracts thousands of visitors to the open gardens to see the birds, and made a great sequence: close-ups of joyous faces with hummers in the foreground, lots of shots of hummingbirds in slow motion at the feeders and key shots of birds setting off across the water on the journey.

The airport at Corpus Christi nearby has a very sophisticated doppler weather radar which has been shown to be able to pick up and track groups of hummingbirds out into the gulf. This was something we were very keen to film, so permission had

Hanging feeders with sugar water for the ruby-throated hummingbirds

been sought and granted well in advance. Accessing the huge ray dome was not easy, involving a climb up several ladders, loaded with the filming gear, in 35°C heat, before going into the huge dome, which was even hotter. The radar beams were turned off, to save us from frying, but the antennae kept rotating and I got some great shots by getting the wide-angle lens in really close to the mechanisms. The monitors in the control centre, with the faces of the operators reflected in the on-screen images, helped us to tell the fascinating migration story. No one knows where many of the birds go once they are out of the 20-km range of the radar. The last shot is a time lapse of the dome from outside, as the sun sets and the incredible migration of these tiniest of birds begins.

Hummingbirds are tiny and very fast so filming them in the wild is going to be a challenge They rely on a continuous supply of nectar to fuel their high-speed life style and need to feed every ten minutes at least, so a readily available supply of nectar-rich flowers is vital for their survival. Their wings can beat at up to 80 beats per second with a heart rate of up to 1,200 beats a minute, they consume double their body weight in nectar a day and - to survive the night without food -they go into a state of torpor, when their body temperature drops from 40° C to 18° C and their heart rate goes way down, to 100 beats per minute. They need extreme in-flight dexterity in order to reach hard-to-access flowers, and are the only birds able to hover, fly backwards and even upside down. I cannot wait to capture them on the high speed camera.

Steep forests at Tandayapa

Rufous-tailed hummingbird

Tandayapa is a rainforest lodge on the western side of the Andes, about one hour's drive from Quito. Like many of the lodges in Ecuador, it is situated in a fantastic area of rainforest in which to view and film birds, especially hummingbirds. Huge tropical trees cling to the steep slopes that plunge into deep, humid valleys, and these dark forests support hundreds of bird species, especially hummingbirds with their exotic names: purple-throated woodstar, sparkling violet ear, western and Andean emerald, violet-tailed sylph, purple-bibbed white tip, white-booted racket tail, rufous-tailed hummingbird and green violet ear. These are just a few of the hundreds of hummingbird species that occur only in the Americas, mostly in the tropics, although one – the Rufous Hummingbird – goes right up to Alaska in the summer.

Our rooms at the lodge are quite basic but we're used to that and they are perfectly adequate for a week's stay. The great thing about these lodges is that they do encourage hummers to visit by putting out hanging tubular feeders, filled with sugar water, giving wonderful opportunities to film the birds at close range. It's desirable in most instances (unless you are talking about them) to frame the feeders out of shot. This is where the Phantom high-speed camera really comes into its own; running at 700 frames per second you would only need the bird in frame for half a second to give you 14 seconds on screen. That, in fact, is often all you get, so fast are these little gems. These cameras are very forgiving in that you can use lenses from other camera systems, in my case Nikon.

My favourite lens is the 50–300 zoom, which gives you a very wide range of framing options, everything from a reasonable wide-angle to a good close-up. It also has very close focus ability of less than three metres. Having to change lenses is time consuming and will more than likely cause the subject to fly off. When I need really stunning close-ups from slightly further away, or if the subject is a little more timid, I use a Nikon 500 mm lens, a big beast but stunning quality. As a matter of interest, the body of the Phantom camera cost £110,000 when we were using it in 2011, plus £25,000 each for the hard drives, of which we had two. Add the lenses, monitors and so on, and you're looking at £200,000.

The recording system is very complex and every night, Max, our Austrian camera technician, would download all my material to various storage systems with safety backups, freeing up the hard drive capacity for the next day's shooting. Max would often work well into the night, as systems can't just be left running, and any technical issues needed to be dealt with straight away. Max's room was like a sorcerer's cave, full of computers, cables and flickering lights. I suspect my job was more enjoyable.

Part of the fascination of filming is the constant need to work round problems or think up innovative shots that haven't been tried before. Because the birds here are so used to people, we have the chance to try different camera set-ups. The tiny purple-throated woodstar turned out to be real star. He was very inquisitive about any new flowers that we brought in to our filming area, on the balcony overlooking the forest. I hit on the crazy idea of putting a flower right in front of the camera, fitted with a wide-angle lens. The little red bloom was set just four inches in front of the lens, with the forest in the background. If we could only get the bird to visit the flower for a second, we would have a shot. Because I needed a large depth of focus to get the flower and the forest sharp, I couldn't run the camera at too high a frame rate – the faster the

MP and the Phantom high-speed camera, fitted with the 50-300 mm zoom lens

A camera set up for the tiny purple-throated woodstar

*Sword-billed hummingbird, with the longest
bill of any bird in relation to its body*

shutter speed, the more light you need – so a larger aperture in turn means less depth of focus. I went for a compromise of 200 frames, 8x slower than normal, and needed the bird in shot for a second to give eight seconds on screen. Using a trick of the trade, I dribbled a little sugar water into the flower to tempt the bird in. I still needed the sun to be reasonably bright to give some detail to the forest background and added a little light to the flower from a special daylight torch. Quite a few things to get right, then, not least having the bird come into frame in the first place. I could do nothing about that: all I could do was be ready and focus all my concentration on that flower.

The thing about the Phantom is that it is running all the time, recording to a caching system. At 1,000 frames, you have maybe five seconds to decide if you want to keep the shot and, because it's just a continuous loop systems, switch the camera off, before it overrides what has just been recorded. At least at 200 fps you have about 25 seconds in which to make that decision and save the shot. It's a waiting game, then, and you can't afford to be distracted by all the other birds zooming around, all the other shots you could be getting.

In a split second, before you can blink, the little woodstar, not much bigger than a bee, could be at the flower and gone again. At least, because the camera is running, you never miss the beginning of a shot, and this is a massive advantage.

The little bird is definitely interested, hovering nearby, then in a flash he's there, takes a quick feed and is gone in a second. I think it's worked. A quick replay on the monitor (another massive advantage over film) shows the bird come into shot, the forest sharp in the background, and flying out of frame right. It's perfect.

The forest here is stunning, with early morning mist slowly burning off in the deep valleys. It makes for great time-lapse shots, setting the scene in these mysterious woodlands, mostly inaccessible with their precipitous slopes. It's been a productive week; we've got many different hummers feeding at various species of flower and some display flights, and shots for a montage sequence of different species preening and bathing, to show how important it is to keep plumage in perfect condition.

One of the most amazing and least known birds in the world is, without doubt, the sword-billed hummingbird. Its bill, relative to its body length, is the longest of any bird. It is found in high-altitude cloud forest in Ecuador, Colombia, Bolivia, Peru and Venezuela, most usually at around 2,500–3,000 metres.

We are spending a week at Guango, a rainforest lodge at 2,700 metres, just on the other side of the Papallacta Pass, a well-known spot for the sword-billed and many other high- altitude species. One, the Ecuadorian hillstar, which I'm sad to say we are not due to film on this occasion, lives only on the slopes of the volcanoes Chimborazo and Quilotoa and on the paramo (rough grassland) in between, at up to an astonishing 5,200 metres. They feed on the bright orange flowers of a shrub called chuquiraga, perching at them rather than hovering, to save energy in the thin, cold air. We are filming the swordbill, though, an equally fascinating and exciting bird which, thanks to its enormously long bill, can access flowers that other hummingbirds cannot, namely the Passiflora (passion flower) and the trumpet-like white blooms of the datura. This is going to involve a lot of 'wait and see' photography, standing around in anticipation of action, with no need for a hide as the birds are very used to people. Swordbills are known as 'trap line' feeders, visiting – in a regular patterned sequence – a circuit of food plants spread over quite a large area, possibly with fewer but larger flowers. After one visit, it could be another two hours before a bird revisits the flowers that you have chosen to watch. Other hummingbirds are territorial, feeding around and aggressively guarding one or several bushes with many flowers and set close together.

The first morning is dull and overcast but this, after all, is cloud forest so sunny days can be a rarity. The light will only permit me to use 75 fps 3x slow motion @ f5.6 and at 1,000 ISO. Within half an hour, the first swordbill zooms up to the datura flower and hovers just inches from it. What an incredible bird it is, the bill glistening like polished pewter in the damp air. It drops beneath the drooping trumpet of the datura, then flies up, thrusting its 12-cm bill deep into the corolla. It feeds for a second then drops, hovers and is away. Paul and I are very excited to have our first shot of the swordbill, and now it's a waiting game for the next visit.

The only problem with working at these forest lodges is that they often have other visitors bent on getting their own photographs, which has a big impact on the success of our filming. If another photographer is nearby, firing off flashguns, then our shot will be ruined, for sure. But, as the old saying goes, 'If you can't beat 'em, join 'em!', and a break in filming at least gives me a chance to get stills of the hummingbirds myself, often needed for publicity purposes.

Just below the lodge is a fast-flowing river which is known to have torrent ducks living on it, highly specialised waterfowl which are supremely adapted to live in these fierce waters. They are slender and fast, leaping from rock to rock and swimming and diving against powerful currents to snatch their invertebrate prey from beneath boulders.

A male torrent duck dives into the white water

The male and female are completely different, the male being predominantly grey and white while the female is grey and chestnut. Just before breakfast, while the light is too bad for filming, I creep down the slippery trail through the forest, hearing the roar of the river. I'm excited at the possibility of seeing a new species of waterfowl. The riverbank is treacherous, with huge, slippery boulders, but there is a little track from which it's possible to scan the rushing waters. At first, there's nothing to be seen, then a pair comes round the bend, flying low over the white water and landing just above me before jumping up onto a boulder. Despite the poor light, I quickly grab a few shots, knowing that they may be the only ones I get. The birds slip back into the torrent and I get a shot of the male skittering across the surface before hopping up onto another semi-submerged rock. I get a somewhat better shot, not close - about 20 metres - but it's something.

After breakfast back at the lodge, I set up the camera at the datura flowers and the wait for the swordbill goes on. It's much brighter than yesterday morning, so I am hopeful of getting better slow-motion at 500 fps. Very soon I get my first close-up shot: the bird zooms into frame, has a quick hover, then plunges that amazing steely bill up to the hilt into the datura, reaching nectar that no other hummingbird can reach. This is starting to look very good, and over the next two hours I get several more visits in good light. There is now a sequence at the flower, but to complete the story I need more shots of him in the forest, perched, resting, taking off, landing and preening. The bird uses its tiny feet to scratch and preen as the bill is too long to use for that.

It's now gone very quiet, the wind has got up and it looks like rain, so we pack in and break for lunch. Paul goes up to the pass to hunt for fresh datura flowers and I go back into the forest to try for perched shots of the swordbill, but the light is dismal and soon it's raining heavily. I take the film gear under the lodge verandah and try for slow-motion raindrops on vegetation, but it's really too dark. The sound of vehicles approaching along the gravel drive is, as I feared, a great crowd of birders, and very soon there are flashguns going off all over the shop. I'm glad it's foul weather and I'm not missing the chance to shoot anything.

Paul gets back from the pass at around 3.30 p.m. after being stuck in horrendous traffic due to an accident in the pouring rain. Some of the driving here is suicidal, and the police station compound at Papallacta seems to have more smashed-up cars in its compound every day, serving as a grizzly reminder of the risks of driving on these tortuous mountain roads.

Before dinner we spend some time looking through the day's swordbill footage. It's amazing to be able to see everything - the slow motion hovering and some more feeding shots – on a high definition monitor on the same day. Not so long ago you had to wait several weeks until you got home with the exposed film, then endure a nail-biting wait until it was processed and viewed in Bristol.

The last few days have produced more great footage of the swordbill feeding on datura, the take-offs and landings from favourite perches that we needed, and interesting behaviour with other species like the chestnut-breasted coronet and long-tailed sylph, as well as preening and some aggressive interaction around flowers. These shots will all help to build montage sequences on preening, bathing and aggression.

It's just after dawn and we're heading up to the Papallacta Pass. The valleys are misty, though the tops of the mountains look clear. We are going beyond the pass, at 4,000 metres, up a very rough boulder-strewn track which will take us to 5,000 metres; our tired and underpowered 4x4 doesn't like it and, like us, is struggling for oxygen. Several times it stalls and is reluctant to go again, like a very tired donkey. Max is making a short 'making of' film as we go, involving a lot of stopping and starting, shooting the vehicle bouncing through frame, then getting shots driving over, or close to, the camera placed on the road. We eventually grind to a halt at the end of the track, which actually leads to a transmitting station, and are treated to the most breathtaking viewpoint: the towering snow-capped volcanoes of Antisana and, further away, Cotopaxi loom out of the crisp air of the Andes. Today is my 65th birthday and I am quite overwhelmed by the grandeur of what is laid out before me. How lucky I am to be here.

Looking across to the volcanoes
Antisana and Cotopaxi

It's now a case of trying to get footage of this spectacular vista to set the scene for the fact that some hummingbirds live and breed at these high altitudes. The film gear still needs to be taken another few hundred metres on foot to the highest point. I'm breathless and have to stop several times on the way before selecting a spot and setting up the tripod for the panning shots, which will reveal this stunning range of mountains and volcanoes and the mysterious misty valleys beyond. It's so difficult to do justice to a place like this on film, to convey the sense of being there, experiencing the crisp thin air, seeing the mountains stretching away into the distance, the strange plants and birds like the secretive seed snipe and elusive Andean teal, of which we get only glimpses.

Having completed, for now, our high-altitude filming, we drop down to the northeastern edge of the Andes, towards the headwaters of the Amazon basin and a much more tropical location than we've been used to these last few weeks. Driving through impressive areas of cloud forest with precipitous roads dropping down into lush valleys, we arrive mid-afternoon at the Wild Sumaco lodge, home to a completely different range of hummingbird species. I instantly take a liking to the place. It has a large decking that looks out over the forest with comfortable cabin accommodation and many species of hummingbirds that are new to us: Gould's jewelfront, golden-tailed sapphire, wire-crested thorntail and the elusive white-tipped sicklebill, a species that is high on our hit list to film.

Golden-tailed sapphire

Having unpacked the gear and settled in, we went with Jim, the very pleasant and helpful American owner, to check out the patch of heliconias, the preferred food plant of the sicklebill, with large, showy red-and-orange flowers. After standing around for a while we do get a glimpse of one but it's very dark among the flowers and it's not going to be easy. Back at the decking area I spend time watching the flowering shrubs which are attracting many species, including the wire-crested thorntail which immediately grabs my attention. It is tiny, a lovely, iridescent deep green with a fine little crest and long tail. The female is very plain and is sitting quietly when, suddenly, the male erupts from his perch and flies in front of her, performing a high-speed aerial dance, side to side, swinging his fanned-out tail then flying rapidly, vertically, up and down and returning to his perch. The whole performance is over in less than six seconds. If this happens again it will be stunning. At 500 fps it will be nearly two minutes of mind blowing action, and we're pretty sure this has never been filmed before. I do love these 'firsts'.

Chestnut-breasted coronet

The evening is glorious, warm and pleasant after the chill of the high-altitude locations. I think how much I love the tropics as we sit out with a beer watching the light fade over the forest, the soundtrack an amazing chorus of strange birds and insects. After dinner I spend the evening getting the film gear prepared for a full day tomorrow. Max has downloaded all the footage from the cameras hard drives so I have full capacity of one hour's filming time.

We have an early breakfast and by 6.45 a.m. I'm set up by the stand of heliconias, just 100 metres from my room, and although the light is not brilliant I hope it will improve. After an hour there's no sign of the sicklebill, but I do get a couple of shots of a golden-tailed sapphire feeding in amongst the blooms. Time passes and, frustratingly, there's still no sign of the sicklebill. We do know it comes here so we just have to be patient and stay alert.

By 10.30 a.m. I decide to pack in and go up to the area where the thorntails are displaying. It's a much more open location so the chances of getting action in good light are a great deal higher. There are sparkling violetears here, too – they're one of the commoner medium-sized hummingbirds, very aggressive between themselves and to other birds, so there's always a lot of action when they are around. The female thorntail is in her usual spot and it's not long before a male springs from his perch and displays in front of her. I'm on the 50–300 mm zoom lens to get the establishing shots first, so I've made a start. After a brief lunch I'm straight back to the action. The morning was sunny, but it's now hazy, although still bright and perfect conditions for filming. The birds don't like the heat of a full sun, and neither do I.

The next couple of hours are amazing, with lots of display action from the thorntails. I get great coverage: medium shots and big close-ups and from different angles, which will help with cutting the sequence, as well as shots of take-offs and landings, which are vital to get in and out of a sequence. I also get shots of preening, in between bouts of display. I cover it at different speeds from 150–500 fps, as you never quite know how it's going to look, and action can always be speeded up if it appears too slow. It's actually very funny to watch and will be an unexpected highlight of the film, something that wasn't scripted for. By 4.30 p.m. the light is getting marginal and half an hour later I decide to call it a day, meaning that Max can get on with downloading the hard drives for viewing later on. It's been a very productive day and I feel sure that we have a fascinating two or three minute sequence on a very little known bird.

The sicklebill is visiting the heliconia patch regularly between 3.30 and 5.00 p.m. each day, so I make sure that I'm there in good time. I'm not using a hide, just keeping

Heliconia flowers, the favourite food plants of the sickle-billed hummingbird

A male wire-crested thorntail

very still, allowing me to watch for any slight movements which show he is around. Each day I am picking up a few shots and even a few close-ups on the 500mm lens, which shows the bird's strangely-shaped bill very well. We use the mini-jib arm to do tracking shots around the flowers and vertical tilts up the flowers to establish the plants in some detail, then, further into the forest, we find a big stand of heliconia that we can use for an establishing shot.

The mornings I am spending on polishing up the thorntail sequence, the more shots the better, and I'm also working on a fly-catching sequence with the sparkling violet ear. Hummingbirds do catch quite a few insects as part of their diet, especially when feeding young. There is a perch in the lower part of the canopy which the bird uses on a regular basis to watch for flies and mosquitoes, quite tiny ones, and he will launch himself at anything that comes within a metre. This is quite a challenge. It's easy enough to get the take-off and landing back on the perch, but less easy to get the actual 'snap' of the bill as it catches the insect. I get some medium shots but there's not much to be seen of the insect. I have to get the close-up to make the sequence complete. I keep trying and persistence pays off, as I do eventually get a few that work, starting wide on the zoom lens and crashing in to the close-up as it hits the insect at 200 fps.

Hummingbirds are one of the largest bird groups with over 320 species, the largest of which is the giant, found along the full length of the Andes on the western and

A sparkling violetear, one of the most common hummingbird species

eastern slopes. It is about the size of a starling and weighs up to 24 grams, ten times the weight of the smallest species, the bee hummingbird. It has correspondingly larger wings, around 20 cm long, which beat at a slow speed, 15 beats per second, to support the larger body in the thin air at higher altitudes.

We have been put in contact with a local couple, Carmen and Mitch, who live in a hacienda just outside Quito in an area called Tumbaco, and whose large garden attracts giant hummingbirds. On the way back from another location, San Isidro, we call on them to check out the situation. It sounds too good to be true but, sure enough, they have a large decked area with feeders and giants are coming to them. We make arrangements to come back with the filming gear early in the morning.

It's just after 6.00 a.m. as we weave our way through the chaos of Quito's traffic, horrendous even at this time of the morning, but we still manage to get to Carmen's fabulous garden by 7.00 a.m. They have a very large dog called Koomah, a type of husky, who loves to follow you around and be part of the action but I don't get too friendly as I suspect he has fleas. The giants are around already, supping the sugary liquid from the feeders, and I set up the Phantom slow-motion camera and fit the 500mm lens for close- ups. The birds are quite timid so I start off well back from the feeder at about ten metres. I need to get slow-motion hovering shots to show the size of the wings and the slow-beating action, adapted to cope with the thin air – we are at about 3,000 metres here. A quick playback in the viewfinder confirms the speed I am using is about right, 300 fps gives one wing beat per second when played back, although I will go as slow as the light levels permit, perhaps 500 or even 1000 fps.

Paul heads out after lunch looking for fresh flowers and returns with sprays of bright orange trumpet vines, surely irresistible to a hummingbird? I put them up in his territory and set up the camera in great anticipation of a visit, and I don't have to wait long. Within minutes this impressive bird is there, visiting each flower in turn, thrusting his long bill deep into the corolla to drain the nectar. For the next visit I fit the 500mm lens and change my angle slightly. As it's sunny, I'm able to run at 1,000 fps, which really shows the wingbeats beautifully. At this setting the shutter speed is just a two-thousandth of a second and everything is absolutely pin-sharp. The giant obliges with another visit, I have got myself in a little closer and a few more big close-ups wrap up a very useful sequence.

Our time in Ecuador is coming to an end and it's been a wonderful experience. I love hummingbirds for their diversity, tenacity and adaptability, we have achieved most of the sequences that we set out for, and we've got a few bonuses, too. We're going home for a month now and will be back out in the New Year, to Brazil, for another sizzling array of these most stunning little birds with apt, jewel-like names – Brazilian ruby, amethyst woodstar, white-chinned sapphire and ruby topaz – for truly jewel-like birds. I can hardly wait.

Campbell albatross in flight

11 To the Antarctic at last

As we pull out of Bluff Harbour, escorted by the pilot boat, I think of the long journey ahead of us, more than 2,000 miles through possibly the stormiest ocean in the world. I'm excited by what lies ahead as the pilot turns away and we head south out into the open sea. The Antarctic is the last great wilderness on the planet and this is the realisation of a long-held desire to go there.

Our route will be via New Zealand's sub-Antarctic islands of Auckland and Campbell, then Macquarie Island, down to Cape Adare on the Antarctic mainland and moving on south through the Ross Sea to Ross Island in McMurdo Sound. I had many reasons for wanting to make this trip, not only for the amazing wildlife and stunning scenery, but also for the opportunity to visit the cabins of Captain Robert Falcon Scott and Sir Ernest Shackleton. This is not always possible due to ice conditions; if the sea ice is fast against the shore, it is impossible to land, and sometimes the sea ice in the Ross Sea can be sufficient to prevent the ship from getting south at all.

Because of the very short window of opportunity in the Antarctic summer, January and February are the only departure dates for this 30-day trip. Leaving in January is perhaps better for birdlife, with the penguins having small chicks, but there would probably be more ice and a lower chance of landings so far south. The February trip gives a greater likelihood of open water and greater landing opportunities. As I'm particularly keen to get to the historic huts, this is the voyage I choose. Our expedition ship is run by Heritage Expeditions of Christchurch, New Zealand. It's not a big vessel, only 70 metres long, and carrying just 50 passengers. The company fleet was built in Finland, ice-strengthened and originally built for research in the Arctic.

The Snares Islands are stark silhouettes as we pass them at dawn, 250 km south of Bluff and home to millions of seabirds, especially sooty shearwaters, Buller's albatross and the endemic Snares crested penguins. Landings are not permitted as this is a strictly controlled sanctuary. Normally it's possible to cruise the coastline by zodiac but today the swell is unforgiving and we press on south.

Albatross are now our constant companions and I spend much of my time at sea on the stern deck, mesmerized by these iconic birds. Effortlessly they glide and bank over the ocean, soaring high before dropping down to slice through the spray that breaks over the waves. There are several species with us: Buller's from the Snares Islands, white-capped and wanderers from the Auckland Islands and southern royals from Campbell Island. They are all magnificent and I can't get enough of them.

After a day at sea we land at Enderby Island, the northernmost point of the Auckland Islands. It is wild and rugged, battered by storms for much of the year and home to a large and important colony of Hooker's sea lions. These are the rarest sea lions in the world and the Auckland Island group is their stronghold.

The precipitous cliffs of the north coast have breeding pairs of the charismatic light-mantled sooty albatross, while on the open grassland there are several pairs of royal albatross. To the south of the bay, the tidal pools and kelp beds provide food and shelter for the little flightless Auckland Island teal.

Sailing south, the rugged interior of Auckland Island looms out of the mist at 659 metres. Earlier colonizers left behind their domestic animals after failed attempts at farming this wild place, and this has had a lasting and destructive influence on its wildlife. Pigs, rats, cats and mice have all been responsible for the demise of ground-nesting species like pipits, snipe and teal. Only those species nesting on pest-free offshore islands have survived the onslaught. Adams Island, which measures just 30 by 7 km, has a population of 5,000 Gibson's wandering albatross, while Disappointment Island to the north, only 4 by 1 km, is the main breeding site for white-capped albatross with c.90,000

Right: The flightless Auckland Island teal
Below: The large colony of hookers sea lions in Sandy Bay, Enderby Island. The recently born pups are at the top of the beach, away from the rampaging bulls

A white-capped albatross on its nest, Auckland Island

King penguins, Macquarie Island

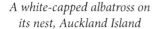

pairs. These two islands are off limits to visitors, apart from researchers keeping a close eye on population numbers; any accidental introduction of alien species would be catastrophic for these populations and measures on board ship are strictly enforced by a Department of Conservation officer that travels with us. When going ashore to tightly controlled landing zones, boots and clothing are thoroughly checked for seeds, soil particles and the like, both before and after landing.

We were able to land at the western end of Carnley Harbour and walk up the steep and densely vegetated hillside to over 200 metres, where white-capped albatross breed. They sat tightly on their single eggs, their pedestal nests sheltered in thick tussock grass on the cliffs. We could only look longingly across to Adams Island with its unattainable population of the beautiful Gibson's wandering albatross.

Macquarie Island, another sub-Antarctic island and Australian territory, lies 700 km to the south of the Auckland Islands. It is a World Heritage site which supports the total world population – about 800,000 – of royal penguins, many hundreds of thousands of king penguins and tens of thousands of elephant seals. Since the early 1800s, when the first whalers and sealers arrived here, the island has been plagued by introduced predators: rats and mice which escaped from the ships, cats introduced to control them, then rabbits introduced for food which escaped and proliferated, causing untold damage to the vegetation, and by extension to the ground-nesting habitat of petrels and shearwaters. From 1985–2000, there was a mass eradication of cats, with over 12,500 culled, but this led to an increase in the rat, mouse and rabbit population. Finally, in 2008, came a concerted effort to rid the island of these pests by means of poisoned bait dropped by helicopter. By 2012 the island was virtually pest-free, with hunting teams scouring the island to mop up any stragglers. The island was finally declared pest-free in 2014. I visited Macquarie in that year and again four years later, and could already see a remarkable improvement in the vegetation and the numbers of ground-nesting birds. It is so satisfying to see such an amazing reversal of the damage done by previous generations. Where there is a strong will to achieve change, it can be done.

As we leave Lusitania Bay with its 250,000 king penguins, we have 1,000 km of some of the wildest and deepest ocean on the planet to pass through en route to Cape Adare, at the entrance to the Ross Sea and the Antarctic continent. Captain James Ross discovered Cape Adare in 1841 but the first expedition to overwinter on the Antarctic continent was the Southern Cross expedition, led by Carsten Borchgrevink, in 1898–1900. The restored hut on the Cape is visible as we pass by but, frustratingly, a landing is impossible due to extensive shore ice. The Cape also has the largest Adélie penguin colony in the Antarctic, with more than 220,000 pairs, and up on the plateau recent discoveries show an old colony, now abandoned, that had been there for 2,000 years.

The ship enters the Ross Sea with another 650 km to run before Ross Island, site of the huts of Scott and Shackleton. The weather is fair and the seas calm. We have left the Albatross behind and are now escorted by snow petrels and Antarctic skuas.

Even though it is midsummer, the temperature hovers around freezing point and any increase in wind will send it plunging to –10 to –20°C in a very short time. Midwinter temperatures here can go down to –60°C. Ross Island is dominated by the 3,794- metre active volcano Mount Erebus, along with its sister Mt Terror. Both of these volcanoes were named back in 1841 by Captain James Ross, who borrowed the names of his two ships. He also discovered what was called the Great Ice Barrier and renamed it the Ross Ice Shelf, as it is still known today. With a total area of 480,000 sq. km – the size of France – and stretching 800 km south towards the Pole, it measures between 15 and 50 metres high at the face, and with 90% of the ice below the surface, is up to 500 metres thick. Captain Ross said at the time that they had 'as much chance of sailing through that as through the cliffs of Dover.'

Cape Crozier and the Ross Ice Shelf

As we approach Cape Royds, we can see that the little bay where we hope to land for Shackleton's hut is choked with ice, so we have to take the ship around the peninsula to Black Sand Beach. We land by zodiac, almost walking over snoozing Weddell seals, their dappled grey-and-white coats looking almost like the snow and volcanic sand on which they are lying. Standing alone on the top of a little hill, looking south, I'm filled with awe as I stare over the endless snowy wastes stretching to the horizon. I am struck by the enormity, magnificence and beauty of this desolate place and think of the incredible achievements and sacrifices of those early explorers. A 40-minute walk takes us over a moonscape of kenyte, volcanic scoria and rock, then we get our first sighting of Shackleton's hut, down the slope and tucked into the hillside, surrounded by the most southerly Adélie penguin colony in the world. The hut is in remarkable condition, lovingly restored and regularly checked by New Zealand's Antarctic Heritage Trust. It was prefabricated in England, brought in on Shackleton's ship Nimrod and assembled on its present site. Fifteen men lived and worked in this 10 x 5.8-metre space. Only eight people are allowed into this amazing monument at any one time – and then only for a short period of 20 minutes – and boots have to be thoroughly cleaned of abrasive material before entering.

Stepping into this place makes the hairs on your neck stand on end: everything is exactly as it was back in 1908 when it was first assembled. It is a strange feeling, after reading about all the expeditions, actually to be here, seeing the tables and chairs and the bunks where these men lived and slept, the shelves sagging with tins of biscuits, tinned meats, salt and flour. Sat in the middle is Mrs Sam's coal-fired stove that provided heat and the means to bake bread, cakes and pies for the ravenous men.

Setting out on an expedition into the unknown, in ferocious conditions, more than a century ago, Shackleton came very close to making it to the Pole. On approaching

Shackleton's hut at Pony Lake, Cape Royds

Mrs Sam's stove   *The interior of Shackleton's hut*

their goal he realized rations for the party were running dangerously low: they could have made it, and were just 97.5 miles short, but would almost certainly have perished on the return journey. He famously wrote in a letter to his wife, 'Better a live donkey than a dead lion.' They all got back to the hut without loss, just in time to meet their ship, *Nimrod*, due to head north on 1 March, although the men, including Shackleton, were in poor condition due to meagre rations and bouts of dysentry from eating tainted meat.

Landing at Cape Evans, just 13 km southeast down the coast from Cape Royds, we come to the much larger *Terra Nova* expedition hut, also in a remarkable state of preservation due to the cold, dry conditions. This is a much bigger building, as 25 men lived and worked here over an Antarctic winter. It, too, was prefabricated in England and brought out on the ship. It has double walls, packed with dried seaweed for insulation, unlike the *Discovery* expedition hut built in 1902 at Hut Point, which was so cold that the men preferred to stay on the anchored ship nearby.

Inside the *Terra Nova* hut, it seems that the men left only yesterday and that time has stood still since. There are the work benches covered in scientific paraphernalia, glassware, test tubes and measuring apparatus, the bunk beds still with the sealskin sleeping bags and, in the corner, the darkroom of Herbert Ponting, who produced stunning photographs of the wildlife, landscapes and expedition members. Even though roll film had been invented 20 years earlier, Ponting preferred to use glass plates, for their superior quality. Part of the work of the expedition was to study Antarctic animals such as orcas, seals and penguins, all of which Ponting tried to photograph. On one occasion, while trying to photograph orcas from an ice floe, he narrowly escaped with his life after the animals tried to smash the floe and pitch him into the water.

Similar rules apply at this cabin as at Shackleton's, though here 12 people at a time are allowed inside. Alongside the hut are the stables for the ponies that were used, unsuccessfully, to haul sledges; there are stalls still full of hay and on the walls hang

Scotts Hut at Cape Evans, base for the
Terra Nova *expedition, 1910–1913*

Interior of hut at Cape Evans

halters and bridles. All too soon our brief but highly emotional visit is over, and we walk out through the door used in 1912 by Scott, Oates, Evans, Bowers and Wilson as they left, never to return.

My once-in-a-lifetime journey to this starkly beautiful and historic region has all too quickly come to an end, but the ship must turn north to escape the ice which is already forming on the sea. It is 24 February as we cruise at 9 knots up the western side of the Ross Sea towards Cape Adare, passing *Terra Nova* Bay. We had hoped for a landing on Inexpressible Island but heavy swell made this impossible. This was the site where Scott's Northern Party of Geologists were forced to overwinter after the *Terra Nova* was unable to pick them up due to pack ice. Even though they had an emergency sledge with supplies, they were forced to dig an ice cave just 3.7 x 2.7 metres in a snow drift, in which the six men spent what must have been a miserable winter, battered by gales and living on meagre rations. When the supplies ran out, they were forced to eat penguins and seals, which were scarce, and all suffered from frostbite, hunger and dysentery. The ship's doctor, George Murray Levick, said, 'The road to hell might be paved with good intentions but it seemed probable that hell itself would be paved something after the style of Inexpressible Island.'

Our ship, Akademik Shokalskiy, *in ice*

Cape Adare with heavy pack ice

As we pass the bleakness of Cape Adare it becomes obvious that, yet again, we will be unable to land due to sea conditions with a northwest wind and heavy swell. The good news is that, thanks to being slightly ahead of schedule, we are going to make a slight detour to the northwest to try for a landing at the rarely visited Balleny Islands. Travelling over a calm sea at 12 knots towards the most southerly of the group, Sturge Island, we had wonderful sightings of wildlife that had been lacking in the Ross Sea. Humpback and minke whales close to the ship, leopard seals on ice floes and Southern fulmars, with Cape, snow and giant petrels. Our first sighting of the island is of huge cliffs looming out of the mist, then massive glaciers pouring into the flat calm sea. It's a privilege to get so close to these remote islands that are normally surrounded by pack ice.

Passing Buckle and Young Islands, we attempt to make landings by zodiac but it's impossible due to heavy shore ice. As we cruise around Sabrina Island, one of the smallest of the group, we get good views of Adélie and chinstrap colonies, with leopard seals waiting menacingly in the heavy swell for any inattentive penguins. A pod of eight orcas close by is impressive when seen from water level and they, too, are keeping an eye out for penguins. I do feel somewhat vulnerable in a six-metre zodiac with such powerful mammals nearby.

It's mid-afternoon on 28 February as the ship rounds the north end of Young Island, which is shrouded in cloud and mist. We set a course of 78 degrees - our next landfall will be Campbell Island, 900 nautical miles to the north, and it will take four

250

Adélie penguins on pack ice near Cape Adare

days at 10 knots to get there. Let's hope we get calm weather, as storms – quite apart from being dangerous – make it impossible to go on deck, ruining any chance of albatross photography.

As we travel north and get back into the albatross zones, we first see light-mantled sooty albatross and, as we approach the Antarctic convergence, the meeting of the warm waters of the sub-Antarctic to the north and Antarctic waters to the south, we notice a few wanderers, their presence betrayed by a fin whale and humpbacks close to the ship. These are extremely rich waters for krill and squid, which form a large part of the diet of many species of albatross and other seabirds, such as petrels and prions. As we travel steadily north, crossing the convergence, the bridge instruments registering staggering depths of 5,000 metres, we saw Southern royals and white-capped joining the sootys and the occasional black-browed, giving me wonderful photographic opportunities as they closely followed the ship. Many albatross species are in severe decline due to long-line fishing in the southern oceans; as the baited hooks are reeled out, the birds take the bait, are dragged down and drowned. Campbell Island, now just over 800 km away, is sometimes called the albatross capital of the world. It has six species nesting on its wild uplands and precipitous cliffs: Campbell, black-browed, grey-headed and light-mantled sooty, along with small numbers of two of the great albatrosses, the Antipodean and the Southern royal. Campbell Island is the main breeding ground for the royal, with a population estimated at 8,400 pairs.

It's dawn on 4 March and a low, red sun lights up the entrance to Perseverance Harbour on Campbell Island, New Zealand's southernmost sub-Antarctic territory, 660 km south of Bluff. It's good to be at anchor after four days of heavy seas. This will be another first for me, an opportunity to visit the colony of southern royal albatross up on Col Lyall. Going ashore by zodiac, we start the one-hour trek up to the colony, entirely on a painstakingly constructed boardwalk to protect the unique native vegetation. Walking through dense rata forest, I catch glimpses of the endemic Campbell Island snipe, only rediscovered on nearby Jacquemart Island in 1997.

Yellow-eyed penguins, the rarest of the 17 penguin species, are more often heard than seen, as they call to their youngsters hidden in these dark dwarf forests. Breaking out onto open moorland-type country, we get our first glimpses of the huge nests of the royals, white specks in the distance amongst the massive tussock grasses. We're too late for the impressive carpets of huge blooms that occur in December and January in the high sub-alpine fell fields, though there are a few examples left of the emperor daisy (*Pleurophyllum speciosum*), paper daisy (*helichrysum*), Campbell Island carrot (*Anisotosum latifolia*) and some small pink, purple and white gentians.

Reaching the ridge, we can see the true size of a great albatross as it sits calmly on its massive nest. Just off the boardwalk at Col Lyall is a zone where it is possible to go off track and approach the nests, but to no closer than five metres. There is so much going on here: up on exposed ridges, groups of sub-adults are 'gaming', practising their display skills, although they are not mature and ready to breed until they are around eight years old. Those on the ground attract others that are circling nearby, which come in low and at great speed to land, wing flaps fully down. It's the most wonderful experience to be so close to these charismatic birds and, with so much action, a photographer's dream. 99% of the population breed here, about 8,400 pairs, with 100 or so in the Auckland Islands 270 km to the northwest. Most are biennial nesters due to the length of the breeding cycle: 79 days of incubation and up to 250 days for the youngster to fledge.

Some of the birds now have small chicks, just 2–3 weeks old, being closely brooded for up to 42 days by the parent bird. The weather here, though it is midsummer, can be atrocious, with fast-moving weather fronts, sudden squalls, snowstorms and fierce winds. The other parent is away fishing and it could be a month before it returns to relieve its partner, travelling huge circumpolar distances in search of food. After 42 days, when the chick is large enough to be left alone, both parents go to sea to bring back increasingly large meals for the chick. If one of the adults is killed at sea, it is impossible for the remaining parent to provide enough food for the rapidly growing chick and it will surely perish.

Albatross have to cover vast distances in their search for food, mostly fish and squid taken from the surface, which brings them close to fishing fleets in the most productive areas of the ocean. Tens of thousands have perished in lines and nets over the past 20 years or more, bringing some populations close to extinction. Thankfully, due to the research efforts of many agencies, effective mitigation measures are being put in place. The toll on the albatross and seabirds of the world is being reduced by simple measures such as setting lines at night, when the albatross are less active, so-called tori lines – bird-scaring devices consisting of cables festooned with an array of dangling streamers – and weighted hooks, which make the bait sink more quickly. Fortunately, the royal albatross is one of the more timid around fishing vessels and its population appears to be stable.

Like the Auckland Islands, Campbell Island had a farming community many years ago which left behind its livestock, rats and cats. These caused devastating losses to the ground-nesting species such as the Campbell Island teal, snipe and albatross. The

Campbell Island snipe

Above: Purple flowers of the mega-herb **Pleurophyllum speciosum**, *looking down to Northeast Harbour, Campbell Island*
Below: Royal Albatross sub-adults display on a ridge

Royal albatross adult with two-week-old chick

cattle and sheep were eliminated in the 1980s and 1990s, and in 2001 a rat eradication programme using poisoned bait dropped by helicopter finally rid the island of those invaders. The vegetation has responded and endemic snipe have recolonised the island from its offshore island stronghold. The flightless teal, at one time thought extinct, but found on offshore Dent Island in 1972, was bred in captivity, then reintroduced to the rat-free island in 2004. They are now breeding successfully and their future seems assured on Campbell.

My journey to the Antarctic and sub-Antarctic islands has been as memorable an experience as I hoped, and more. These are without doubt some of the remotest and yet most vulnerable outposts of the planet. I'm leaving, not knowing if I will ever return, but I very much hope I will.

Campbell albatross off Campbell Island

978-184995-147-0 £18.99

...*a fascinating insight into the numerous threats faced by some of our most vulnerable wildlife and the resourcefulness of those who dedicate their lives to protecting it. These are uplifting tales of hurdles overcome, crises averted and disasters prevented.* Extract from **Foreword** by **Mark Rose, Chief Executive Officer, Fauna & Flora International**

...*it's wonderful to hear any tales of animals that have been saved, and of the fantastic individuals who go to great lengths to help them.* **The Weekly News**

...*this book shows that it's possible to turn the tide of species decline. It's full of conservation success stories, valuable lessons and inspiration for the future.* **Wildlife World**

...*The knowledge, experience and raw passion for conservation that Dr Smith possesses is exuded in 'bucket loads' ... coupled with factual up to date information on the plight of some of the world's most endangered species. ...a supremely interesting read...* **ECOS**

978-184995-435-8 £18.99

THIS IS THE FIRST BOOK FOR OVER 50 YEARS ENTIRELY DEVOTED TO ALL
MONGOOSES. IT PROVIDES A COMPREHENSIVE AND THOROUGH OVERVIEW
AND DESCRIBES THE MOST UP-TO-DATE AND SCIENTIFICALLY-SOUND
INFORMATION ABOUT ALL 34 MONGOOSE SPECIES.

MONGOOSES OF THE WORLD HIGHLIGHTS THE CURRENT CONSERVATION
STATUS OF EACH MONGOOSE SPECIES AND DESCRIBES THE THREATS
THAT THEY FACE. THE ROLE THAT MONGOOSES HAVE PLAYED IN HUMAN
CULTURE, MYTHOLOGY AND FOLKLORE IS ALSO DESCRIBED.

*The book is pleasantly easy to read and gives the reader information on the
evolution of the mongoose, their lifestyle and behaviour ... their diet, breeding
and principal predators. ...is well laid out and amply supplied with lovely
colour photographs, maps and tables. ...I must admit to having thoroughly
enjoyed this book.* Wildlife Detective – the blog of Alan Stewart

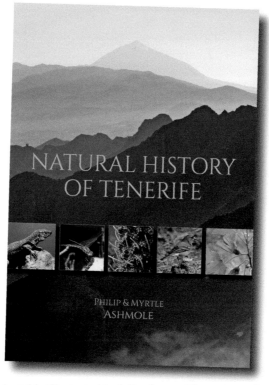

978-184995-225-5 £35.00

...The whole is lavishly illustrated in full colour, with so many close-ups of key plants and selected animals, that it pretty-well doubles as a field guide for the general naturalist or botanist. ... I cannot recommend this too highly to all naturalists visiting Tenerife who will be much indebted to them for how this cannot but really open their eyes to the island's biodiversity.
Biodiversity & Conservation

...remarkable book. An excellent map at the beginning of the book displays the physical features and natural habitats on Tenerife. The book is a botanist's dream, detailing hundreds of different plants... ...is a reference book that must be unparalleled in its field. In my opinion its value extends beyond the normal reference book because of its usefulness to the visitor to the island in finding and sharing the joys of its wildlife. I consider it a must for any Tenerife tourist with an interest in nature. Wildlife Detective – The blog of Alan Stewart

***** **Amazon review**

Just what I needed for Tenerife visits. Very thorough guide to the natural history of the island. The photos are excellent and well described. The book gives anybody who loves this fascinating place a superb tool to dig deeper and understand it more. Thanks to both the authors on a job well done

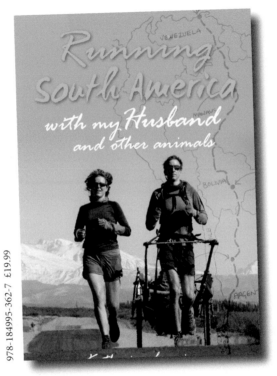

978-184995-362-7 £19.99

RUNNING MARATHONS BACK-TO-BACK, SLEEPING BY THE SIDE OF THE
ROAD, GIVING PRESENTATIONS TO REMOTE SCHOOLS THAT HAD NEVER
BEEN VISITED BY THEIR OWN KINSFOLK – LET ALONE A PAIR OF GRINGOS
EMERGING BAREFOOT FROM THE FOREST SPATTERED IN BRICK-RED AMAZON
MUD AND PULLING A BRIGHT ORANGE BAMBOO TRAILER; THIS IS THE
REMARKABLE STORY OF PERSONAL ENDURANCE THAT GIVES AN ENGROSSING
INSIGHT INTO THE PEOPLE AND WILDLIFE OF SOUTH AMERICA

*A feat of extraordinary courage and determination which transports [you]
on a wild journey through deserts and forests, in the face of extreme dangers
and physical hardship.* Sir Ranulph Fiennes

*...reading Katharine's powerful and exciting book about her remarkable
adventure is certainly a white-knuckle experience. It takes you deep into the
heart of a mysterious continent where you are invited to watch the landscape
unfold on a human scale one step at a time. It is a thrilling account punctuated
by bizarre encounters with incredible native wildlife...* Daily Express

*...Katharine relates the story of the run in fascinating details and with frankness
and humour. She is also...a quality artist, which is demonstrated in the beautiful
sketches of wildlife throughout the book. ...is an enthralling book and without
doubt one of the best I have read.* Wildlife Detective, The blog of Alan Stewart

978-184995-342-9 £25.00

Richard Sale and Per Michelsen

The Arctic

THIS IS A CELEBRATION OF THE ARCTIC WILDERNESS BY AN ACKNOWLEDGED
EXPERT AND FEATURES THE WILDLIFE THAT LIVES THERE – THE TERRESTRIAL
AND MARINE MAMMALS, THE BIRDS, INSECTS AND PLANTS

*...a true celebration of the Arctic Wilderness... ...is essential reading for both Arctic
'aficionados' and ordinary travellers to the Arctic, anyone indeed, with real interests
in the future of the physical and human environment of the hugely extensive and
beautiful wilderness of the Arctic.* **ECOS**

*This is an extremely well laid-out book, written by Richard Sale and with photos by
Per Michelson on almost every page helping the reader to understand the subject under
discussion. To read it was a fascinating experience... ...absolutely fascinating... ...
illustrated by amazing photographs... Reading the book I was in awe at the vast knowledge
of the author. This is not a book about one aspect of the Arctic but of a wide range of
complex topics. The compilation of such a book, and its photographic illustrations, are a
credit to Sale and Michelsen.* **Wildlife Detective, The blog of Alan Stewart**

Whittles Publishing, Dunbeath, Caithness, Scotland, KW6 6EG
Tel: 01593 731333; info@whittlespublishing.com; www.whittlespublishing.com